Governance and Citizenship in Asia

Series editors

Kerry J Kennedy, Centre for Governance and Citizenship,
The Education University of Hong Kong, Hong Kong, Hong Kong
Sonny Shiu Hung Lo, Centre for Governance and Citizenship,
The Education University of Hong Kong, Hong Kong, Hong Kong

Aims and Scope

This series explores how citizenship is shaped by social, political, cultural and historical contexts and how it may be moulded to serve the nation state in the age of globalization. In these publications we see how governance relates to all aspects of civic life, including politics, public policy, administration, civil society and the economy, as well as the core values of society.

Titles cover themes including public trust and trust building, the role of civil society, citizens' rights and obligations, citizenship identities including those related to gender, class and ethnicities. Authors explore how young people are shaped by democratic and traditional value systems and the importance of citizenship challenges in the Asia Pacific region.

Research collaborations in this interdisciplinary series probe questions such as: What are the links between 'good governance' and new forms of citizenship? What is the role of citizenship education as a tool in state formation and the development of active citizenship cultures? How do we explain the distinctive features of governance and citizenship in Asian societies?

Through these publications we see that citizenship is an integral part of 'good governance' and that such governance ultimately enriches citizenship. Scholarly investigation and academic dialogue in this series describe the interdependence and mutuality of governance and citizenship.

More information about this series at http://www.springer.com/series/11911

Sicong Chen

The Meaning of Citizenship in Contemporary Chinese Society

An Empirical Study through Western Lens

Springer

Sicong Chen
Graduate School of Education
Tohoku University
Sendai, Miyagi
Japan

ISSN 2365-6255 ISSN 2365-6263 (electronic)
Governance and Citizenship in Asia
ISBN 978-981-10-6321-3 ISBN 978-981-10-6323-7 (eBook)
https://doi.org/10.1007/978-981-10-6323-7

Library of Congress Control Number: 2017950027

Printed on acid-free paper

This Springer imprint is published by Springer Nature
The registered company is Springer Nature Singapore Pte Ltd.
The registered company address is: 152 Beach Road, #21-01/04 Gateway East, Singapore 189721, Singapore

For Tomoko

Foreword

I welcome this fascinating, timely and significant academic work. Sicong Chen has written a book that will be of value to academics and professionals around the world.

It is extremely important for us to know more about what is happening in Chinese society and education system. China is characterized and interpreted in diverse ways. It is a powerful international force and at times it portrays itself as a developing country. It is a socialist country and it has a high-profile market economy. It is unified and hugely varied. It has a turbulent past and is currently relatively stable. Whether or not it is accurate to claim that it was Napoleon who referred to China as a sleeping giant who when she wakes will shake the world is less important than the sense that quotation is correct: the country is now of immense significance. To be content with our current level of knowledge and understanding about China would be foolhardy. Sicong Chen adds valuably to a growing field of scholars who are exploring China and who are illuminating key issues about education.

This book takes an impressively focused position by using a Western lens to analyse key developments. This is a difficult thing to do well. Of course, terms such as 'west' and 'east' are both geographically and conceptually positioned. A map of the world with China at the centre would see the USA as being in the east. Not all countries in the east or west necessarily share similar characteristics: China is not Japan; Germany is not the USA. And those who live in the East or West are not necessarily 'eastern' or 'western'. The 'west' is as fluid as any other place. Further, if we embark on anything that approaches comparative research it is important not to simply use a conceptual net to capture what one likes or does not like; it is not simply for one 'side' to learn from the other; but rather to illuminate through analysis of what might be considered to take the form of blurred distinctions. Our attachment to diversity should not be represented as fragmentation; our commitment to consensus should not lead us to naïve positions about uniformity. Sicong Chen navigates these choppy waters with skill.

On the basis of an impressively wide ranging literature review and an in-depth empirical study, Sicong Chen has drawn attention to key ideas and issues.

His fluency in languages has enabled him to take a precise interest in *gongmin*, developing its meaning in relation to ideas relevant to being human, the city, the state and public matters. By contrasting and comparing official views of *gongmin* (through government announcements and media statements) with nonofficial media statements and with the perceptions of university students and migrant workers, there is a sense of an embryonic pluralism that is closely connected but distinct from established debates about citizenship. It is fascinating that the empirical parts of the work are based on data collected in Guangdong Province. This province, at some distance from Beijing and bordering Hong Kong, is, of course, not representative of the whole of China but it is a place where there is potential for some fascinating discussions and analyses of education about—and for—engagement in contemporary society. The differences and similarities between and within official and respondent positions, contextualized over time, is fascinating. There are connections made in this work with key ideas of Confucianism, Maoism and modern socialism. There is a subtle, nuanced argument that allows for the development of a singularly Chinese form of education that is nevertheless connected to characterisations that are to be found in other countries. The existing forms of political education, moral education and ideological education are likely to develop in the face of changing social and economic circumstances and the changing nature of beliefs and perceptions which in part emerge from an increasingly internationally mobile population.

China is developing its own way forward. In all regions and countries, a struggle for meaning and good practice for a socially just world is taking place. The use of a Western lens, the focus on *gongmin*, the careful discussion of valuable empirical work and perhaps above all the recommendations for an 'inclusive, active and justice-oriented citizenship going below and beyond nation-state' makes this book essential reading.

Ian Davies
University of York, UK

Preface

This book is written at a time of mounting official interest in citizenship education, increasing dynamics between state and society, and growing citizenship awareness and practice in society in contemporary China. Taking into account the state factor and placing the focus on society, the book investigates the meaning of the Chinese term *gongmin*—equivalent to 'citizen'—in nonofficial media discourses and in university students' and migrant workers' perceptions in Guangdong Province. The meaning of the term is examined through the analytical lens of Western citizenship conception theoretically constructed with three dimensions: the extent dimension about identity, the content dimension about rights and responsibilities, and the depth dimension about participation. By laying out the complex details of how the meaning of the term resembles and deviates in and between collective social discourses and individual citizens' understandings with reference to state discourses, the book makes clear that there is discrepancy in the meaning of *gongmin* between state and society and that the meaning varies in society in contemporary China.

This is a study cutting across topics of Chinese citizenship, East–West citizenship and citizenship education. Drawing upon the empirical findings, the book considers the potentials and limits of the term *gongmin* for citizenship practice in society and the implications for state–society relation in contemporary China. Furthermore, by connecting and comparing citizenship conceptions in East and West, the book serves as an intercultural communication and search for the possibility of common ground for Eastern and Western citizenship conceptions. Beginning with the official interest in citizenship education, the book suggests at the end improvements for Chinese citizenship education to develop inclusive, active and justice-oriented citizenship going below and beyond nation-state.

Sendai, Japan Sicong Chen

Acknowledgements

This book is the culmination of my research on Chinese citizenship and citizenship education in my doctoral years and early academic career. It is adapted with substantial revision from my doctoral thesis which itself could not be done without the support and help of many people. In particular, I am deeply indebted to my supervisors Yasumasa Hirasawa, Ryoko Kimura and Beverley Yamamoto for their professional guidance, constant encouragement and wholehearted support during the doctoral research process and thesis writing.

Study II of my doctoral thesis and this book received financial support from Osaka University Scholarship for Short-Term Overseas Research Activities 2011. It subsidized my 3-month stay (March–May 2012) as academic visitor in the Centre for Citizenship and Governance, Hong Kong Institute of Education (HKIEd, now The Education University of Hong Kong), and my fieldwork in Guangdong Province during the period. I would like to express my gratitude to the members of the centre, particularly to Yan-Wing Leung and M. Ramesh for accepting my visit request and to Kerry John Kennedy for inspiring discussions. My thanks also go to the university staff and student assistants for helping me conduct the research in their universities and to the factory owners for allowing me to carry out the investigation in their factories. I would also like to thank the university students and migrant workers who kindly participated in the study.

I am also grateful to the Global COE Program of Osaka University for providing me travel subsidy to report some findings at the International Conference on 'Governance and Citizenship in Asia: Paradigms and Practices' in HKIEd on 18–19 March 2011. Some findings of this book were also presented at the 9th CitizED International Conference in Tokyo on 13–15 July 2013 and at the 11th CitizED International Conference at National Institute of Education of Singapore on 2–4 June 2015. Findings of Study I of this book has been reported in a journal article in 2013 under the title 'The discrepancy of meaning of citizenship between the state and society in China: implications for citizenship education and its policymaking', *Education, Citizenship and Social Justice*, 8(3), 263–275. I gratefully acknowledge the publisher's permission for me to include the content in this book.

I also owe a great many personal debts of gratitude to my families in China and Japan for their unconditional support. My deepest appreciation goes to my wife Tomoko, who has been a constant source of inspiration and support in every way.

I was lucky to have Springer's Lawrence Liu's encouragement for the book writing journey and Lay Peng Ang's assistance during it. I deeply appreciate the book series editors' and the reviewers' generous and constructive comments and suggestions. Responsibility for what is written in this book remains my own.

Contents

Abbreviations

CCP	Chinese Communist Party
CPPCC	People's Political Consultative Conference
HEI	Higher Education Institution
HRS	Household Registration Status
NGO	Non-Governmental Organization
NPC	National People's Congress
PC	People's Congress
PRC	People's Republic of China
WTO	World Trade Organization

Chinese Terms

aiguo	爱国
canjia	参加
canyu	参与
chengxin	诚信
daode	道德
Daode yu fazhi	道德与法治
Datongshu	大同书
fengxian	奉献
gong	公
gongmin	公民
Gongmin daode jianshe shishi gangyao	公民道德建设实施纲要
gongmin jiaoyu	公民教育
Gongmin zizhi pian	公民自治篇
guo	国
guojia jimi	国家机密
guomin	国民
Guomindang	国民党
hao gongmin	好公民
hukou	户口
jiaoyu	教育
jiaqiang gongmin yishi jiaoyu	加强公民意识教育
jilü	纪律
jingye	敬业
kuoda gongmin youxu de zhengzhi canyu	扩大公民有序的政治参与
lixiang	理想
min	民
minban gaoxiao	民办高校

mingli	明礼
Nanfang dushibao	南方都市报
Pinde yu shehui	品德与社会
Pinde yu shenghuo	品德与生活
putong gaoxiao	普通高校
putonghua	普通话
qimeng gongmin yishi	启蒙公民意识
qinjian	勤俭
quanli	权利
quanyi	权益
ren	人
renmin	人民
Renmin ribao	人民日报
shehuizhuyi hege gongmin	社会主义合格公民
shehuizhuyi minzhu fazhi, ziyou pingdeng, gongping zhengyi	社会主义民主法治、自由平等、公平正义
shequ jianshe	社区建设
shi	市
shijie gongmin	世界公民
shimin	市民
shoufa	守法
si	私
siren	私人
Sixiang pinde	思想品德
Sixiang zhengzhi	思想政治
tianmin	天民
tuanjie	团结
wei renmin fuwu	为人民服务
wenhua	文化
wenhua quanli	文化权利
wenming suzhi	文明素质
Wudu	五蠹
Xin sanzijing	新三字经
Xinminshuo	新民说
yiwu	义务
youshan	友善
zeren	责任
zhanlue zhuti	战略主题
zhiqingquan, canyuquan, biaodaquan, jianduquan	知情权、参与权、表达权、监督权
ziqiang	自强

Chapter 1
Introduction: Citizenship, Education, East and West

This introductory chapter introduces three tendencies in relation to citizenship education and citizenship in contemporary China as the background against which this book is written. It puts forward the purpose of this study and explains its position in three wider research areas: education, East–West citizenship, and Chinese citizenship. The research framework and key findings are also laid out before an outline of the following chapters in the book.

Background: Three Tendencies

Citizenship education (*gongmin jiaoyu*), hardly found in the vocabulary of the Chinese Communist Party (CCP) in the first half century of its rule over China since 1949, began to appear in state discourses since the 2000s. The need to 'boost citizenship awareness education' (*jiaqiang gongmin yishi jiaoyu*) is openly expressed as a way to establish 'socialist democracy, rule of law, liberty, equity, fairness and justice' (*shehuizhuyi minzhu fazhi, ziyou pingdeng, gongping zhengyi*) in the CCP Seventeenth National Congress Report delivered by then General Secretary Hu Jintao in 2007 (Hu 2007). This is observed to be 'the first time' ever that citizenship education is officially 'lifted…to such a high level' (Tu 2011, p. 431). Following the tone set by the CCP, the same expression is found in the national plan for education in the decade of 2010s, under the heading of 'strategic theme' (*zhanlue zhuti*) and for nurturing 'socialist qualified citizens' (*shehuizhuyi hege gongmin*) (PRC State Council 2010).

It is apparent from the above illustrations that the official expression of citizenship education is well confined within the socialist ideology. What do citizenship and relevant concepts, such as democracy and justice, mean in the socialist sense? To what extent does citizenship awareness education differ, if any, from the long-standing political, moral and ideological education in the CCP regime? The authorities give neither immediate nor systematic answers to these direct and

S. Chen, *The Meaning of Citizenship in Contemporary Chinese Society*,
Governance and Citizenship in Asia, https://doi.org/10.1007/978-981-10-6323-7_1

important questions. After all, the expression of citizenship education is not necessarily a favourite of the CCP. The term 'citizenship awareness education' curiously disappeared in the subsequent CCP Eighteenth National Congress Report delivered by Hu Jintao as well in 2012; and Wan's (2004, p. 355) observation that there is no official curriculum subject title containing 'citizenship' in school of any kind or level remains as valid today as then, particularly at the compulsory level.

Nevertheless, the expression of citizenship education in state discourses, however vague, ambiguous, volatile and ephemeral, indicates that citizenship education has grabbed attention or interest from the party-state.[1] This change came alongside other two broader tendencies: first, the party-state's policies and governance are more and more shaped by demands from society which, second, has witnessed increased citizenship awareness and practice in recent decades. I shall give an overview of these two broader tendencies in turn.

The fundamental force pushing the party-state to meet societal demands and even allow citizens to participate in the policymaking process is arguably the change of its legitimacy ground. By legitimacy ground I mean the reason whereby the CCP can continue to claim itself as the ruling party, and the party-state can exercise what Simmons (2001, p. 155) called 'the exclusive moral right' to impose duties on group or person within it and coercively enforce the latter to obey it. Wave after wave of political purges in the name of class struggle peaking in the 10-year turmoil of Cultural Revolution (1966–1976) exposed to the society 'the irrationalities of the communist system in such an extreme form' (Shirk 1993, p. 14). They heavily damaged the CCP's ruling legitimacy based primarily, though not exclusively, on socialist and communist ideology. To restore the regime from the verge of political and economic collapses, the CCP has adopted market economy since the 1980s, with the rhetoric of 'socialism with Chinese characteristics' to try to reconcile the theoretical conflict between classical socialism and the market. The democracy movements in the late 1980s ending up being cracked down by the authorities further alienated the public from the official socialist ideology. Standing at the vantage point of the 1989 crackdown and from the perspective of Chinese youth, Rosen (2004) observed that as 'abundant evidence' suggested, the CCP 'had lost its ideological legitimacy in the eyes of Chinese youth' before 1989, and the post-1989 regime 'recognized that old appeals to a discredited ideology had become counter-productive, and that a renewal of popular support required goals that could only be assessed using criteria based on performance' (p. 172). He noted that this performance-based legitimacy is projected through making policies both satisfying citizens' needs at the individual level and building a prosperous and powerful China at the collective level.

It would be mistaken to consider that the party-state has since entirely placed its ruling legitimacy on performance and abandoned its ideological leading role in socialism and towards communism. The clinging of 'socialist' to concepts such as citizenship, democracy and justice as shown at the beginning of this chapter

---

[1]The use of 'party-state' in this book does not mean that it treats party and state as one entity but implies that, following Zheng's (2010, Chap. 5) disaggregation, as two separate political organizations, the party dominates the state and speaks in the name of the state.

demonstrates that socialist ideology is still vividly present in state discourses. Performance hence does not replace, but is better seen as mixing with, socialist ideology in what Teets et al. (2010, p. 17) called 'a complex cocktail of legitimacy'. In addition to the political-ideological element in this 'cocktail', there is also a political-cultural element, which is paternalism based on Confucianism, a ruling legitimacy familiar in Chinese history and picked up by the CCP regime to rule and satisfy societal needs like a father to his son (Fairbrother 2014).

If meeting societal needs is a direct result of grounding legitimacy on performance, then opening the door for citizens to engage in politics and policymaking is an indirect and direct one. Demands from citizens are not necessarily political; and meeting economic, social and cultural demands does not make political engagement necessary. Yet in contemporary Chinese context the approach—i.e. market economy—employed by the party-state to satisfying other-than-political demands requires, ironically, citizens' involvement in policymaking. It is in this sense that I call political engagement an indirect result of performance-based legitimacy. The adoption of market economy to unleash production capacities for economic needs encouraged social agency in the market and necessitated more decisions to be effectively made in society and at the local level. As the market economy develops and issues facing the party-state become 'fast-moving and complex' than before, the authoritarianism of the party-state is further 'fragmented', pushing it not only to delegate responsibilities to the market and society, but also to consult social actors in the policy process (Mertha 2010, p. 72). A concrete example of the party-state's decentralization of the role of decision-making and governance to citizens is the village elections for village committees formally mandated nationwide in 1998. Luo (2014) noted that both in official literature and academic studies, the official purpose of village elections is considered as an 'instrumental' way to 'solve the political anarchy' after the former commune system undermining peasants' incentive for production was 'left with no authority' in the market economy (pp. 13–4).

Allowing citizens to influence and take part in the policy and governance process becomes a direct result of performance-based legitimacy when it is precisely what citizens demand, as witnessed in recent decades. In addition to top-down designed political participation such as the abovementioned formal village elections and informal policy consultancy, there have been top-down unintended participation, such as workers' protests for law implementation by using legal knowledge promoted by the state, and bottom-up social initiatives, such as urban homeowners' associations (Perry and Goldman 2007b). In between these top-down and bottom-up engagements exist 'policy entrepreneurs'—prominently 'disgruntled or disenfranchised officials, the media, and NGOs [non-governmental organizations]'—who were previously prohibited from but now are either 'sought out' or 'sometimes grudgingly tolerated, sometimes enthusiastically welcomed' by the regime for policy advice (Mertha 2010, pp. 72–3).[2] Furthermore, in spite of, and

[2]Such tolerance and welcome, however, should not be taken for granted. For instance, the party-state recently tightened control over NGOs through more law and regulation. For a news report on the recent move by the Chinese authorities, see 'New Chinese law tightens control over NGOs' at http://www.aljazeera.com/news/2017/01/china-ngo-law-170101083414954.html (accessed 25 April 2017).

perhaps as a result of, the remarkable economic growth since the introduction of market economy, contemporary China is plagued with a wide range of new and old issues, from spatial and class inequality to environmental destruction and ethnic unrest. These issues have triggered diverse patterns of conflict, resistance and protests by and among citizens who often demand policy response from the authorities, as recorded and traced in Perry and Selden's (2010) edited volume.

While there are social demands for having a say in governance once monopolised by the party-state, the absolute leading role claimed by the CCP reminds us that such demands are confined. Yet they do not necessarily challenge against the CCP's rule. Indeed, drawing on the studies in Gries and Rosen's (2010) edited volume on Chinese politics in state, society and market, Teets et al. (2010) concluded that 'most protest and contestation in China is not driven by the desire for regime change but instead for better access to the government policy-making and implementation process' (p. 13). Similarly, Wright (2010) discussed that 'there is substantial evidence that the popular unrest that has spread since the early 1990s does not denote widespread dissatisfaction with the ruling regime' and that, by reviewing existing surveys on Chinese public opinion, 'popular support for the CCP-led political regime is strong' despite demographic and geographic variations (pp. 12–9). Whether this popular regime support is derived from the party-state's fulfillment of its multi-stranded legitimacy and what goes wrong is not its policy intention but implementation in citizens' eyes as Teets et al. (2010) reasoned, or from the party-state's successful adaptive responses to changing economic and social conditions in relation to different social groups as Wright (2010) detailed, the absence of direct political challenge in society against the party-state helps prevent the tension between state and society in policy and governance from collapse, leaving space and opportunities for both the CCP regime to maintain its legitimacy and social forces to exert influences on the running of the state. In short, the Chinese state-society relation has been dynamized.

Of equal significance to the increasing involvement from society in the policy and governance process is that this involvement is increasingly demanded as rights by citizens. Referring to the grassroots political changes, whether intended by the top such as village elections or initiated from the bottom such as the growing number of NGOs, Goldman (2005) observed that

> One of the major changes in the last two decades of the twentieth century was a growing sense of rights consciousness, particularly of political rights. Initially articulated by intellectuals, this rights consciousness gradually spread to the population in general – workers, peasants, the growing middle class, and religious believers. (p. 2)

Rights and participation are key components of citizenship, at least in Western citizenship conception (the focus of Chap. 2). The increased rights consciousness and participation among Chinese citizens testify the development of citizenship awareness and practice in contemporary Chinese society (to be detailed in Chaps. 4, 5 and 6).

In summary, the overview above outlined three tendencies in contemporary China as the background against which this book is written:

(1) The mounting, albeit ambiguous and uncertain, official interest in citizenship education;
(2) The increasing, but not necessarily deadlocked, dynamics between the party-state and society in policymaking and governance; and
(3) The growing citizenship awareness and practice in society.

Purpose of the Book

The three background tendencies bear implications for two scenarios. First, in the case that the party-state continues to show interest in citizenship education through expression and promotion, it would be hard for the party-state to have the say on all, since the content and outcome of citizenship education would rely increasingly upon support and engagement by citizens in society. Second, even if citizenship education turns out to be little more than an ephemeral rhetoric in the state discourse, the growing citizenship awareness and practice in society could still turn into pressure upon the party-state for policy response and change regarding citizenship education.

In whichever scenario the three tendencies suggest that citizenship in society has become a critical factor in the development of citizenship education in China. Questions such as how is citizenship interpreted and narrated in society, how is citizenship actually taught and learnt in and beyond schools, and how is citizenship practiced by citizens are important variables in the extent to which the party-state can advance its vision of citizenship education on one hand and ordinary citizens can influence the course of citizenship learning and practice on the other hand. In particular, what does the Chinese term *gongmin*, which is the legal equivalent and the most popular translation of 'citizen', mean in contemporary Chinese society is a prerequisite variable for the questions above. The meaning of the term, however, remains unexplored in a direct, empirical and systematic manner in the literature on Chinese citizenship, which I shall review later in this chapter.

At the beginning of his classic work *Keywords*, Williams (1990) introduced that in the course of his study on culture and society, he found that the discourses of culture and society are inevitably and significantly shaped by a vocabulary of 'a shared body of words and meanings in our most general discussions' (p. 15). This awareness prompted him to conduct the unique inquiry into the change and variation of the meanings of a list of keywords to '[bind] words in certain activities and their interpretation' and 'open up issues and problems' (p. 15). Chinese citizenship and citizenship education similarly cannot escape from but is shaped by a Chinese vocabulary in public discourses. It also deserves a keyword inquiry. The term *gongmin* is certainly a keyword in the Chinese vocabulary repertoire for citizenship description, discussion and negotiation, contributing to the cognitive construction and scope of citizenship learning, teaching, perception and practice in society. Moreover, the meaning of *gongmin* in society can serve as a vantage point both to observe and assess the party-state's stance on citizenship and to explore and identify the potentials and limits of citizenship development in society. In a broader sense, citizenship is perceived as a concept not necessarily unitary but possible to be understood and interpreted differently and even distinctly in diverse political, social, cultural and economic contexts. The inquiry into the Chinese term in Chinese society carries implications for cross-context citizenship and citizenship education observation and comparison.

This book empirically examines what the term *gongmin* means in contemporary Chinese society. It explores what words and connotations it binds and what issues that open up. This is not an etymological study of *gongmin* as defined in dictionaries, but an empirical record and interpretation of its 'present meanings, implications and relationships' (Williams 1990, p. 23) in Chinese society with reference to the past, the party-state and the West. In this sense, this book is a direct response to Wong's (1999) call for comparative analysis of what citizenship meant to Chinese people in order to 'avoid easy assumptions inferred from European practices about what "citizenship" has meant in Chinese contexts' and to 'recognize the appropriateness, or even necessity, of using a term that Chinese themselves began to use a century ago' (p. 117).

Before further introducing the study itself, I shall explain its position in three related areas—education, the concept of citizenship, and Chinese citizenship. The following section will state the educational intention behind this study on Chinese citizenship after a consideration of the relationship between education and citizenship in nation-states.[3] Turning from within to across nation-states and from political to sociocultural contexts, there will be a section highlighting the nature of the concept of citizenship to clarify the East–West approach, namely investigating Chinese citizenship through Western analytical lens, in this book. What follows will be another section giving an overview of the literature on Chinese citizenship and identifying two research gaps that this book helps to bridge.

Education and Citizenship

Education in this book is considered in the broad sense, covering both school education and varied educational activities in the wider society known as public pedagogy. The latter is a form of education and learning taking place in a wide range of sites, including other-than-school institutional sites such as museum, informal sites such as media and popular culture, and sites of activism such as social movement, and containing the potential, similar with school education, for both reproduction and resistance (Sandlin et al. 2010). Citizenship is indeed the original

[3]The hyphenated nation-state implies neither that one state necessarily has only one nation nor that a nation necessarily claims for forming a state, but serves as an indication that modern state is built in the name of nation, which, as Hobsbawm (1992, pp. 18–23) traced, bears political and ethnical meanings in modern times.

concern in the study of public pedagogy, because it influences, and thus is suggested as an approach in addition to school education for, the development of citizenship elements such as national identity and social engagement (Sandlin et al. 2011).

In a discussion of the possibility of extending liberal civic culture to societies outside liberal democracies, Kennedy (2004) noted that 'citizenship education is the province of nation-states and not some supra-national authority' (p. 18). This observation arguably can be extended to modern school education in general and to the intra-national level. That is, modern school education is the province of nation-states and not some intra-national authority. It is for sure that the nation-state is not the only player in education, especially given that education is increasingly marketised and exposed to the influences by the flow of capital, people and ideas below and beyond nation-states in contemporary times. Yet in many states, the national government remains the predominant authority having the legitimate power in school education nationwide.

Indeed, it is treated as a 'historical fact' that nationwide school education systems were established and led by modern states in the process of nation building since the nineteenth century from Europe, Japan and the North Americas and later to other parts of the world (Green 1997, p. 9). Modern public and universal school education contributed to and functioned in the nation building in several ways. Socially, it served as the way of 'equalizing the capacity of all citizens to avail themselves of the rights to which they are entitled' (Bendix 1977, p. 124). Economically, it was 'the least specialized, the most universally standardized' approach of 'generic training' to producing and reproducing workforce demanded by the paralleling industrialization (Gellner 2008, p. 26). Politically, it was used as a tool to turn the masses—in the case of democratic states, by the masses in theory yet still by the elites in reality due to the difficulty of direct democracy in modern times—to a certain kind of citizenry matching particular political doctrine adopted by the nation-state at certain time (Heater 2004a). This political function of education to 'convey' certain image of citizenship is not confined to Western countries but shared in modern nation-states including Asian ones (Kennedy and Fairbrother 2004, p. 296).

While education as social entitlement and its role in industrialization are new in modern times, its political function, which is often carried out through citizenship education, is not. By tracing the history of education for citizenship, Heater (2004b) revealed that

> Whether in city-state or nation-state, republic, principality or empire, citizenship has throughout history been a legal and political status accorded by the state to the individual and a bond of loyalty owed by the individual to the state. Citizenship education has accordingly sought to induct the individual into that status and to clinch that bond… [I]n both theory and practice, it has often been thought natural, prudent and necessary for the state to make provision for a form of citizenship education in its own image. (p. 194)

State control on citizenship education in particular, and on school education in general, is typical, if not universal, in Asian contexts. In his elaboration of the leading role of the state in education and the role of education in state formation, Green (1997) focused on the model of 'developmental state', the 'defining characteristic' of which is 'the dynamic, shaping role played by the state leadership and bureaucracy in relation to civil society' and the representatives of which in the second half of twentieth century include Singapore, Taiwan and South Korea in Asia (p. 11). Education in these cases has two distinguishing features: the absolute centrality of government planning in education and the emphasis of moral and social education in national curriculum (Green 1997). If measured by the two features, education in China is no different from its Asian counterparts, given the persistent official planning amply illustrated by the educational plan for the 2010s mentioned at the beginning of this chapter, and the stress of moral education which will be detailed in Chap. 3.

The state-oriented social, economic and political functions of modern education have been questioned by neoliberalism, postmodernism and globalization since the second half of the twentieth century (Green 1997). Although this skeptic view may be, as Green (1997) contended, neither 'universally shared' nor 'the dominant belief' around the world (p. 10), it at least reminds us that state-controlled education is not free of challenge. Indeed, Heater (2004a) observed that 'the state control and manipulation of the educational system was achieved only gradually and against considerable opposition' in modern times (pp. 79–80). Similarly, in her classic study of the social origins of modern state education systems in England, France, Denmark and Russia, Archer (1979) discussed that it was 'the interaction of dominant and assertive groups' that brought about the 'autonomous emergence' of integration of education to the state in each of the four cases; and the integration could also be contributed to by 'external intervention' in forms of 'conquest, colonization or territorial redistribution' in other cases (p. 144). Whether autonomous or intervened, that modern state education system is a result of domestic or/and foreign power contestation suggests that state control on education—and politically on what kind of citizenship to develop—should not be taken for granted but is subject to challenge when power balances change. This dynamic arguably also applies to the case of citizenship education in contemporary China, given the dynamics between state and society in the making of policies including educational ones, and the growing citizenship awareness and practice in society which creates public pedagogical discourses and sites for citizenship learning and practice.

This book sets off from and for education. Understanding that citizenship education carries out political functions under state control yet not without power contestation, it puts forward a particular model of citizenship education and gives suggestions for developing it in the Chinese context based on the empirical evidence from the investigation of the meaning of citizenship in this book. This model balances rights and responsibilities of citizenship, promotes inclusive citizenship so that no one is detained or deprived of rights and responsibilities because of age, class, gender, ethnicity, religion or ability, facilitates active and justice-oriented citizenship participation in social and political affairs, and encourages understanding and practice of citizenship that goes below and beyond nation-state. It is important to acknowledge that this model is only one among many in the contested terrain of citizenship and citizenship education. The primary intention of this book is not to justify this model of citizenship education or counter its criticisms, though the development of key ideas behind this model will be traced in Chap. 2. Nor is it intended to analyze and calculate whether the party-state would adopt and implement the model or not. Rather, drawing upon the meaning of citizenship in society, this book suggests what needs to be done to achieve this model of citizenship education in and beyond schools in contemporary Chinese context. The ideas underpinning this model are primarily derived from citizenship theory and discussion in the West, which it is often depicted to be socially and culturally different and even distinct from China or the East.

Understanding Citizenship: The East–West Approach

The concept of citizenship in Western discourse can be understood in narrow and broad terms. In modern times its narrowest understanding is one shaped on the juridical-legal basis, dedicating formal status, rights, obligations, allegiance and protection of state members under the authority of laws. 'Legal definitions of citizenship', as Janoski (1998) noted, 'seem to short-circuit citizenship because they remain the realm of passive rights and do not extend into active rights of political and social democracy' (p. 239). Thus citizenship in a broader sense is defined by its practice, activeness and agency. Citizenship as political engagement was observed as early as in ancient Greek *polis*, exclusively enjoyed by privileged men at the time. After civil and political citizenship being legally universalized as the product of revolutionary political struggles and the significance of social substance in achieving civil and political citizenship under the market influence rising to the surface in modern times, citizenship began to be theoretically extended to and analyzed in the socioeconomic sphere. Bryan Turner placed social practice at the centre of modern citizenship to highlight the 'dynamic social construction' under 'unequal distribution of resources in society' (1993, pp. 2–3), distinguishing modern citizenship as 'social citizenship' from classical or pre-modern citizenship as 'political citizenship' (2006, p. 150). The universalization of modern citizenship, however, was confined within state boundaries and accompanied with a monolithic image of citizen projecting the dominant culture in the nationalized state. In contemporary context that '[t]he partial break up of previously assumed homogenous national culture has opened questions of cultural inclusion and exclusion' (Stevenson 2001b, p. 3), the concept of citizenship has been further linked to and increasingly pronounced in the cultural sphere. Cultural citizenship, on one hand, explores the cultural factors and resources behind issues of identity, belongingness, membership and public participation. On the other hand the idea of cultural citizenship deconstructs and diversifies modern citizenship in the respects of ethnicity, gender, religion, age and ability beyond and below the nation-state level, in the attempt to turn citizenship into an more inclusive concept for the public recognition and participation of minorities excluded from the modern homogenized national culture (e.g. Stevenson 2001a).

Chap. 2 will elaborate the conceptual evolution of citizenship in the Western context. What the brief outline above makes clear and is important at this point is that citizenship is a fluid, contested and constructed concept as demonstrated by its conceptual evolution and expansion, and that citizenship in contemporary Western discourse is understood and analyzed in multiple spheres, from legal to political, social and cultural.[4] In other words, citizenship is not simply about legal membership of political community according to its narrowest definition, but is in the broadest sense about the political, social and cultural relationship of individual and community—be it local, national or global. Citizenship so understood inevitably bears different meanings to different people in different contexts. In such fluidity and uncertainty, citizenship conceptions help define each other. A necessary and effective way to study and identify citizenship conception in one context is through the lens of citizenship conception in another context.

This book examines the meaning of citizenship in contemporary Chinese society through the analytical lens of three-dimensional Western citizenship based on the conceptual clarifications by Isin and Turner (2002) and Delanty (2000). The three dimensions are the extent dimension about identity, the content dimension about rights and responsibilities, and the depth dimension about participation (Fig. 1.1). Chap. 2 will detail the elements of each dimension by further drawing on English-language citizenship theories and discussions primarily developed in the Western context and addressing Western societies. It is in this sense that I call the analytical lens 'Western'. This approach inescapably falls into the East-West binary, given that China is traditionally counted as part of 'the East' antithetical to 'the West' in either geopolitical or sociocultural sense. Although the adoption of market economy has significantly confused the substance of China as a socialist state, communism, which is the Cold War opposition of the West defined as liberal democracy, is still its official ideology. In social and cultural respects, China—more broadly, East Asia and even Asia—is often posited on the opposition side to the West, such as in the arguments of the collectivist (Hofstede et al. 2010) or relationalist East (Lee 2004) as opposed to the individualist West.

The sociocultural East–West dichotomy is a modern creation. Geographically covering 'from China to Mediterranean', the East, as Said (2003) unveiled, was 'made' (p. 6) by European powers in modern times as 'one of its deepest and most

Fig. 1.1 The three-dimensional Western analytical lens of citizenship

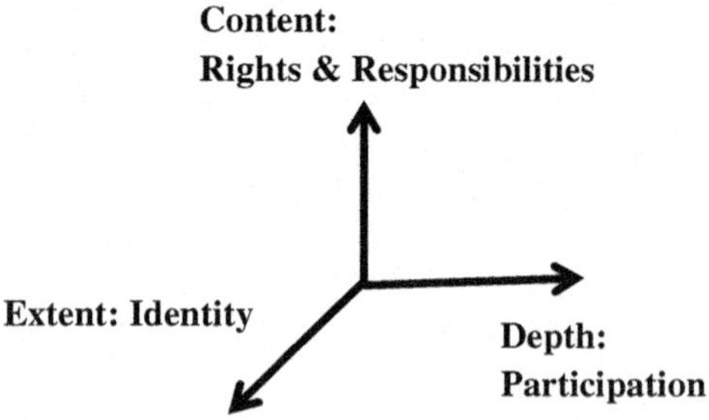

[4]There are also advocates for an environmental sphere in the concept of citizenship which considers the relationship between human beings and the nature. But for the reasons that concern about the nature is not new to human history, though it is indeed unprecedentedly heightened by modern human activities, and that it is less controversial than other spheres, the environmental sphere of citizenship is not discussed and examined in this book.

recurring images of the Other' (p. 1) to define the West 'in a position of strength, not to say domination' (p. 40). Helpfully complementing Said's theory of orientalism by and for the West, Bonnett (2004) argued that the West is not only a Western invention; it is also 'deployed' by non-Western actors to define their own superior images of the Self (p. 11). Examples are spiritual Asia vis-à-vis soulless West in Tagore's and Kakuzo Okakura's work, and hard-working Asia vis-à-vis decadent and indulgent West by contemporary supporters of so-called Asian values (Bonnett 2004). Furthermore, the dichotomous East-West creation often conceals the differences within each category. While both Europe and the United States are often counted as parts of the West—especially during the Cold War (Therborn 2006), 'current societal changes in Europe [at the start of the twenty-first century] cannot be understood in terms of Americanization' (Delanty 2006, p. 4). Likewise, '[t]here is no common tradition in Asia to define the Great Books of the East' (de Bary 1990, p. 42, cited in Therborn 2006, p. 31).

The investigation of Chinese citizenship through the lens of Western citizenship in this book has no intention to perpetuate the constructed and overgeneralized East–West dichotomy, let alone persuade the superiority of East or West. It sees the East–West binary, following Bonnett's (2004) treatment of the idea of the West, as 'a category, an intellectual resource, that helps map out the big picture; that gives coherence and statue to what, otherwise, can appear eclectic and tendentious opinion' (p. 6). This book contributes to the 'big picture' of the concept of citizenship with an East–West communication.

Understanding Chinese Citizenship: Two Gaps

Since the late twentieth-century citizenship studies have become 'a de facto field in the humanities and social sciences' (Isin and Turner 2002, p. 1), with 'exponential growth in scholarship on citizenship education both within and across nations' (Arthur et al. 2008, p. 5). As part of these global tendencies, there have also been increased studies on Chinese citizenship and citizenship education in recent decades. Our understanding of citizenship in the case of China substantially benefits from three clusters of research in scholarly English literature.

The first cluster includes studies with a conscious and explicit focus on Chinese conception of citizenship, some tracing its historical and cultural roots (Perry 2008, 2009; Wong 1999) and unraveling its modern formation (Culp 2007a, b; Fogel and Zarrow 1997; Guo and Guo 2015; Harris 2002; Harrison 2000; Mitter 2011), while others recording its contemporary construct (Keane 2001; Li and Wu 1999) and examining its legislative evolution (Ni et al. 2010). A seminal contribution in this cluster is Goldman and Perry's (2002) edited volume *Changing Meaning of Citizenship in Modern China*, which extensively touches all the aspects above. Literature in this cluster provides philosophical, historical, social, cultural and legislative accounts on the conceptual construct of citizenship in China.

Offering insights of citizenship in the party-state perspective, the second cluster is research on a variety of public policies in relation to citizenship. There is a growing body of research on the intentions, policies, curricula, textbooks and pedagogies of citizenship-related education (e.g. Chen and Reid 2002; Fairbrother 2004; Feng 2006; Kennedy et al. 2014; Law 2006, 2011; Lee 1996, 2001; Lee and Ho 2008; Li 2011; Li et al. 2004; Mitter 2012; Rose 2015; Tse 2011; Tse and Lee 2003; Zhan and Ning 2004; Zhao and Fairbrother 2010; Zhong and Lee 2008; Zhu and Feng 2008). A much larger body of literature in a more general context of political, social and cultural citizenship policies and on state-society relation also contributes to our understanding of the party-state's stance on citizenship (e.g. Chen 2014; Diamond and Myers 2001; Gries and Rosen 2010; Liu 2007; O'Brien 1990; Perry and Goldman 2007a; Whyte 2010).

The third cluster of research provides empirical evidence of citizenship in society. It involves an increased number of empirical studies recording public political opinions (e.g. Liu 1996; Tang 2005) and citizenship-related awareness, practice, predicaments and struggles in society (e.g. Fong and Murphy 2006; Goldman 2005; Guo and Guo 2015; Ho and Edmonds 2008; Perry and Selden 2010). Particular concerns have been paid to migrant workers and their children (Kwong 2011; Lee 2007; Li 2015; Ngok 2012; Solinger 1999), villagers (Li 2010; O'Brien and Li 2006), young people (Chan 2000; Chen 2011; Fairbrother 2003; Fong 2004; He 2015; Law and Ng 2009; Li 2009; Pan 2011; Tu 2011), and ethnic minorities (Shih 2002; Zhao 2010). The three clusters are nicely cut across by the collective effort of the recent special journal issue edited by Guo and Xia (2016), which highlights the relevance of traditional values in the state-constructed citizenship, the appeal to Confucian culture in citizenship-related class, and the interaction between citizenship institution and practice about peasant workers.

Among the existing literature on Chinese citizenship, there is, however, little empirical research directly and systematically inquiring into the meaning of citizenship or *gongmin* in contemporary Chinese society. While the historical and official respects of Chinese conception of citizenship, including those of the term *gongmin*, have been studied, what *gongmin* means in contemporary society is little explored and, consequently, it remains unanswered as to whether, and if so in what way, the social meaning of *gongmin* follows or deviates from the meaning of the term in historical and official perspectives.[5] Of equal importance is that, although citizenship awareness and practice in contemporary Chinese society has been empirically and increasingly studied, the literature leaves unexplored the extent to which the Chinese term *gongmin* used and understood in Chinese society embraces or, using Williams's (1990, p. 15) word, 'bind[s]' elements and concepts often drawn from Western citizenship conception and taken for granted in the study of the Chinese case. In short, there are two research gaps in the literature on Chinese citizenship: the lack of research on a systemic comparison of the meaning of the Chinese term *gongmin* with Western citizenship conception; and the lack of empirical research on the meaning of *gongmin* in contemporary society in comparison with that in historical and official perspectives. This book helps to close the two research gaps.

[5]In this book the phrase of 'social meaning of *gongmin*' is used as an alternative expression of meaning of *gongmin* or citizenship in society, bearing no implication of social citizenship as a counterpart to political or cultural citizenship.

Research Framework and Data

Citizenship, as shown above, is a constructed and context-sensitive concept. Perceived in the same vein in this book, the Chinese term *gongmin* could mean different things to different people. Language, following Fairclough (2001), is a form of social practice produced and interpreted in close relation to a power struggle in society. The complication of language and power exists at both individual and collective levels. The meaning of *gongmin* in society at the collective level can be seen as the public opinion on the term. Blumer (1948) reminded us that, 'in the process of forming public opinion, individuals are not alike in influence nor are groups that are equal numerically in membership alike in influence'; on the contrary, 'differences in prestige, position, and influence that characterize groups and individuals in the functional organizations of a society are brought into play in the formation of public opinion' (p. 545). In other words, putting the state factor aside, there is power imbalance between social sectors and actors in the formation of the collective meaning, and power struggle in the individual production and interpretation of the meaning, of *gongmin* in society. It is beyond the scope of this book, indeed nearly impossible, to undertake a comprehensive examination across the whole Chinese society. Rather, bearing the complication of language and power in mind, the book spotlights social sectors and actors of distinct and distant social position and power to examine the meaning of *gongmin* at both individual and collective levels as an attempt to explore the variation of the meaning. It is a study not for generalization but for variation.

Taking into account the state factor and placing the focus on society, this book looks into the meaning of *gongmin* at two social levels, the collective or macro level and the individual or micro level, which are investigated, respectively, by two sub-studies conducted in Guangdong Province (Fig. 1.2). Considering newspapers as a window onto the public opinion in society, Study I analyzed and compared 2257 articles and 2744 articles containing the term *gongmin*, respectively, from an influential nonofficial newspaper and from the CCP's mouthpiece newspaper in the

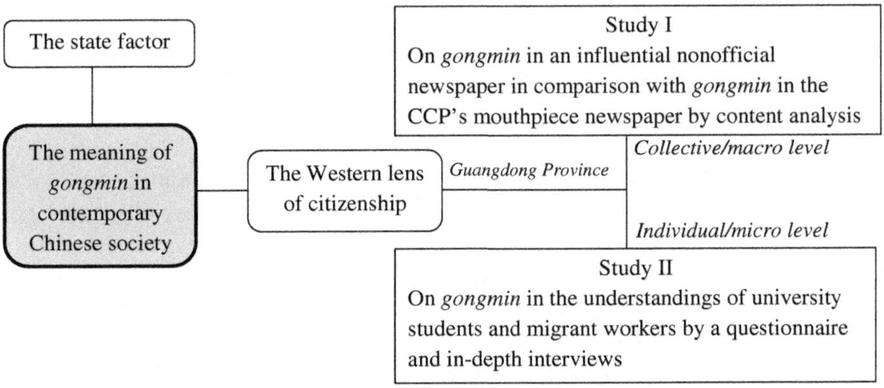

Fig. 1.2 The research framework

period between October 2007 and August 2010, to uncover the meaning of the term at the collective/macro social level with reference to the state discourse. Study II investigated the understandings of the term *gongmin* by migrant workers and university students through a questionnaire survey (294 student and 226 worker respondents) and in-depth interviews (11 student and 11 worker interviewees) conducted in 2012 to disclose the meaning of *gongmin* at the individual/micro social level. Details of the data collection and analysis of the two sub-studies are in the Appendix of the book.

Key Findings and Implications

This study found that there is a discrepancy in the meaning of *gongmin* between state and collective social discourses, the former more likely to express the term in relation to responsibilities and participation while the latter more likely to refer to *gongmin* in terms of rights. Nor is the meaning of *gongmin* in the same mould in society. In the content dimension about rights and responsibilities, similar with the meaning at the collective social level, rights outweigh responsibilities in university students' understanding of *gongmin*, while the two aspects are relatively balanced in the view of migrant workers. Notwithstanding, the two social groups do share the concern about personal interest when considering *gongmin*'s responsibilities. In the depth dimension about participation, while the participatory connotation is weak in the collective social meaning, political participation by *gongmin* enjoys not only a higher expectation but also a deeper understanding—in the sense of taking actions not within but beyond existing rules and for the sake of not just us but others—from students than from workers. There are also similarities and differences between the two social groups regarding the extent dimension about identity in the meaning of *gongmin*. The most salient similarities are their overwhelming approvals of 'Chinese *gongmin*' as legal identity and *gongmin* as collective social identity, and their strong acceptance of the identity of *gongmin* at national and global levels. The main distinctions are that 'Chinese *gongmin*' defined in terms of ethnicity and culture is likely to be embraced by workers but opposed by students, and that students also perceive *gongmin* as an independent identity and as a dual, simultaneously active and subordinate, entity vis-à-vis the state, while for workers *gongmin* is largely a collective social identity and a subordinate identity in the face of the state.

The empirical findings bear implications for citizenship in Chinese society. Notably, university students' and migrant workers' shared cognition of *gongmin* as legal identity shows their potential to jointly advance citizenship discourse and practice based on the recognized legal identity. This potential, however, faces some obstacles. Their understandings of *gongmin*'s rights and responsibilities seem to be constrained by their socioeconomic and sociopolitical resources and experiences; and the gap between their understandings of *gongmin*-state relation and *gongmin*'s political participation could hinder *gongmin* to serve as a shared identity for their joint political participation in contemporary times.

There are also implications for Chinese state-society relation, East–West citizenship, and Chinese citizenship education. First, the discrepancy between the collective social and state discourses empirically reveals that the meaning in contemporary Chinese society is not in full convergence with the party-state's stance. This supports the observation that the Chinese state-society relation has been dynamized. More specifically, while the party-state is unlikely to face immediate pressure from university students and migrant workers for political rights in the name of *gongmin*, not only could there be social forces to claim them through the term given the salient connection between *gongmin* and political rights at the collective social level, but students would be easier than workers to join those social forces via the vehicle of the term *gongmin* in challenging the party-state's stance on citizenship political participation. Also, the clear *gongmin*-rights connections at both social levels, and the concern about personal interest in students' and workers' understanding of *gongmin*'s responsibilities, suggest that the party-state's recent strategy to indoctrinate clichéd socialist virtues with the help of the term *gongmin* would hardly work if those virtues override citizens' rights and personal interest. Second and for East–West citizenship, the legal element in the term *gongmin* found to be fully recognized in society can function as a starting point for dialogue between citizenship debates in Western democracies and discussions of *gongmin* in China. The findings also make clear that neither liberal citizenship nor civic republican citizenship—two Western citizenship traditions—alone is adequate to fully represent the meaning of *gongmin* in contemporary Chinese society, which is yet to clearly reflect, but does have etymological legacies to develop, ideas such as multi-layered and justice-oriented citizenship emerged from contemporary conceptual reconfiguration of citizenship in the West. Third, drawing upon the empirical evidence, the book provides eight suggestions for Chinese citizenship education to develop inclusive, active and justice-oriented citizenship going below and beyond the nation-state.

Organization of the Book

The following chapters are divided into two parts. Containing two chapters, Part I constructs the Western lens for the examination of the meaning of *gongmin*, and gives a detailed account of the state factor in the meaning of *gongmin* in contemporary China. Specifically, Chap. 2 concentrates on the concept of citizenship in the West, sorting out its historical roots, modern formation and contemporary reconfiguration. It concludes with an explanation on the importance of Western citizenship as an analytical lens in the study of Chinese citizenship. Shifting the context from the West to China, Chap. 3 explains the Chinese terminology of citizen and the official use of *gongmin*, discusses the official stance on citizenship through a review of relevant policies including school citizenship-related education, and at last highlights and illustrates the contemporary state-society dynamics.

With the state factor in the background, Part II unveils the meaning of *gongmin* in contemporary Chinese society through the constructed Western lens. Chapter 4 concentrates on *gongmin* as identity in society, elaborating the conditions for the identity of 'Chinese *gongmin*', the identity of *gongmin* vis-à-vis state and society, and the capacity of *gongmin* as multileveled identity. Chapter 5 turns to the content dimension, examining the rights and responsibilities attached to the social meaning of *gongmin*. Chapter 6 details the meaning of *gongmin* in the dimension about participation, assessing its connections with civic and political participation in Chinese society. The social implications of the meaning of *gongmin* in the three dimensions are also addressed in the above three chapters respectively. Chapter 7 amalgamates the theoretical (Chaps. 2 and 3) and the empirical (Chaps. 4, 5 and 6) chapters, situating the social meaning into the three wider research areas of Chinese citizenship, East–West citizenship, and Chinese citizenship education. Chapter 8 as the concluding chapter compensates for the limits of this empirical study with a consideration of the prospect of changes to the found meaning, and suggests necessary future work for further understanding the term *gongmin* in contemporary Chinese society.

References

Archer, M. S. (1979). *Social origins of educational systems*. London: Sage.

Arthur, J., Davies, I., & Hahn, C. (2008). Introduction to the Sage handbook of education for citizenship and democracy. In J. Arthur, I. Davies, & C. Hahn (Eds.), *The Sage handbook of education for citizenship and democracy* (pp. 1–10). London: Sage.

Bendix, R. (1977). *Nation-building and citizenship*. California: University of California Press.

Blumer, H. (1948). Public opinion and public opinion polling. *American Sociological Review, 13* (5), 542–549.

Bonnett, A. (2004). *The idea of the West: Culture, politics and history*. New York: Palgrave Macmillan.

Chan, C. (2000). The political pragmatism of Chinese university students at the dawn of the twenty-first century. In S. Zhao (Ed.), *China and democracy: Reconsidering the prospects for a democratic China* (pp. 207–232). New York: Routledge.

Chen, S. (2011). Developing global citizenship: The effect of studying abroad. *International Journal of Development Education and Global Learning, 3*(3), 45–64.

Chen, X. (2014). *Social protests and contentious authoritarianism in China*. New York: Cambridge University Press.

Chen, Y., & Reid, I. (2002). Citizenship education in Chinese schools: Retrospect and prospect. *Research in Education,* (67), 58–69.

Culp, R. (2007a). *Articulating citizenship: Civic education and student politics in Southeastern China, 1912–1940*. Cambridge, MA: Harvard University Asia Center.

Culp, R. (2007b). Synthesizing citizenship in modern China. *History Compass, 5*(6), 1833–1861. doi:10.1111/j.1478-0542.2007.00478.x.

Delanty, G. (2000). *Citizenship in a global age: Culture, society and politics*. Buckingham: Open University Press.

Delanty, G. (2006). Introduction: The idea of a post-Western Europe. In G. Delanty (Ed.), *Europe and Asia beyond East and West* (pp. 1–7). Oxon: Routledge.

Diamond, L., & Myers, R. H. (Eds.). (2001). *Elections and democracy in greater China*. New York: Oxford University Press.

Fairbrother, G. P. (2003). The effects of political education and critical thinking on Hong Kong and Mainland Chinese university students' national attitudes. *British Journal of Sociology of Education, 24*(5), 605–620. doi:10.1080/0142569032000127161.

Fairbrother, G. P. (2004). Patriotic education in a Chinese middle school. In W. O. Lee, D. L. Grossman, K. J. Kennedy, & G. P. Fairbrother (Eds.), *Citizenship education in Asia and the Pacific: Concepts and issues* (pp. 157–174). Hong Kong: Comparative Education Research Centre, The University of Hong Kong.

Fairbrother, G. P. (2014). The Chinese paternalistic state and moral education. In K. J. Kennedy, G. P. Fairbrother, & Z. Zhao (Eds.), *Citizenship education in China: Preparing citizens for the "Chinese century"* (pp. 11–26). New York: Routledge.

Fairclough, N. (2001). *Language and power* (2nd ed.). Essex: Longman.

Feng, A. (2006). Contested notions of citizenship and citizenship education: The Chinese case. In G. Alred, M. Byram, & M. Fleming (Eds.), *Education for intercultural citizenship: Concepts and comparisons* (pp. 86–105). Clevedon, England: Multilingual Matters.

Fogel, J. A., & Zarrow, P. G. (Eds.). (1997). *Imagining the people: Chinese intellectuals and the concept of citizenship, 1890–1920*. New York: M. E. Sharpe.

Fong, V. (2004). Filial nationalism among Chinese teenagers with global identities. *American Ethnologist, 31*(4), 631–648.

Fong, V., & Murphy, R. (Eds.). (2006). *Chinese citizenship: Views from the margins*. Oxon: Routledge.

Gellner, E. (2008). *Nation and nationalism* (2nd ed.). New York: Cornell University Press.

Goldman, M. (2005). *From comrade to citizen: The struggle of political rights in China*. Cambridge, MA: Harvard University Press.

Goldman, M., & Perry, E. J. (Eds.). (2002). *Changing meanings of citizenship in modern China*. Cambridge, MA: Harvard University Press.

Green, A. (1997). Education and state formation in Europe and Asia. In K. J. Kennedy (Ed.), *Citizenship education and the modern state* (pp. 9–26). London: Falmer Press.

Gries, P. H., & Rosen, S. (Eds.). (2010). *Chinese politics: State, society and the market*. Oxon: Routledge.

Guo, Z., & Guo, S. (Eds.). (2015). *Theorizing Chinese citizenship*. Lanham, MD: Lexington Books.

Guo, Z., & Xia, Y. (2016). Introduction. *Journal of Chinese Political Science, 21*(4), 413–415. doi:10.1007/s11366-016-9434-y.

Harris, P. (2002). The origins of modern citizenship in China. *Asia Pacific Viewpoint, 43*(2), 181–203.

Harrison, H. (2000). *The making of the Republican citizens: Political ceremonies and symbols in China 1911–1929*. New York: Oxford University Press.

He, R. (2015). Identifying with a "rising China"? Overseas Chinese student nationalism. In E. Vickers & K. Kumar (Eds.), *Constructing modern Asian citizenship* (pp. 314–340). Oxon: Routledge.

Heater, D. (2004a). *Citizenship: The civic ideal in world history, politics and education* (3rd ed.). Manchester: Manchester University Press.

Heater, D. (2004b). *A history of education for citizenship*. Oxon: Routledge.

Ho, P., & Edmonds, R. L. (Eds.). (2008). *China's embedded activism: Opportunities and constraints of a social movement*. Oxon: Routledge.

Hobsbawm, E. J. (1992). *Nations and nationalism since 1780* (2nd ed.). Cambridge: Cambridge University Press.

Hofstede, G., Hofstede, G. J., & Minkov, M. (2010). *Cultures and organizations: Software of the mind: Intercultural cooperation and its importance for survival* (3rd ed.). New York: McGraw-Hill.

Hu, J. (2007). Report to the Seventeenth National Congress of the Communist Party of China (in Chinese). http://cpc.people.com.cn/GB/64162/64168/106155/106156/6430009.html. Accessed November 26, 2016.

Isin, E. F., & Turner, B. S. (2002). Citizenship studies: An introduction. In E. F. Isin & B. S. Turner (Eds.), *Handbook of citizenship studies* (pp. 1–10). London: Sage.

Janoski, T. (1998). *Citizenship and civil society: A framework of rights and obligations in liberal, tranditional, and social democratic regimes*. Cambridge: Cambridge University Press.

Keane, M. (2001). Redefining Chinese citizenship. *Economy and Society, 30*(1), 1–17. doi:10.1080/03085140020019061.

Kennedy, K. J. (2004). Searching for citizenship values in an uncertain global environment. In W. O. Lee, D. L. Grossman, K. J. Kennedy, & G. P. Fairbrother (Eds.), *Citizenship education in Asia and the Pacific: Concepts and issues* (pp. 9–24). Hong Kong: Comparative Education Research Centre, The University of Hong Kong.

Kennedy, K. J., & Fairbrother, G. P. (2004). Asian perspectives on citizenship education in review: Postcolonial constructions or precolonial values? In W. O. Lee, D. L. Grossman, K. J. Kennedy, & G. P. Fairbrother (Eds.), *Citizenship education in Asia and the Pacific: Concepts and issues* (pp. 289–301). Hong Kong: Comparative Education Research Centre, The University of Hong Kong.

Kennedy, K. J., Fairbrother, G. P., & Zhao, Z. (Eds.). (2014). *Citizenship education in China: Preparing citizens for the "Chinese century"*. New York: Routledge.

Kwong, J. (2011). Education and identity: The marginalisation of migrant youths in Beijing. *Journal of Youth Studies, 14*(8), 871–883. doi:10.1080/13676261.2011.607435.

Law, W. W. (2006). Citizenship, citizenship education, and the state in China in a global age. *Cambridge journal of education, 36*(4), 597–628. doi:10.1080/03057640601049322.

Law, W. W. (2011). *Citizenship and citizenship education in a global age: Politics, policies, and practices in China*. New York: Peter Lang Publishing.

Law, W. W., & Ng, H. M. (2009). Globalization and multileveled citizenship education: A tale of two Chinese cities, Hong Kong and Shanghai. *Teachers College Record, 111*(4), 851–892.

Lee, C. K. (2007). *Against the law: Labour protests in China's rustbelt and sunbelt*. Berkeley: University of California Press.

Lee, W. O. (1996). Changing ideopolitical emphases in moral education in China: An analysis of the CCP Central Committee documents. *Asia Pacific Journal of Education, 16*(1), 106–121. doi:10.1080/0218879960854261 4.

Lee, W. O. (2001). Moral education policy in China: The struggle between liberal and traditional approaches. In M. Bray & W. O. Lee (Eds.), *Education and political transition: Themes and experiences in East Asia* (2nd ed., pp. 201–219). Hong Kong: Comparative Education Research Centre, The University of Hong Kong.

Lee, W. O. (2004). Emerging concepts of citizenship in the Asian context. In W. O. Lee, D. L. Grossman, K. J. Kennedy, & G. P. Fairbrother (Eds.), *Citizenship education in Asia and the Pacific: Concepts and issues* (pp. 25–35). Hong Kong: Comparative Education Research Centre, University of Hong Kong.

Lee, W. O., & Ho, C. H. (2008). Citizenship education in China: Changing concepts, approaches and policies in the changing political, economic and social context. In J. Arthur, I. Davies, & C. Hahn (Eds.), *The SAGE handbook of education for citizenship and democracy* (pp. 139–157). London: Sage.

Li, B., & Wu, Y. (1999). The conception of citizenship in People's Republic of China. In A. Davidson & K. Keekly (Eds.), *Globalization and citizenship in the Asia-Pacific* (pp. 157–168). Hampshire: Macmillan Press.

Li, J. (2009). Fostering citizenship in China's move from elite to mass higher education: An analysis of students' political socialization and civic participation. *International Journal of Educational Development, 29*(4), 382–398. doi:10.1016/j.ijedudev.2008.10.001.

Li, L. (2010). Rights consciousness and rule consciousness in contemporary China. *The China Journal, 64*, 47–68.

Li, M. (2011). Changing ideological-political orientations in Chinese moral education: Some personal and professional reflections. *Journal of Moral Education, 40*(3), 387–395. doi:10.1080/03057240.2011.596342.

Li, M. (2015). *Citizenship education and migrant youth in China*. New York: Routledge.

Li, P., Zhong, M., Lin, B., & Zhang, H. (2004). Deyu as moral education in modern China: Ideological functions and transformations. *Journal of Moral Education, 33*(4), 449–464. doi:10.1080/0305724042000315581.

Liu, A. P. L. (1996). *Mass politics in the People's Republic: State and society in contemporary China*. Colorado: Westview Press.

Liu, S. (2007). Social citizenship in China: Continuity and change. *Citizenship Studies, 11*(5), 465–479. doi:10.1080/13621020701605776.

Luo, T. (2014). *Village economic autonomy and authoritarian control over village elections in China: Evidence from rural Guangdong Province*. Ph.D. thesis, The London School of Economics and Political Science, London.

Mertha, A. (2010). Society in the state: China's nondemocratic political pluralization. In P. H. Gries & S. Rosen (Eds.), *Chinese politics: State, society and the market* (pp. 69–84). Oxon: Routledge.

Mitter, R. (2011). Classifying citizens in nationalist China during World War II, 1937–1941. *Modern Asian Studies, 45*(2), 243–275. doi:10.1017/S0026749X1100014X.

Mitter, R. (2012). Educating citizens through war museums in modern China. In V. Benei (Ed.), *Manufacturing citizenship: Education and nationalism in Europe, South Asia and China* (pp. 129–142). Oxon: Routledge.

Ngok, K. (2012). Migrant labour, urban exclusion and social harmony in China. *Journal of Poverty and Social Justice, 20*(3), 247–260. doi:10.1332/175982712x657073.

Ni, S., Cheng, L., & Sin, K. K. (2010). Who are Chinese citizens? A legislative language inquiry. *International Journal for the Semiotics of Law - Revue internationale de Sémiotique juridique, 23*(4), 475–494. doi:10.1007/s11196-010-9167-8.

O'Brien, K. J. (1990). *Reform without liberalization: China's National People's Congress and the politics of institutional change*. New York: Cambridge University Press.

O'Brien, K. J., & Li, L. (2006). *Rightful resistance in rural China*. New York: Cambridge University Press.

Pan, S. (2011). Multileveled citizenship and citizenship education: Experiences of students in China's Beijing. *Citizenship Studies, 15*(2), 283–306. doi:10.1080/13621025.2011.549730.

Perry, E. J. (2008). Chinese conceptions of "rights": From Mencius to Mao—and now. *Perspectives on Politics, 6*(1). doi:10.1017/s1537592708080055.

Perry, E. J. (2009). A new rights consciousness? *Journal of Democracy, 20*(3), 17–20.

Perry, E. J., & Goldman, M. (Eds.). (2007a). *Grassroots political reform in contemporary China*. Cambridge, MA: Harvard University Press.

Perry, E. J., & Goldman, M. (2007b). Introduction: Historical reflections on grassroots political reform in China. In E. J. Perry & M. Goldman (Eds.), *Grassroots political reform in contemporary China* (pp. 1–19). Cambridge, MA: Harvard University Press.

Perry, E. J., & Selden, M. (Eds.). (2010). *Chinese society: Change, conflict and resistance* (3rd ed.). London: Routledge.

PRC State Council. (2010). Outline of China's national plan for medium- and long-term education reform and development 2010–2020. http://www.gov.cn/jrzg/2010-07/29/content_1667143.htm (in Chinese) and http://planipolis.iiep.unesco.org/upload/China/China_National_Long_Term_Educational_Reform_Development_2010-2020_eng.pdf (in English).

Rose, C. (2015). Going global? National versus post-national citizenship education in contemporary Chinese and Japanese social studies curricula. In E. Vickers & K. Kumar (Eds.), *Constructing modern Asian citizenship* (pp. 83–104). Oxon: Routledge.

Rosen, S. (2004). The state of youth/youth and the state in early 21st-century China: The triumph of the urban rich? In P. H. Gries & S. Rosen (Eds.), *State and society in 21st-century China: Crisis, contention, and legitimation* (pp. 159–179). New York: Routledge Curzon.

Said, E. W. (2003). *Orientalism*. London: Penguin.

Sandlin, J. A., O'Malley, M. P., & Burdick, J. (2011). Mapping the complexity of public pedagogy scholarship. *Review of Educational Research, 81*(3), 338–375. doi:10.3102/0034654311413395.

Sandlin, J. A., Schultz, B. D., & Burdick, J. (2010). Understanding, mapping, and exploring the terrain of public pedagogy. In J. A. Sandlin, B. D. Schultz, & J. Burdick (Eds.), *Handbook of public pedagogy: Education and learning beyond schooling* (pp. 1–6). New York: Routledge.

Shih, C. (2002). *Negotiating ethnicity in China: Citizenship as a response to the state*. London: Routledge.

Shirk, S. L. (1993). *The political logic of economic reform in China*. Berkerley: University of California Press.

Simmons, A. J. (2001). *Justification and legitimacy: Essays on rights and obligations*. Cambridge: Cambridge University Press.

Solinger, D. J. (1999). *Contesting citizenship in urban China: Peasant migrants, the state, and the logic of the market*. California: University of California Press.
Stevenson, N. (Ed.). (2001a). *Culture and citizenship*. London: Sage.
Stevenson, N. (2001b). Culture and citizenship: An introduction. In N. Stevenson (Ed.), *Culture and citizenship* (pp. 1–10). London: Sage.
Tang, W. (2005). *Public opinion and political change in China*. California: Stanford University Press.
Teets, J. C., Rosen, S., & Gries, P. H. (2010). Introduction: Political change, contestation, and pluralization in China today. In P. H. Gries & S. Rosen (Eds.), *Chinese politics: State, society and the market* (pp. 1–21). Oxon: Routledge.
Therborn, G. (2006). Post-Western Europe and the plural Asias. In G. Delanty (Ed.), *Europe and Asia beyond East and West* (pp. 24–44). Oxon: Routledge.
Tse, T. K.-C. (2011). Creating good citizens in China: comparing Grade 7–9 school textbooks, 1997–2005. *Journal of Moral Education, 40*(2), 161–180. doi:10.1080/03057240.2011.568098.
Tse, T. K.-C., & Lee, J. C.-K. (2003). China: Defending socialism with Chinese characteristics. In M. Williams & G. Humphrys (Eds.), *Citizenship education and lifelong learning: Power and place* (pp. 103–117). New York: Nova Science Publishers.
Tu, Y. (2011). Citizenship with Chinese characteristics? An investigation into Chinese university students' civic perceptions and civic participation. *Frontiers of Education in China, 6*(3), 426–448. doi:10.1007/s11516-011-0140-4.
Turner, B. S. (1993). Contemporary problems in the theory of citizenship. In B. S. Turner (Ed.), *Citizenship and social policy* (pp. 1–18). London: Sage.
Turner, B. S. (2006). Citizenship East and West: Reflections on revolutions and civil society. In G. Delanty (Ed.), *Europe and Aisa beyond East and West* (pp. 148–160). Oxon: Routledge.
Wan, M. (2004). Ethnic diversity and citizenship education in the People's Republic of China. In J. A. Banks (Ed.), *Diversity and citizenship education: Global perspective* (pp. 355–374). San Francisco: Jossey-Bass.
Whyte, M. K. (Ed.). (2010). *One country, two societies: Rural-urban inequality in contemporary China*. Cambridge, MA: Harvard University Press.
Williams, R. (1990). *Keywords: A vocabulary of culture and society*. London: Fontana Press.
Wong, R. B. (1999). Citizenship in Chinese history. In M. Hanagan & C. Tilly (Eds.), *Extending citizenship, reconfiguring states*. Rowman and Littlefield: Lanham, MD.
Wright, T. (2010). *Accepting authoritarianism: State-society relations in China's reform era*. California: Stanford University Press.
Zhan, W., & Ning, W. (2004). The moral education curriculum for junior high schools in 21st century China. *Journal of Moral Education, 33*(4), 511–532. doi:10.1080/0305724042000327993.
Zhao, Z. (2010). *China's Mongols at university: Contesting cultural recognition*. Lanham, MD: Lexington Press.
Zhao, Z., & Fairbrother, G. P. (2010). Pedagogies of cultural integration in Chinese citizenship education. In K. J. kennedy, W. O. Lee, & D. L. Grossman (Eds.), *Citizenship pedagogies in Asia and the Pacific* (pp. 37–52). Hong Kong: Comparative Education Research Centre, The University of Hong Kong.
Zheng, Y. (2010). *The Chinese Communist Party as organizational emperor: Culture, reproduction and transformation*. New York: Routledge.
Zhong, M., & Lee, W. O. (2008). Citizenship curriculum in China: A shifting discourse towards Chinese democracy, law education and psychological health. In D. L. Grossman, W. O. Lee, & K. J. Kennedy (Eds.), *Citizenship curriculum in Asia and the Pacific* (pp. 61–73). Hong Kong: Comparative Education Research Centre, The University of Hong Kong.
Zhu, X., & Feng, X. (2008). On the development of citizenship education outlook in China. *Frontiers of Education in China, 3*(1), 1–21. doi:10.1007/s11516-008-0001-y.

Part I
The Western Lens and the State Factor

Chapter 2
Evolving Citizenship Conception in the West

The purpose of this chapter is to trace the evolution of the concept of citizenship in the West and, by doing so, construct the dimensions and elements of the Western analytical lens to be used in the examination of the meaning of citizenship in contemporary Chinese society later in this book. The construction is based on English-language scholarly literature on citizenship in the Western context. Labelling the lens as 'Western' entails no implication of any indispensible particularity of Western citizenship against citizenship conceptions in other contexts. The concept of citizenship in the West is far from univocal and unanimous, whether historically or contemporarily. Its complex and often contested variations are, however, not the focus of this chapter, though some will be taken into account. This chapter is to trace the conceptual evolution of Western citizenship, marking and explaining where it is from, in what shape it has been, and in what direction it is now changing. In so doing, it unpacks the components of Western citizenship at the vantage point of early twenty-first century. Specifically, the first three sections will deliberate, respectively, its historical roots, modern formation and contemporary reconfiguration, with a particular focus on the societal conditions behind. The last section will connect the analytical lens to the study of this book, explaining the importance of the Western perspective in understanding the concept of citizenship in general and Chinese citizenship in particular.

Pre-modern Citizenship

The idea of citizenship in Western thought is widely accepted to have its historical roots as long ago as in ancient Greek and Roman times. Ancient Greeks handed down citizenship as active political participation in the name of civic virtue while later Romans offered citizenship as legal status with entitlements (Walzer 1989).

Against the background of citizenship practice in ancient Greek city-state or the *polis*, Aristotle defined citizen as a member of the political community who rules

S. Chen, *The Meaning of Citizenship in Contemporary Chinese Society*,
Governance and Citizenship in Asia, https://doi.org/10.1007/978-981-10-6323-7_2

and is ruled by others, actively and collectively participating in the political community to make and obey decisions with mutual respect (Pocock 1995). At the heart of Aristotelian citizenship is the 'basic moral calibre' to 'common weal' through active political participation (Heater 1999, p. 45). As a result of such conception practiced in Greek city-state and theorized by Aristotle, citizenship replaced biological relations to be the social bond; and collective participation in political deliberation for community was desired beyond personal material goods (Shafir 1998). Shafir (1998) called these 'a double process of emancipation': 'the liberation of a portion of humanity from tribal loyalties and its fusion into a voluntary civic community' and 'the transcendence of the instrumental sphere of necessity…into the sphere of freedom' (p. 3).

What should be noted is that both in theory and in reality, not all but only a few in the city-state were able to practice in the political community the freedom of ruling and being ruled in the name of citizen. In Aristotle's normative account citizenship was reversed for those in the categories of 'a male of known genealogy, a patriarch, a warrior, and the master of the labour of others (normally slaves)' (Pocock 1995, p. 31). In other words, citizen was 'a leisured, propertied elite', freed from the private sphere looked after by women and slaves and accordingly able to 'study or participate fully in public affairs' (Heater 1999, p. 46).

Citizenship defined in ethical and active terms—which is the source of what is now called the civic republican tradition of citizenship (Heater 1999)—had a close link to the societal conditions of the *polis* wherein it was practiced. Featuring small-scale population and intimate social connections between citizens, or in Walzer's (1989, p. 213) words, 'the minimal range of social differentiation', ancient Greek city-state was 'not merely a collection of individuals' but 'an organic society' in which citizens as members engaged with each other in public affairs for 'the mutual benefit of the individual and the community' (Heater 1999, pp. 44, 55).

Citizenship conception altered as societal conditions changed. The extension of citizenship to defeated subjects in the expanded Roman Empire resulted in 'a large and heterogeneous population' (Walzer 1989, p. 215), which in turn contributed to the emergence of the other tradition than the civic republican one in Western thought of citizenship. Without the unity and trust between homogeneous citizens as in ancient republican times, the moral commitment to and active involvement in community were gradually replaced by loyalty to legal institutions, which protected citizens in communities of strangers across the Empire by rights under a common law. In such circumstances, citizen of the Roman Empire was perceived less as active participant in public affairs but more as 'passive recipient of specific rights and entitlements' under the protection of law; and citizenship became 'a legal status rather than a fact of everyday life' (Walzer 1989, p. 215).

The break from active political participation, however, did not strip Roman citizenship of the political nature of citizenship apparent in the Greek one. Rather, as Pocock (1995) explained, it is the meaning of political that was altered by Roman citizenship through the notion of law. Unlike Greek citizen who ruled and was ruled by others, Roman citizen did not have access to the making of imperial law applying to and governing them. Yet by appealing to the law that conferred rights on him, Roman citizen in effect involved in 'the process of adjudication, and litigants, witnesses, compurgators, pleaders and so forth' that functionalized and effectively determined the law (Pocock 1995, p. 39). In this sense, Roman citizenship maintained the nature of being a political institution for deliberation and negotiation as of Greek citizenship. Also resembling Greek citizenship, Roman citizenship remained a privilege enjoyed by adult men and off limits to women and slaves.

Citizenship as a legal status at the state level 'was then eclipsed in the West by the various feudal and religious statuses of the medieval Christian world' (Smith 2002, p. 106). Yet *qua* members of various voluntarily-formed and self-governing guilds, citizens in medieval cities still enjoyed certain rights of self-governance and exercised active involvement in the public affairs of the guild (Isin 2002a). In the same time medieval citizenship showed some unprecedented features. As various guilds—seen by Isin (2002a) as 'the most important technology of citizenship in the struggle of various groups for dominance in the city' (p. 128)—competed for rights in medieval cities, citizenship rights became claims to be won through active contestation and struggles, as opposed to rights as passive entitlement like in the Roman Empire. This development arguably helped pave the way for the establishment of democracy and the universalization of citizenship rights in the late eighteenth century marked by the French Revolution.

Modern Citizenship

The concept of citizenship underwent its modern transformation into what is now called liberal citizenship, which, viewed from the contemporary vantage point, is not only one of the two traditions of citizenship (the other one is civic republican citizenship) influencing citizenship debates, but also the 'dominant' form of citizenship at least in the West (Heater 1999, p. 4).

Like Greek, Roman and medieval citizenship, modern liberal citizenship also came along under certain societal conditions. Powered by industrialization, the eighteenth and nineteenth centuries of Western Europe witnessed the rise of capitalism and the growing and prevailing power of the market which necessitated individual freedoms. It experienced subversions by the bourgeoisie against the monarchs and aristocrats for civil and political rights. With the intellectual support of English liberalism flourishing in the seventeenth century and the practical experience of British Civil War and American Revolution (Heater 1999), the 1789 French Revolution became the tipping point of those subversions. It gave birth of modern democratic state in which subjects were turned into citizens; law-protected rights were open to formerly excluded groups; and a 'direct relation' between citizens and the state was established 'so that all citizens as individuals possess equal rights before the sovereign, national authority' (Bendix 1977, pp. 89–91). Marked by this unprecedented direct citizen–state relationship, French Revolution, as Heater (1999) noted, 'first established the principle and practice of citizenship as the central feature of the modern socio-political structure' (p. 4). In short, what features modern liberal citizenship is equal and universal citizenship status and rights, grounded on the idea of individual liberty and bounded within the sovereign state.

The routes to modern citizenship are argued to be not identical in Western states, at least among Britain, Germany, France and America. Critically arguing that the equal and universal entitlement of citizenship was actually a 'ruling class strategy' from above to reconcile demands for rights below, Mann (1987) demonstrated that in Britain modern citizenship was employed by the ruling class—first the monarch and aristocrats and later the bourgeoisie—as a liberal strategy to incorporate lower classes through the welfare state, while in Germany modern citizenship served as an authoritarian strategy for the German monarch to settle down demands from lower classes with substantial social rights yet superficial political rights. As a criticism to Mann's argument, Turner (1990) pointed out that perceiving citizenship solely as strategy from above renders citizenship a completely passive institution, obscuring the reality that in some cases, such as France and America, citizenship was actually the result of active struggles from below. He complemented that, although it is true that citizenship was passively bestowed from the top in Britain and Germany, the two cases can be further distinguished from a public/private perspective as the former locating citizenship in the public arena while the latter constraining citizenship in the private arena. Likewise, while French and American citizenships were obtained through active struggles from below, the former required active public engagement while the latter focused on the private realm of individuals (Turner 1990). Departing from Mann's differentiation of modern citizenship formation, Turner (1990) suggested that there were four routes to the establishment of citizen–state relationship and hence four types of citizenship in modern times: British passive and public citizenship, German passive and private citizenship, French active and public citizenship, and American active and private citizenship.

Whether initiating from above or below and whether ending in public or private realm, modern citizenship formation was not only an extension of citizenship rights to former subjects but also a separation of citizenship rights itself. Based on the English experience, Marshall (1998) offered a classical three-element classification of citizenship rights, which were 'blended' in pre-modern times but 'parted company' and separately, if neither necessarily nor sequentially, developed under the status of citizenship from the eighteenth to the twentieth century (pp. 94–5). They are civil rights 'necessary for individual freedom', political rights 'to participate in the exercise of political power' and social rights covering 'from the right to a modicum of economic welfare and security to the right to share to the full in the social heritage and to live the life of a civilized being according to the standards prevailing in the society' (Marshall 1998, p. 94).

While civil and political rights have been extended, albeit at varying paces, to formerly excluded groups in modern Western democracies, it does not necessarily mean that subject-turned modern citizens are able or willing to directly and actively participate in state affairs on a par with Ancient Greek citizens. Even in republican France where citizenship featured active and public characteristics and Rousseauian desire for direct popular governance at the state level was high, Greek active citizenship was not restored. This is because, as Smith (2002) remarked, 'in modern large-scale republics, there has simply been no practical alternative to extensive reliance on representative systems of self-government, except for effective abandonment of any meaning self-governance at all' (p. 107). After all, when the bourgeoisie led the struggles to universalize civil and political rights, their primary purpose was to secure their individual freedoms in the market other than political participation per se. For modern citizenship, individual freedoms are the end to be met through means such as 'the odd duty' of taxpaying for rights protection by the state in return, and the right to 'rouse itself from the quiet pursuit of private affairs and rebel' in cases that the state trespasses on or fails to protect individual freedoms (Heater 1999, pp. 6–7). In a word, political participation is perceived no more than a means to meet the end of individual freedom. In this sense, modern citizenship is 'apolitical' (Smith 2002, p. 108).

Civil and political rights alone cannot live up to the idea of modern citizenship. That is, as Marshall (1998) revealed, civil and political rights are in effect 'an aid, and not a menace, to capitalism and the free-market economy' as 'a system, not of equality, but of inequality', while 'citizenship, even in its early forms, was a principle of equality' (pp. 102–5). Behind the universalized civil and political rights lie certain necessary social resources and capabilities for supposedly equal modern citizens to exercise those rights. The theory and practice of social rights—such as education, minimum wage and health care—under the legal and equal status of citizenship were thus introduced as an attempt to eliminate or at least alleviate inequalities in social resource and capability. The struggles and contests in the distribution of often finite social resources gave unprecedentedly significant rise to the social dimension in modern citizenship, leading Turner (2006) to claim that distinct from classical 'political citizenship', modern citizenship is 'social citizenship' in essence (p. 150). Moreover, as citizenship now covers issues not only in relation to the state but also to the market, the public and the private life (Janoski 1998), how to secure civil and political rights for individual liberty on one hand and social rights for social equality on the other hand continues to be a key question in contemporary citizenship debates.

One important social feature of modern citizenship is the development of the idea of nation and the attendant national identity and nationalism, and its influence on citizenry solidarity. The term 'nation' in its classic Roman usage connoted community of people of the same decent, either geographically or culturally but not politically (Habermas 1995, p. 258). Politicizing the idea of nation and defining it in 'universalist, rationalist, assimilationist, and state-centred' terms, the French bourgeoisie employed it to mobilize the population at large against the monarch and aristocrats and, through the French Revolution, to establish the self-determining sovereign nation whose membership was institutionalized in the political and legal form of citizenship (Brubaker 1998, pp. 139–42). This process resulted in what Hobsbawm (1992, p. 19) meant 'the equation nation = state = people' or what Delanty (2000, p. 91) called 'the coupling of nation and state' in modern political vocabulary. Following the invention and institutionalization of nation-state came the emergence of exclusive nationalism out of the internal defence of the nascent nation-state and its later external expansion (Brubaker 1998, p. 143). Viewed on the state and citizenship side, Habermas (1995) remarked that the emerged nationalism 'founded a collective identity that played a *functional role* for the implementation of the citizenship that arose in the French Revolution'; while national identity served as the 'socio-psychological connection' for, yet 'was never conceptually tied to', modern liberal citizenship (p. 259, original emphasis).

First introduced into modern political discourse through French revolution (Shafir 1998, p. 16), the idea of nation and nationalism experienced conceptual transformation in the late nineteenth century (Hobsbawm 1992). Brubaker (1998) neatly pointed out the cause behind and the result of this transformation:

> [The expansive and aggressive political-ideological nationalism directed abroad] contributed to the later emergence, during the Napoleonic period, of a German counternationalism in which ethnocultural motifs came to play an important role. Revolutionary expansion, itself driven by political nationalism, thus engendered ethnocultural nationalism: the 'crusade for liberty' elicited in response the myth, if not the reality, of a 'holy war' of ethnonational resistance. (p. 144)

This alternative and ethnocultural nationalism was rooted in the German 'particularist, organic, differenctialist, and *Volk*-centred' perception of nationhood (Brubaker 1998, p. 139), echoing the classic usage of nation in their connection to culture. Yet, ethnocultural nationalism is significantly modern in the sense that it was constructed upon the French experience of the politicized nation and thus was charged with the demand of self-determination often, if not always, in the form of independent state.

Unlike political nationalism based on acquirable political ideas, ethnocultural nationalism presupposes ascriptive and distinct ethnic and cultural homogeneities among people of the claimed nation. But similar to political nationalism, ethnocultural nationalism arguably also functions as the socio-psychological bond among modern citizens, whether it is viewed by Anderson (2006) as an imaginary construct, thanks to modern technology and apparatus, or it does involve distinctly recognizable 'ethnic core' like in pre-modern cultural communities, as argued by Smith (1989).

The equations of nation with state and people of the nation with citizen of the state, together with the conceptual transformation of nation and nationalism, complicated the answer to the question of who is a citizen in modern discourse. While in modern nation-state citizenship continues to be a legal status, it tends to, though not necessarily in theory and not always in practice, bear implications of ethnocultural homogeneities such as common homeland, common culture (typically language), and common descent (Smith 1989, p. 344). In other words, in its modern conception citizenship as legal membership of the state is often associated with national membership based on assumption of cultural and ethnic homogeneities.

So far our journey on the conceptual evolution of citizenship in the West has gone from ancient Greek and Roman citizenship, briefly through medieval citizenship, to modern liberal citizenship. As these variations are the grounds for the contemporary conceptual development of Western citizenship, it is helpful to highlight the key connections and distinctions between them before we continue the journey to contemporary times.

Modern citizenship can be seen as a continuity of the Roman experience of citizenship in the sense that both serve as a legal status entailing certain law-protected rights. Yet, it should be noted immediately that such similarity makes sense only with reference to the Greek republican citizenship. While both the modern theory and the Roman practice treat citizenship as a legal status, modern citizenship inspired by the liberal idea of social contract—through which citizens as independent individuals submit themselves with consent to the authorities in exchange for protection of their rights—is fundamentally different from citizenship subject to the arbitrariness of Roman emperor. The difference in source of authority further determines that rights negotiated and equally shared by all independent and equal citizens, at least in theory, in modern nation-state—developed from medieval experience of rights contestation between guilds in cities—are distinct from rights of subject bestowed by emperor. In addition to the above distinctions, the contents of rights have also been considerably expanded in modern times, compared with ancient citizenship rights, or indeed privileges.

In spite of these important differences, modern liberal citizenship shares the feature of passivity with Roman imperial citizenship, as it does not necessarily entail active political participation in the name of virtue which is the essence of the civic republican tradition of citizenship. Though modern citizens legally have the right to political participation and do sometimes actively participate in political community to protect or claim for rights, for modern citizenship political participation serves as the means to ends rather than itself the end. Modern citizen in this sense is similar to what Pocock called 'legal being' when he discussed the imperial citizenship in comparison with 'political being' of classical citizens in ancient republican Greece and Rome (Pocock 1995, p. 34). By 'political being', Pocock (1995) indicated citizens that emancipate themselves from individual possessions or 'thing' so as to politically engage with others, which itself is an end or 'the ideal'; by contrast, 'legal being' means citizens only engaging with others through and for possessions or 'things' which are material or 'the real' (pp. 34–5). The focus on 'the real' rather than 'the ideal' in the modern conception renders the nature of civic virtue required by modern citizenship different from that by the ancient republican citizenship. As mentioned above, political engagement in everyday life as 'the ideal' is required in the name of virtue in the Aristotelian model of citizenship. For modern citizenship, however, virtue as duty such as taxpaying and voting becomes the means of access to 'the real' and individual liberty secured by rights.

While the ideas of liberty and democracy, which are the backbone of modern Western citizenship, may not be commonly espoused across the globe, citizenship as legal status has been institutionalized in most, if not all, modern nation-states (Isin and Wood 1999, p. 5), including China.[1] Some nation-states follow the

[1]How citizenship is legally defined in China is explained in Chap. 3.

principle of jus sanguinis which offers the legal membership at birth to those born to parent with the legal status, while others apply the principle of jus soli which grants the status to those born in it (Heater 1999, p. 80). The change of legal citizenship is often eligible based on criteria varying in different states, such as a certain length of legal residence. The worldwide recognition of citizenship as legal status offers a common ground for citizenship discussion at a time that contemporary societal conditions and developments have brought modern citizenship into question.

Contemporary Reconfiguration

Citizenship, as demonstrated in the above sections, is a fluid, contested and constructed concept, altering along changing societal conditions. Modern citizenship formed in particular historical context is thus inevitably reconfigured in contemporary settings featuring postmodernization and globalization which pose serious challenges to modern citizenship. This reconfiguration is a constructing process as the history of the evolution of the concept suggests, and is in a contesting manner given that not only may the elements of the concept come into conflict (such as civil vs. social rights), but also there are contrasting ideas in the conceptual legacies of citizenship, notably the civic republican and the liberal traditions. Rather than placing the focus on the details of contemporary contestation and construction, in this section I intend to depict the changing landscape of the concept in contemporary times by highlighting in what way modern citizenship is challenged by, and in what direction the concept is evolved under, the two contemporary forces of postmodernization and globalization identified by Isin and Turner (2002). It is this contemporarily reconfigured Western citizenship that serves as the analytical lens for the examination of citizenship in the Chinese case.

The contemporary citizenship reconfiguration departs from and draws on its pre-modern and modern legacies, which—to oversimplify—include political participation and civic virtue from ancient Greek citizenship, legal status and law-protected rights from ancient Roman citizenship, and national identity from modern citizenship. This summary corresponds with Delanty's (2000, p. 126) definition of citizenship containing four components of rights, responsibilities, participation and identity. Similarly, Isin and Turner (2002) suggested that citizenship has 'three fundamental axes, extent (rules and norms of inclusion and exclusion), content (rights and responsibilities) and depth (thickness or thinness)' (p. 2). A synthesis of these categories creates three dimensions of citizenship: (1) content about rights and responsibilities, (2) extent about identity, and (3) depth about participation. In what way are these dimensions reconfigured by contemporary postmodernization and globalization? This is the question to be addressed below.

Citizenship in Postmodernization

Postmodernization, either as the ideological movement of postmodernism or as the historical process towards the condition of postmodernity, is, in the simplest terms, a departure from modern society. Any discussion of postmodernization thus has to start from a consideration of modern society. For some the departure is merely the continuity of modern society, while for others, such as Crook et al. (1992), it is 'a genuinely new historical configuration' (p. 1).

Modern society featured at least two transformations from pre-modern society. One was the rationalization of human experience into calculable and impersonal knowledge; and the other was, inspired by the first one, the universalization of ideas and values attempting to bind together differentiated units of social structure (Crook et al. 1992). The former gave rise to modern science, while the latter gave birth to bureaucratic administration. Postmodernization, according to Crook et al. (1992), is the extension 'to extreme levels' of both the universalization of modern social organization with rationalized and centralized management, and the differentiation of modern social structure with increased specialization and complexity (p. 32). Calling the former extension 'monocentric organization' and the latter 'hyperdifferentiation', Crook et al. (1992) argued that the contradiction of the two renders the former 'untenable', breaking down modern established principles and categories and leading to uncertainty and unpredictability (pp. 34–5).

The collapse of modern principles and categories is, in a sense, the failure of the modern grand narrative of universality. Such failure is illustrated in Pathak's (2006) account on modern values, although he did not position himself as a postmodernist but aimed to 'humanize modernity' (p. 161). Pathak (2006) observed that, while modernity bears core values such as 'freedom, criticality, democratization, openness and optimism for the future' which are desirable and undeniable for human beings, it may induce 'arrogance and violence' in practice (pp. 23–6), in the sense that modernity could become a kind of Western cultural imposition which universalizes certain understandings and behaviours in the name of rationality, consequently disregarding social, cultural and religious differences and obscuring the heterogeneity in the actual world. This critique of modernity implies that paralleling the fall of modern and supposedly universal grand narrative is the rise of attention to difference and particularity in the hyperdifferentiated postmodern society.

This shift poses challenges to modern universal citizenship at least from two directions. First and within individual nation-states, it breaks up the modern monolithic image of citizen projecting the dominant culture in the nationalized state, opening up questions of cultural inclusion and exclusion (Stevenson 2001). Ethnic, gender and religious groups excluded or marginalized from mainstream discourses of modern citizenship increasingly demand group identity to be recognized and group-differentiated rights to be guaranteed in the name of citizen (Isin 2002b, pp. 122–3). The concept of citizenship is hence turned to be a contested terrain not merely for social resources as since its modern formation, but also for cultural recognition and representation in contemporary debates. In other words, the postmodern shift opens the cultural sphere in the concept of citizenship, bringing in cultural rights seen by Norman and Kymlicka (2003) as 'a fourth wave of citizenship rights…to the accommodation of cultural difference' (p. 218). Second and across nation-states, modern liberal citizenship with a bundle of rights is perceived in the postmodern vein as little more than a Western construct. Citizenship study is thus required to be contextualized by considering specific historical, political, social and cultural conditions. In other words, citizenship is now less seen as a meta-narrative but more as a context-sensitive narrative that is constructed and can only be properly understood in specific contexts. Corresponding to citizenship reconfigured in this way, citizenship education is increasingly considered not context-free but dependent on 'cultural norms, political priorities, social expectation, national economic development aspirations, geopolitical contexts and historical antecedents' (Kennedy 2004, p. 17).

While the attention to citizenship particularities helps prevent the 'arrogance and violence' of modern citizenship, overemphasizing them risks of falling into relativism and closing the door of mutual understanding and interaction between perspectives and conceptions of citizenship. This is arguably undesirable and indeed impossible, especially given that globalization—the other contemporary force to be discussed later—is the sharing context from which no contemporary citizenship conception can escape. There is thus appeal that 'we should concentrate on how globalization… affects human beings, regardless of the differences in terms of culture, values or religion' (Brunn and Jacobsen 2000, p. 11, cited in Kennedy 2004, p. 19). How to avoid violence at one extreme and relativism at the other has been an imperative yet unsettled issue in the face of contemporary conflicts ranging from politics and economics to culture and religion. Kennedy (2004) suggested the search for 'common values' in citizenship and 'a common core of citizenship knowledge and insights' for citizenship education (p. 17). By contrast, viewing the existence of common values as 'assumption that…is not necessary a conclusion' (p. 116), Byram (2006) argued for intercultural citizenship able to communicate, understand and evaluate different perspectives while acknowledging cultural relativity. The present study on the meaning of citizenship in Chinese society through the analytical lens of Western citizenship conception is in effect an intercultural communication about citizenship. The two, as will be compared in detail in Chap. 7, are indeed found to share some common values, such as rights as an inherent part of citizenship.

The postmodern hyperdifferentiation not only breaks up modern universal and monolithic construct of citizenship, but also alters both modern socioeconomic-based political culture and modern bureaucratic political participation through representation. By dismantling modern class composition and destabilizing modern sociopolitical conditions, social hyperdifferentiation, according to Crook et al. (1992), produces a new type of politics based on sociocultural, other than modern socioeconomic, allegiance as witnessed in the generational specificity and occupational diversity in contemporary social activism and movements in Western democracies. Featuring self-organized action and suspicion against established elites and centralized state apparatus (Crook et al. 1992, p. 148), this new type of politics highlights the significance of individual citizens in postmodern citizenship participation.

The altered nature of political culture and participation is reflected by the contemporary focus on the agency and activeness of citizenship, an aspect implicit in modern liberal citizenship conception. Viewing citizenship practice in connection with citizenship rights, Isin and Wood (1999) suggested that citizenship should be seen not only as a politico-legal concept about status but as a sociological concept about practice. The two aspects, they explained, are 'not mutually exclusive but constitutive' because rights attached to status are not only often first claimed through, but also guarantee for, citizenship practice (p. 4). Citizenship in this sense is perceived as practice through which citizens, especially those of minority groups, struggle for rights ranging from long concerned civil, political and social rights to cultural rights coming to the surface in postmodernization as discussed above.

Citizenship practice is pronounced not only for rights but also as civic virtue. The idea of active citizenship originating from the civic republican tradition of citizenship is revived by scholars as a response to the allegedly diminished public participation in Western democracies by citizens 'losing the desire, the will and the means to be active citizens' (Crick 2010, p. 16). Echoing the civic republican tradition, the idea expresses the necessity of active participation by citizens in community and politics on moral grounds. But the contemporary revival contains distinct variations, from being restored by classic civic republicans as the essence of citizenship, to being treated by communitarians as an instrumental way to maintain social bonds in hyperdifferentiated postmodern society.

Indeed, civic virtue or what Roche (1992, p. 49) called 'duties discourse' has gained momentum in contemporary citizenship discussion, paralleling, if not replacing, the modern discourse of rights dominating liberal citizenship. One illustration is the treatment of social and moral responsibility, together with political literacy and community involvement, as the three key strands of citizenship education proposed in the Crick Report (Crick 1998) which led to the formalization of the subject in national curriculum in England in 2002. The rise of concern over responsibility is arguably also in line with the postmodern context. Postmodernist focus on particularity of individual and society needs to be supported and sustained by mutual respect; and given the resistance against and the reduced capacity of authority and establishment in postmodern society, citizens are on one hand demanded by the New Right to bear more personal responsibilities usually at the expense of rights, social rights in particular, and on the other hand required by the Left to take more social and moral responsibilities to challenge against and help remove inequalities in society.

Perceived as either a responsibility, a right itself, or a means to protect and claim for other rights, citizenship agency or participation has been a recurring theme in contemporary citizenship debates. While its importance is recognized, how far should it go remains an open question. Citizenship participation, following Zukin et al. (2006), comes into two descriptive categories: political participation such as voting that 'has the intent or effect of influencing…the making or the implementation of public policies', and civic participation such as volunteering that is 'organized voluntary activity focused on problem solving and helping others' (pp. 5–7). Normative accounts of citizenship political and civic participation—that is what citizens are desired to do—can be found in contemporary theories of good citizenship.

From the political perspective and in the context of multicultural American society, Banks (2008) developed a fourfold escalating typology of citizenship:

(1) Legal citizenship: citizen that has legal rights and obligations but keeps away from political participation;
(2) Minimal citizenship: citizen that conventionally votes in elections;
(3) Active citizenship: citizen that takes action beyond voting to actualize existing laws and conventions; and
(4) Transformative citizenship: citizen that takes action to actualize values and moral principles beyond conventional authority.

Similarly, in the American context but more in civic circumstances, Westheimer and Kahne (2004) identified three escalating progressive conceptions of good citizenship:

(1) Personally responsible citizen: with good characters such as honest, responsible and law-abiding, this kind of citizen acts responsibly in community, paying taxes, obeying laws and willing to volunteer if needed;
(2) Participatory citizen: as active member in community, this kind of citizen possesses know-how and takes leadership in organizing community effort to accomplish collective tasks within established systems and community structures; and
(3) Justice-oriented citizen: by critically assessing social, political and economic structures, this kind of citizen challenges established systems that reproduce injustice, making effort to solve social problems and improve society.

The most progressive models of good citizen in these two typologies, transformative citizenship and justice-oriented citizenship, share some common features. Similarly, referring to citizens pursuing justice even if breaking existing rules, they go beyond the active citizenship and participatory citizenship which take yet keep actions within established systems, to say nothing about the passive minimal citizenship and personally responsible citizenship. This echoes Almond and Verba's (1965) differentiation between the roles of subject and citizen vis-à-vis government and law. According to them, subject participates after general policy has been made, while citizen engages and exerts influence on policymaking; and subject 'appeals' by following existing rules to government accountability, while citizen 'demands' by challenging current norms (p. 169). As a consequence, the competence of subject is 'administrative' matter of 'being aware of…rights under the rules', as opposed to the competence of citizen that is 'political' one of 'participating in the making of the rules' (p. 169). It can be discussed that Banks's (2008) active and Westheimer and Kahne's (2004) participatory citizen who participates within established systems—such as monitoring government, engaging in local community affairs, and appealing to authority for intervention in the case of abuse of established rights—plays the role of what Almond and Verba (1965) called subject. By contrast, a transformative and justice-oriented citizen engaging in public affairs to challenge existing unjust rules and make new just rules—for example, taking part in governmental policymaking and demanding for new rights—is qualified to be called citizen in Almond and Verba's terms.

A transformative and justice-oriented citizen not only makes efforts to remove current unjust norms but also engages in making new rules to 'promote social justice in communities, nations and the world' (Banks 2008, p. 137). Following Streich's (2011) argument that the pursuit for justice should be extended from 'justice for just us' to 'justice beyond just us' (p. 2), a transformative and justice-oriented citizen is expected to promote justice not only for themselves or in-group members but also for others or out-group members.

The idea of transformative and justice-oriented citizenship well corresponds to the postmodern denial of authority and articulation of agency. But admittedly, even active participation within established systems could be a burden for citizens today, since citizen is more often than not just one of many identities held by citizens who in their 'real life' have 'largely vicarious' participation in state affairs and 'too many other things to worry about' such as earning a living (Walzer 1995, p. 156). Nevertheless, serving as a benchmark for what citizens are desired to do in contemporary society, transformative and justice-oriented citizenship manifests the contemporary expectation for citizens to go beyond conventional participation within existing systems to actively engage in public affairs with the commitment to ensure that justice is not curbed by, but prevails beyond, authorized rules.

In summary, bringing particularity and agency to the fore, postmodernization challenges the genericness and passiveness of modern liberal citizenship. It reconstructs contemporary citizenship to be a context-dependent discourse in which citizenship practice is a lively theme.

Citizenship in Globalization

While the wave of postmodernist thought rising since the 1960s might be chronologically earlier than the dramatic spread of globalization theory around the 1990s, the two forces in effect have closely interacted with each other. It is for the purpose of clarifying their particular impacts on modern citizenship that they are separately discussed here. If modernity is 'primarily a discourse of time' in which emancipation, equality and democracy come into sight as utopias at the evolutional end of human history, then the contemporary focus 'has shifted from time to space' (Delanty 2000, p. 83). While postmodernization draws our attention to context and emphasizes the particularity of space, globalization, defined tersely by Delanty (2000) as 'the diminishing importance of geographical constraints' (p. 83), makes possible both 'convergence and divergence' in space (p. 89).

Contemporary globalization, whether as an ongoing process or an existing condition, features an unprecedentedly intense flow of people, capital and information and the attendant interaction, cooperation and interdependence of local economics, politics and cultures on the global scale. Scholarly evaluation of the consequence of globalization varies, involving, according to Delanty (2000), 'strong' and 'weak' arguments (pp. 86–9). On one hand, scholars taking the 'strong argument' side view globalization in the convergent direction as the formation of an integrative, standard and homogenous global culture and even a global society; on the other hand, those on the 'weak argument' side contend in the divergent direction that globalization leads to diversity and fragmentation, either politically, economically or culturally. While the 'weak argument' shares a similar perspective with postmodernists, the 'strong argument' of globalization needs to be differentiated from modernity, given that the latter, as discussed earlier, tended to ignore heterogeneity and violate particularity but the former does not necessarily so. An immediate illustration is that the aforementioned Kennedy's (2004) call to search for common values of citizenship in the globalized world is made with rather than without recognition of diverse and sometimes conflictive understandings of citizenship in specific contexts. Besides the one-way divergent or convergent considerations, globalization is also perceived by some in a dialectical way. Robertson (1992) suggested that 'contemporary globalization in its most general sense' is 'a form of institutionalization of the two-fold process involving the universalization of particularism and the particularization of universalism' (p. 102). The former process means 'the extensive diffusion of the idea that there is virtually no limit to particularity, to uniqueness, to difference and to otherness', while the latter carries 'the idea of the universal being given global-human concreteness' (p. 102).

Whether as a force of convergence or divergence or both, contemporary globalization traverses the boundaries of, and by so doing, confronts and weakens the predominant powers of modern nation-state. Held (1995) pointed out five 'disjunctures' in the contemporary global system that challenge the modern state's autonomy or 'the actual power…to articulate and achieve policy goals independently', and its sovereignty or 'the entitlement of a state to rule over a bounded territory' (p. 100). They are (1) the transcendence of international law from law between sovereign states to law addressing world order such as human rights and human heritages; (2) the internationalization of political decision-making which reflects expanded transnational links and corresponding needs for global governance; (3) the formation of power blocs and military alliances that reduces individual states' autonomy in defence and security; (4) the development of global communication systems that weakens the cultural hegemony of nation-states; and (5) the worldwide spatial reach of production, distribution and exchange that limits state control over economy (pp. 101–34). Drawing these legal, political, security, cultural and economic disjunctures as evidence, Held (1995) concluded that the autonomy, the sovereignty and consequently the powers of modern sovereign state have been eroded.

These disjunctures induce the reconfiguration of citizenship from its modern state-centred conception. First, as opposed to rights and responsibilities of modern citizenship which are determined, protected and enforced by the state, international law applying to all human beings, such as the Universal Declaration of Human

Rights by the United Nations, provides the legal basis for the recognition of citizenship rights and obligations beyond state boundaries. Also, it has become less legitimate for the nation-state to appeal to sovereignty for its infringement of citizenship rights stated in international law, notwithstanding its remaining functional significance in enacting and protecting citizenship rights within its boundaries. Grounded on international law, the increasingly internationalized political decision-making stimulates the idea of political citizenship at the global level. Despite that a world state in which all human beings *qua* global citizens practice political rights like in a democratic state is unrealistic, at least at the time of the early twenty-first century, what Heater (2002) called 'political quasi-world citizenship' is already in place, given the guarantee by international law of political rights at the state level and the evidence of worldwide political activities by citizens across state borders, largely through local and international NGOs (pp. 136–7).

Second, economic globalization, often fuelled by neoliberalism advocating free market without state interference and by market globalism believing in an inevitable and beneficial scenario of global integration of markets (Steger 2009), has impact on the substance and scope of modern social citizenship. It reduces the state's autonomy to allocate and distribute resources, and therefore its ability to fulfil the commitment taken on in modern times to guarantee the social rights of its citizens. Furthermore, by exposing one market to another and accelerating competition and exploitation between them, economic globalization brings economic and social inequality to the global scale. To counter this globalized inequality, there have been worldwide social movements known as 'global justice movement' since the late 1990s, from the regular demonstrations to sites of meeting held by major world economic institutions to the Occupy movements taking place in key financial districts around the world (Steger et al. 2013). These movements, according to Steger et al. (2013), bear the ideology of what they called 'justice globalism', two of whose core concepts are 'equality of access to resources and opportunities' and 'social justice'. These developments require social citizenship, considered by Turner (2006) as the essence of modern citizenship, to expand its conceptual scope from the state to the global in contemporary socioeconomic contexts.

Third, globalization challenges not only the predominant position of the state in modern political and social citizenship discourses, but also the implication of ethnocultural homogeneity attached to modern citizenship. Thanks to technological developments, unprecedented cross- and within-border human and information flows diversify the ethnic and cultural backgrounds of the population in individual nation-states and undermine the nation-state' capability to control cultural narratives. These break down the modern construct in the name of nation of the homogeneous 'us' inside and the alien 'other' outside the state, or, to put it succinctly, the modern equation of nation and state.

Indeed, Delanty (2000) argued that the nation once closely in association with the state has gradually shifted away from the state and instead is 'free-floating' in society; and national identity becomes only one collective identity among others not directed from above but often generating from below (p. 96). The implication of this for the concept of citizenship is that citizenship as legal identity is detaching from national identity in the ethnic and cultural sense, and that citizens could have different ethnic and cultural identities while sharing the same legal state membership. Ong's (1999) study of the cultural logics of transnationality among overseas Chinese gives evidence from the anthropological perspective that in the age of globalization legal citizenship does not necessarily go hand in hand with ethnic and cultural identity. Her study recorded citizens of Southeast Asian states who reclaimed their long assimilated Chinese ethnic identity in business network building and investment in China, and multi-passport holders who used legal citizenship as a strategy to respond to changing political–economic conditions while not necessarily losing their original cultural identity. She coined the term 'flexible citizenship' to reflect the contemporary phenomena of legal citizenship driven by economic accounts and detached from cultural ones.

That detachment opens up the cultural discourse of citizenship, enabling its narratives to be diversified in terms of such as class, ethnicity, gender, religion, age and ability. As an approach to recognizing and accommodating these disclosed cultural differences, Yuval-Davis (1999) suggested that citizenship should be understood as a 'multi-layered' construct, from local to national and to global, to allow 'transversal dialogue', in which 'difference encompasses equality and perceived unity and homogeneity are replaced by dialogues' between inter-affecting collectivities across these layers (pp. 131–2). For the idea of global citizenship, it is important to note that the increased interest on it is not merely from proponents who use it as a way to challenge modern injustice and accommodate diversity in various spheres. It is also taken advantage of by neo-liberalists to glorify individual responsibility and entrepreneurial spirit in the global market and by authoritarian states to increase global competiveness for the sake of national interest. We will refer to the latter case when we consider Chinese citizenship-related education in Chap. 3.

In short, the convergent and divergent forces in globalization considerably erodes, yet not necessarily eradicates, the autonomy and sovereignty of nation-state, the predominant modern political institution, triggering the expansion of the scope of political, social and cultural citizenship beyond nation-state and the corresponding changes with respect to citizenship rights, responsibilities, identity and participation.

It is important to remind us that the separation of discussion of citizenship in globalization and postmodernization in this section does not mean that the influences of the two contemporary forces on the concept of citizenship are always able to be sharply distinguished in reality. For instance, it is hard to claim that the postmodern denial of modern monolithic citizenship and articulation for citizenship particularity and agency is not related to the decline of state powers and the expanding scope of political, social and cultural citizenship resulted from globalization. The contemporary reconfiguration of citizenship is a process under the joint influence of postmodernization and globalization.

Western Citizenship as Analytical Lens

This chapter has so far traced the conceptual evolution of citizenship in the West, from the pre-modern roots to the modern institutionalization, and at last to the contemporary reconfiguration. The connections and changes in the process of evolution confirm that citizenship is a fluid and dynamic concept, subject to contestation, deconstruction and reconstruction according to changing political, economic and social circumstances. The general direction of this evolution can be summarized as from narrow to wide in the extent of citizenship as membership, from less to more in the content of citizenship including rights and responsibilities and from formal to informal in the depth of citizenship regarding participation. It is expectable that as the conceptual evolution goes on, new individuals and groups may be recognized as full citizens in particular political community according to redefined eligibility; new rights and responsibilities may be claimed and attached to citizenship; new forms of citizenship participation may emerge; and even new theoretical dimensions in addition to the extent, content and depth ones may be added to take further advantage of the concept of citizenship for human values such as liberty and justice.[2]

With acknowledgement of ongoing debates and controversies about it and its potential for further evolution, the Western conception of citizenship, viewed from the standpoint of the early twenty-first century, covers at least the following elements: citizenship as legal, local, national and global identities in the extent dimension; citizenship civil, political, social and cultural rights, and legal and moral responsibilities in the content dimension; and citizenship political and civic (non-political) participation in the depth dimension. These three dimensions are by no means isolated from each other. As briefly referred to at some points above, citizens' rights often serve as either the basis or the goal of citizenship participation, which on another occasion may be required as citizens' responsibility. Similarly, on one hand rights and responsibilities that citizens have help to shape their understanding of citizenship identity; and on the other hand their personal identities such as ethnic identity motivate citizens to claim for rights to recognize and preserve those identities often through citizenship practice in the forms of such as appealing, campaign, protest and social movement. In short, the content, extent and depth of citizenship are interdependent to the point of defining and redefining each other.

This book uses the Western conception of citizenship with the three dimensions as the analytical lens to examine the meaning of citizenship in China. While inevitably bearing the modern constructed East–West binary, this approach, as explained in the introductory chapter, allows this study on the East to access and

---

[2]It may sound contradictory to speak of human values given the postmodern denial of grand narrative. There is of course no single and universal definition of the mentioned values. But these values, however understood and interpreted, are at least commonly viewed as important for human beings around the world, from Western democracies to socialist China, which does attach them to citizenship in official documents as shown at the opening of this book.

connect to the intellectual debates in the West so as to help, using Bonnett's (2004, p. 6) words, 'map out the big picture' of the concept of citizenship. Furthermore, this approach bears three important implications for our understanding of the concept of citizenship in general and Chinese citizenship in particular.

First, more rather than less comparisons are needed at a time that the focus on difference and particularity gains momentum as a result of postmodernization. Citizenship is now widely recognized as a constructed concept. This suggests that as Eastern and Western conceptions of citizenship are constructs in respective historical, social, economic, political and cultural contexts, the two are not necessarily understood in the same way as each other. For instance, Lee (2003) observed from the cultural perspective that citizenship in Asia has three features that make it 'fundamentally different' from Western citizenship (p. 21). The three features are as follows: first, emphasis on relationship between individuals and collectives and harmony rather than individual rights and responsibilities; second, the priority of spirituality or one's personal quality over rights and responsibilities of citizens; and third, the focus on the development of individuality and the self rather than individualism or individualization. Leaving aside the question of whether such observation is convincing or not, at least Lee (2003) also noticed that 'the world is dynamic in its interaction and flow of ideas' (p. 22). It implies that even if there are fundamental distinctions between Eastern and Western citizenship conceptions, the two sides are not isolated from but influential to each other—although such influence in the critical perspective is unlikely to be equal, especially given the political and cultural power contestations intensified by globalization. Indeed, as will be shown in the next chapter, Western citizenship was historically not a stranger in the distance but had influence on the modern formation of Chinese citizenship. Arguably, distinction arguments and inevitable mutual influences require more rather than less comparisons between Western and Chinese citizenship conceptions for us to better understand their differences and connections and to share and learn legacies and lessons between the two sides. This book sees China in the mirror of the West, examining to what extent the Western conception of citizenship is embraced by the Chinese term of *gongmin* in contemporary society, without any intention of implying any intrinsic particularity, rightness, completeness or superiority of the Western conception.

Second, while from the postmodernist standpoint there is no universal theory of citizenship because different societies would have their own, it does not mean there is no need to search for common ground between various conceptions of citizenship in contemporary world. It is because that in the process of globalization there are increasing issues such as poverty, conflict, inequality and injustice that cannot be effectively resolved without understanding and cooperation by citizens at local, national and global levels. While the common ground may not exist as Byram (2006) understood, possibility cannot be ruled out either. Looking into Chinese citizenship through Western citizenship is in effect a research for the possibility. Third, China as part of the world is not immune to the contemporary forces of postmodernization and globalization. The Western citizenship conception being reconstructed in response to the two contemporary forces serves as a helpful reference for exploring what Chinese citizenship conception is and, furthermore, in what direction it needs to develop.

Equipped with the Western citizenship elaborated in this chapter as the analytical lens, the following chapters will turn the focus to citizenship in the Chinese context. The book is about the meaning of citizenship in contemporary Chinese society, to which citizenship in the perspective of the state is a key factor. This is partly because citizenship is a concept closely associated with the state as demonstrated in this chapter, and partly due to the central and leading role of the party-state in citizenship issues in socialist China, as the next chapter will show.

References

Almond, G. A., & Verba, S. (1965). *The civic culture: Political attitudes and democracy in five nations*. Boston: Little, Brown and Company.

Anderson, B. (2006). *Imagined communities: Reflections on the origin and spread of nationalism*. London: Verso.

Banks, J. A. (2008). Diversity, group identity, and citizenship education in a global age. *Educational Researcher, 37*(3), 129–139. doi:10.3102/0013189X08317501.

Bendix, R. (1977). *Nation-building and citizenship*. California: University of California Press.

Bonnett, A. (2004). *The idea of the West: Culture, politics and history*. New York: Palgrave Macmillan.

Brubaker, R. (1998). Immigration, citizenship and nation-state in France and Germany. In G. Shafir (Ed.), *The citizenship debates: A reader* (pp. 131–164). Minneapolis: University of Minnesota Press.

Byram, M. (2006). Developing a concept of intercultural citizenship. In G. Alred, M. Byram, & M. Fleming (Eds.), *Education for intercultural citizenship: Concepts and comparisons* (pp. 109–129). Clevedon, England: Multilingual Matters.

Crick, B. (1998). *Education for citizenship and the teaching of democracy in schools*. London: Qualifications and Curriculum Authority.

Crick, B. (2010). Civic republicanism and citizenship: The challenge for today. In B. Crick & A. Lockyer (Eds.), *Active citizenship: What could it achieve and how?* (pp. 16–25). Edinburgh: Edinburgh University Press.

Crook, S., Pakulski, J., & Waters, M. (1992). *Postmodernization: Change in advanced society*. London: Sage.

Delanty, G. (2000). *Citizenship in a global age: Culture, society and politics*. Buckingham: Open University Press.

Habermas, J. (1995). Citizenship and national identity: Some reflections on the future of Europe. In R. Beiner (Ed.), *Theorizing citizenship* (pp. 255–281). Albany: State University of New York Press.

Heater, D. (1999). *What is citizenship?*. Cambridge: Polity Press.

Heater, D. (2002). *World citizenship: Cosmopolitan thinking and its opponents*. London: Continuum.

Held, D. (1995). *Democracy and the global order: From the modern state to cosmopolitan governance*. Cambridge: Polity Press.

Hobsbawm, E. J. (1992). *Nations and nationalism since 1780* (2nd ed.). Cambridge: Cambridge University Press.

Isin, E. F. (2002a). *Being political: Genealogies of citizenship*. Minneapolis: University of Minnesota Press.

Isin, E. F. (2002b). Citizenship after orientalism. In E. F. Isin & B. S. Turner (Eds.), *Handbook of citizenship studies* (pp. 117–128). London: Sage.

Isin, E. F., & Turner, B. S. (2002). Citizenship studies: An introduction. In E. F. Isin & B. S. Turner (Eds.), *Handbook of citizenship studies* (pp. 1–10). London: Sage.

Isin, E. F., & Wood, P. K. (1999). *Citizenship and identity*. London: Sage.
Janoski, T. (1998). *Citizenship and civil society: A framework of rights and obligations in liberal, tranditional, and social democratic regimes*. Cambridge: Cambridge University Press.
Kennedy, K. J. (2004). Searching for citizenship values in an uncertain global environment. In W. O. Lee, D. L. Grossman, K. J. Kennedy, & G. P. Fairbrother (Eds.), *Citizenship education in Asia and the Pacific: Concepts and issues* (pp. 9–24). Hong Kong: Comparative Education Research Centre, The University of Hong Kong.
Lee, W. O. (2003). Conceptualizing citizenship and citizenship education in Asia. *Pacific Asian Education, 15*(2), 8–26.
Mann, M. (1987). Ruling-class strategies and citizenship. *Sociology-The Journal of the British Sociological Association, 21*(3), 339–354. doi:10.1177/0038038587021003003.
Marshall, T. H. (1998). Citizenship and social class. In G. Shafir (Ed.), *The citizenship debates* (pp. 93–111). Minneapolis: University of Minnesota Press.
Norman, W., & Kymlicka, W. (2003). Citizenship. In R. G. Frey & C. H. Wellman (Eds.), *A companion to applied ethics* (pp. 210–223). Oxford: Blackwell Publishing.
Ong, A. (1999). *Flexible citizenship: The cultural logics of transnationality*. Durham, NC: Duke University Press.
Pathak, A. (2006). *Modernity, globalization and identity: Towards a reflexive quest*. Delhi: Aakar Books.
Pocock, J. G. A. (1995). The ideal of citizenship since classical times. In R. Beiner (Ed.), *Theorizing citizenship* (pp. 29–52). Albany: State University of New York Press.
Robertson, R. (1992). *Globalization: Social theory and global culture*. London: Sage.
Roche, M. (1992). *Rethinking citizenship: Welfare, ideology and change in modern society*. Cambridge: Polity Press.
Shafir, G. (1998). Introduction: The evolving tradition of citizenship. In G. Shafir (Ed.), *The citizenship debates: A reader* (pp. 1–28). Minneapolis: University of Minnesota Press.
Smith, A. (1989). The origins of nations. *Ethnic and Racial Studies, 12*(3), 340–367.
Smith, R. M. (2002). Modern citizenship. In E. F. Isin & B. S. Turner (Eds.), *Handbook of citizenship studies* (pp. 105–115). London: Sage.
Steger, M. B. (2009). *Globalisms: The great ideological struggle of the twenty-first century* (3rd ed.). Lanham, MD: Rowman & Littlefield.
Steger, M. B., Goodman, J., & Wilson, E. K. (2013). *Justice globalism: Ideology, crises, policy*. London: Sage.
Stevenson, N. (2001). Culture and citizenship: An introduction. In N. Stevenson (Ed.), *Culture and citizenship* (pp. 1–10). London: Sage.
Streich, G. W. (2011). *Justice beyond "just us": Dilemmas of time, place, and difference in American politics*. Surrey: Ashgate.
Turner, B. S. (1990). Outline of a theory of citizenship. *Sociology-The Journal of the British Sociological Association, 24*(2), 189–217. doi:10.1177/0038038590024002002.
Turner, B. S. (2006). Citizenship East and West: Reflections on revolutions and civil society. In G. Delanty (Ed.), *Europe and Aisa beyond East and West* (pp. 148–160). Oxon: Routledge.
Walzer, M. (1989). Citizenship. In T. Ball, J. Farr, & R. L. Hanson (Eds.), *Political innovation and conceptual change* (pp. 211–220). Cambridge: Cambridge University Press.
Walzer, M. (1995). The civil society argument. In R. Beiner (Ed.), *Theorizing citizenship* (pp. 153–174). Albany: State University of New York Press.
Westheimer, J., & Kahne, J. (2004). What kind of citizen? The politics of educating for democracy. *American Educational Research Journal, 41*(2), 237–269.
Yuval-Davis, N. (1999). The 'multi-layered citizen'. *International Feminist Journal of Politics, 1* (1), 119–136. doi:10.1080/146167499360068.
Zukin, C., Keeter, S., Andolina, M., Jenkins, K., & Carpini, M. (2006). *A new engagement? Political participation, civic life, and the changing American citizen*. New York: Oxford University Press.

Chapter 3
Citizenship and the State in Contemporary China

The state in classical Marxist thought is on one hand destined to 'wither away' in the communist utopia, and on the other hand believed to be necessary in the transitional socialist phase in order to lead, under the communist party and featuring a full range of state intervention in society, the political transition to the utopia. Despite that the Chinese party-state has significantly reinterpreted socialism under the rhetoric of 'socialism with Chinese characteristics', socialism remains the official political ideology in the CCP-ruled China. The party-state hence holds the ideological legitimacy to occupy the central and leading role in society. It indeed exercises the role, albeit at varying degrees in different social sectors and periods. For this reason, the party-state's stance on citizenship is an important factor that should not be ignored in our examination of the meaning of citizenship in Chinese society. To describe and specify the official stance, this chapter will analyze, firstly and generally, official policies in relation to citizenship and, secondly and specifically, citizenship-related education. The chapter will also highlight and illustrate the dynamized state-society relation in contemporary China. But first of all, it is necessary to clarify the Chinese terminology for citizenship, and explain why this book spotlights the term *gongmin* as the Chinese equivalent of the English word 'citizen'.

Gongmin: The Chinese Equivalent of 'Citizen'

In modern Chinese language, there are several Chinese terms in addition to *gongmin* that could be translated into 'citizen', each with 'its own intricate etymology and specific connotations' (Feng 2006, p. 87). In this section, I shall briefly compare these terms and argue that it is important in the contemporary context and appropriate for this book to single out the term *gongmin* as the Chinese equivalent of the modern Western citizen.

When citizenship is understood in the modern sense as the relationship with the nation-state, there are at least four terms used to denote the citizenry within the

S. Chen, *The Meaning of Citizenship in Contemporary Chinese Society*,
Governance and Citizenship in Asia, https://doi.org/10.1007/978-981-10-6323-7_3

Table 3.1 Four Chinese terms translatable to English by 'citizen'

Chinese term	First character	Second character	Literal translation
guomin	*guo* (the state)	*min* (people)	People of the state
renmin	*ren* (human)		Human people
shimin	*shi* (city)		City people
gongmin	*gong* (public)		Public people

nation-state in modern Chinese language (Table 3.1). All of them are terms with two Chinese characters, same on the second ones but different on the first ones which convey distinct nuances.

The term *guomin* (people of the state), according to Goldman and Perry (2002), appeared in pre-Qin texts more than 2000 years ago as a reference to 'inhabitants of rival warring states', was 'adopted' in the Japanese language in the Meiji period (1868–1912) to designate people of the modern institution of nation-state imported from the West, and 'reintroduced' from Japanese into modern Chinese language by reformist Liang Qichao in the late-Qing dynasty at the turn of the twentieth century (p. 4). In the context of internal turmoil and external pressure from foreign powers at the time, Liang used the term to promote what he considered a new kind of citizenship in his serial essay *Xinminshuo* (The New People) published between 1902 and 1906. What Liang aimed to cultivate for was rights-aware, active and self-disciplined citizens contributable to the project of building a powerful and prosper Chinese nation-state to stand up to foreign forces (Goldman and Perry 2002; Nathan 1985; Zarrow 1997). Liang's vision of citizenship, as Goldman and Perry (2002) noted, was 'state-conferred membership', distinct from ideas of building unity among people based on either ethnicity, culture or morality proposed by other reformists in the same period (p. 4).

Associating with Liang's theory of citizenship and soon becoming 'an important part of political discourse' (Harris 2002, p. 191), the term was used not only in the name of *Guomindang* (traditionally translated as the Nationalist Party) founded by Sun Yat-sen, but also to constitutionally designate people owning the sovereignty and holding the legal membership of the Republic of China established in 1912 by the above party which ended its rule on mainland China in 1949. While remaining a familiar term to people in mainland China nowadays, *guomin* was dismissed from the political language after the succeeding CCP established its regime in 1949, and replaced by the term *gongmin*, which we will turn to later, in the constitution of the People's Republic of China (PRC). Harris (2002, p. 196) commented that the substitution served as a means of language differentiation from the Nationalist Party and probably also expressed the recognition of the finite nature of the state suggested by classical Marxism.

Like *guomin*, *renmin* (human people) also has a long history that can be traced back to pre-Qin texts. The 'seemingly neutral' term, as Feng (2006) observed, was 'highly politicised' in the political language of the CCP particularly in the class struggle movements during the Maoist years till the end of the 1970s, and is still used in the name of almost every official institution, from the army to the government and the court at various levels (p. 89). If CCP's dismiss of *guomin* as the designation of state legal membership conveys the classical Marxist belief in the ultimate fate of the state as Harris (2002) speculated, then it is tempting to associate its employment of *renmin*, despite already being part of the political vocabulary of the Nationalist Party, with the communist commitment to emancipating all human beings. But *renmin* is not a term for all people in socialist China. It is an exclusionary category. The term designates the holder of all the powers of the PRC in Article 2 of the latest 2004 amended constitution, but not all legal members of PRC or *gongmin* are considered as the holder of sovereign power or *renmin*. The 'politically prestigious' term of *renmin* (Feng 2006, p. 89) excludes *gongmin* considered as 'enemies of the state' (Goldman and Perry 2002, p. 7), either the so-called bourgeois traitors and counter-revolutionaries during the Cultural Revolution, or people challenging socialist ideology as stated in the current constitution. Although the political exclusionary implication of the term 'seems to be waning gradually' after decades of focus on economic reform (Feng 2006, p. 89), *renmin* remains 'a revolutionary political term rather than a democratic political term' in contemporary China (Ni et al. 2010, p. 486).

Appearing much later than *guomin* and *renmin* in the Chinese language, the term *shimin* (city people), according to Harris (2002), came into use as a 'straightforward result' of the late nineteenth century circumstances in which urban gentry and merchant elites demanded for local self-rule and autonomy in city management in the face of the declining late-Qing dynasty (p. 188). Given this origin, and its appearance not only in the slogans of labour strikes and anti-invasion demonstrations for autonomy and self-rule in the republican China but also in the mobilization for mass protests for democracy during the 1989 pro-democracy movements in socialist China, Goldman and Perry's (2002) observation that the term 'figured prominently in the discourse of twentieth-century political activism' seems persuasive (p. 5). But Harris (2002) cautioned that those 'politically charged moments have not...been typical', and the term 'acquired an air of humdrum administrative convenience, remote from the memory of revolutionary *citoyens*' played by the urban bourgeois in the late eighteenth century West (p. 189). Furthermore, the use of *shimin* by city residents in their demonstrations implied that what they demanded, from civil autonomy to social rights, were indeed privileges attached to the urban residence, and thus expressed a sense of exclusion against the rural population (Culp 2007). In the PRC lexicon *shimin* is often 'just a narrow administrative term' (Harris 2002, p. 197), likely to appear in calls for civic virtue by local government in city management (Goldman and Perry 2002), and in claims for social benefits by urban residents, usually in ignorance of the rural population against the backdrop of the significant inequality between urban and rural in contemporary China described by Whyte (2010) as two societies in one country.

The brief review of the modern use of *guomin*, *renmin* and *shimin* above suggests that each of the three terms shares certain substance with modern Western citizenship. While the term *guomin* conveys a sense of state-centredness, the term *renmin* is left with the mark of political contestedness, and the term *shimin* is associated with ideas of liberty and self-rule. For modern Western citizenship, those aspects are recognized, protected and practiced through the legal institution of citizenship rights and responsibilities. None of the three terms bears the legal connotation in contemporary Chinese language. Although *renmin* does appear in the current constitution, it is short of connection to legal rights and responsibilities which are stated with the term of *gongmin*; *guomin* used to be the constitutional designation of legal state membership in republican China, but it has been replaced by *gongmin* under the current CCP regime. In other words, it is only the fourth term *gongmin* that is given the legal status and associated with legal rights and responsibilities in contemporary China. It is clearly stated in Article 33 of the current 1982 Constitution amended most recently in 2004 as follows:

> All persons holding the nationality of the PRC are citizens [*gongmin*] of the PRC.
> All citizens [*gongmin*] of the PRC are equal before the law.
> The State respects and preserves human rights.
> Every citizen [*gongmin*] is entitled to the rights and at the same time must perform the duties prescribed by the Constitution and other laws.[1]

This constitutional statement places *gongmin* in a similar position as 'citizen' which is legally institutionalized first in the modern West. It is for the reason of this legal similarity that I call *gongmin* the Chinese equivalent of 'citizen' in the section title. Like the concept of citizenship, the term *gongmin* is understood in this book as constructed, having its own etymological evolution (which we will turn soon) not necessarily in the same way as 'citizen' has in the West. This means that the equivalence between *gongmin* and citizen has to be understood in the relative sense. Nevertheless, this relative equivalence provides a shared starting point for contemporary debates and developments about citizenship and citizenship education across the Chinese and Western contexts.

The present constitutional statement about *gongmin* did not exist from the start of the PRC but has emerged a long way. The term was initially introduced into the first constitution in 1954, but it was only in the 1982 Constitution that the term began to be used to designate persons of the PRC nationality. Moreover, it was not until in the latest amendment in 2004 that the connection between *gongmin* and human rights is established. Drawing on the changes in the constitution and other Chinese legislations, Ni et al. (2010) discussed that citizen (*gongmin*) in the contemporary Chinese legislative language is now constructed not only as a legal identity, but also as an independent social identity manifested by the entitlement of private property, the equality before law and the attachment to human rights.

According to the present PRC Nationality Law enacted in 1980, dual legal citizenship is not recognized in China. The acquisition of legal Chinese citizenship

---

[1]The PRC Constitution is originally in Chinese. The Article 33 quoted here is from its English version available on the website of The National People's Congress of the PRC (http://www.npc.gov.cn/englishnpc/Constitution/node_2825.htm, accessed 26 April 2016). Those in square brackets are added by the author to indicate that *gongmin* is the original Chinese term for the 'citizen' in the English version.

follows a combination of the jus sanguinis or extraction principle and the jus soli or birthplace principle (Li and Wu 1999). A child born either in or out of China is eligible to be a PRC citizen if at least one parent is a PRC citizen. The eligibility also applies to a person born in China whose parents are stateless or of uncertain nationality but have settled in China. Given that the latter case is uncommon, legal Chinese citizenship, by and large, follows the jus sanguinis principle.

The term *gongmin* has been brought into public discourse after its first appearance in the 1954 Constitution (Yu 2002). Although it experienced two periods of disuse, one during the Cultural Revolution and the other soon after the 1989 pro-democracy movements in the early 1990s, from the mid-1990s onwards the term has been increasingly mentioned by the CCP leaders and pro-reform scholars against the societal backgrounds of ongoing legal reform, the shift from state-centeredness to market-orientedness, the acceptance of debate over universal human rights, and the growing demands for political reform (Harris 2002). Feng (2006) also observed that there has been 'more and more' legal, official and popular use of *gongmin* to refer to state membership (p. 88). Before we move on further to examine in what topics *gongmin* is used by the authorities, it is pertinent to briefly trace the history of the term to identify the connotations it gained prior to the CCP regime.

Like the terms of *guomin* and *renmin*, the term *gongmin* (public people) also 'finds its roots' in pre-Qin texts, originally the *Wudu* (The Five Vermin) written by legalist philosopher Han Fei (Fielder 2016, p. 170). In that text, *gongmin* served as the antithesis of *siren* (private person). Here contained two dichotomies: *gong* (public) versus *si* (private) and *min* (people) versus *ren* (person). First, given that the character *min* was often used to designate the masses as opposed to the ruler while *ren* was understood as an entity existing in between the sky and the earth in ancient Chinese literature and philosophy, it can be discussed that the term *gongmin* earned the connotation of collectivity, or at least non-individuality, in ancient use. Second, according to Mizoguchi (1995), the character *gong* had two connotations in traditional Chinese literature. One was the connotation of morally preferred publicness or non-privateness as conveyed in the original text, and of impartial sharing, equal division, justice and universality extended in the later use of the character. The other connotation was a public place, such as working and worship place, and also public office and official institution. Mizoguchi (1995) discussed that the first connotation conceptually influenced the second one, the moral preference attached to *gong* not only requiring public offices to act for public interest and justice but also serving as a justification for political intervention by the public for justice if which was not satisfied by monarchical rule. By the character *gong*, the term *gongmin* was equipped with the implications of publicity and moral orientation in public interest and justice.

The term *gongmin* was almost lost in use after pre-Qin times but began to reappear in the writings of late-Qing reformists in the late nineteenth century. In the aforementioned The New People in which Liang Qiqiao prominently elaborated his idea of new citizenry with the term *guomin*, he occasionally referred *gongmin* to the idea of participatory citizenship in the ancient West, and at one point even treated *gongmin* as a 'subset' of *guomin* by considering only participatory *guomin* as *gongmin* (Harris 2002, p. 189). In addition to Liang's The New People, there was the article *Gongmin zizhi pian* (On Self-Government by Citizens) written in 1902 by Liang's mentor Kang Youwei, another key reformist in that period. The two literatures are considered as 'perhaps the most influential work' on citizenship in the transitional China at the threshold of the twentieth century (Harris 2002, p. 189). It was Kang who expressed the term *gongmin* most explicitly at the time. In his above article advocating for local participation, *gongmin* was used to designate participants in local self-government.

Kang's use of the term *gongmin* for self-governance and local participation might be influenced by the Japanese language, given his exile experience in Japan. The Chinese character *gong* is also used in Japanese (pronounced as *kō*). According to Mizoguchi (1995), in contrast to the primacy of the first connotation of *gong* such as justice and universality in Chinese, *kō* in Japanese was prominently understood in the second connotation of *gong*, namely public and official institutions. Mizoguchi (1995) reasoned that this was because of, firstly, the non-conformity of the ideas of justice and universality in Japanese political tradition and, secondly, the fact that Japan imported the character from China mainly through literature in Han and Tang dynasties when the character was more often used in its second connotation. In the Meiji Constitution enacted in 1890, *kōmin* (same Chinese characters as *gongmin*) was used to refer to residents qualified to participate in public and official affairs at local levels (Isaka 1994), reminiscent of the role of *gongmin* in local self-government advocated by Kang. It was possible that the connection of *kōmin* with local participation in Japanese inspired Kang who, amid his relentless search for ideas from foreign experience to reform the problem-ridden late-Qing China, was exiled to Japan in 1898 for five months (Saito 2009) before his work on *gongmin* and local self-government written after his return to China.

For Kang, the entitlement of *gongmin* was conditional. Though regardless of male or female, a *gongmin* 'had to be a resident for years, over twenty years old, of good family, without a criminal record, with a willingness to help the poor and the ability to pay an annual tax of 10 yuan' (Min 1989, p. 139). The entitlement of *gongmin* would allow one to participate in local self-government primarily through voting in the local assembly, which was seen by Kang as a necessary institution to help officials govern and communicate with the common people (Min 1989). To the point that public involvement is concerned, *gongmin* developed by Kang is similar with *guomin* advanced by Liang and *shimin* by urban political activism in modern Chinese language.

Serving as a conditional entitlement for local participation and governance was only one of the two features of *gongmin* portrayed by Kang. He also envisaged *gongmin* beyond the local and even the national, idealistically treating *gongmin* as members of the world and participants in the universal public realm (Harris 2002). In his another work *Datongshu* (Great Harmony) Kang proposed to turn all uninhabited islands to public places wherein *gongmin* would live as residents, implying a vision of *gongmin* disconnected from the state. More explicitly, he once wrote that '[e]very person is born from Heaven, …should not be regarded as a citizen of the state (*guomin*) but as a citizen of Heaven (*tianmin*)' (Kang 1916, cited in Harris 2002, pp. 190–1). As Harris (2002) interpreted, Kang imagined that the state system would be gradually substituted by an expanding and eventually universal public (*gong*) realm in which global citizen (*shijie gongmin*) would practice authority through public discussion. The envision of the end of the state associated with the second feature of Kang's *gongmin* takes us back to the classical Marxist belief mentioned earlier that the state would eventually wither away, reinforcing the speculation of the reason behind the CCP's use of *gongmin* to designate the legal membership of nation-state. While whether Kang was influenced by Marxist theory is beyond the scope of consideration here, Kang's double-featured *gongmin* did reflect the two connotations of *gong* in traditional Chinese literature: *gongmin* as political participants in local self-government echoing *gong* in the sense of public and official institutions; and the utopian image of *gongmin* embodying the commitment to universality and justice associated with *gong*.

This section has justified the use of the term *gongmin* in this book as the Chinese equivalent of the English term citizen on the grounds that both share the legal connotation. The etymology of *gongmin* suggests that up to CCP-ruled China, the term was associated with collectivity and the moral commitment to public good and justice, expected to participate in public affairs and also envisaged to be actors beyond the state in the universal public realm. These historical connotations, however, do not necessarily sustain in the meaning of the term in contemporary times, because citizenship conception evolves according to changing societal conditions, a point demonstrated in the Western context in Chap. 2. In what context is *gongmin* mentioned by the authorities, and more substantially, what policies are promoted in reference to the term by the party-state? This is the question we are to explore in the next section.

The Party-State's Stance on Citizenship

The CCP National Congress opening every five years is seen as 'the most authoritative public event in the politics of China since 1949'; and the report delivered by the party general secretary at the event is 'a consensus document' containing 'ideological themes and policy lines' that are 'the most authoritative expression of the party's policy in the areas they address' (Wang 2012, p. 122). Given that in contemporary China the CCP as the sole ruling party is 'the real policy maker' under 'a dual bureaucracy' with the party 'dominant over' the government (Chan et al. 2008, p. 45), the existing CCP national congress reports are an authoritative source and start to examine the party-state's focus of *gongmin* in policy and its stance on citizenship. Table 3.2 summarizes the times that the term appeared and the subjects with which it was associated in the reports.

Table 3.2 The term *gongmin* in CCP national congress reports

Year (congress no.)	Occurrence	Subject in reference to *gongmin*
1987 (Thirteenth)	4	Legal rights, legal consciousness
1992 (Fourteenth)	0	N/A
1997 (Fifteenth)	4	'Four-have' (having ideal, morality, knowledge and discipline)
2002 (Sixteenth)	3	Political participation, legal rights, morality
2007 (Seventeenth)	5	Political participation, legal rights, citizenship awareness education, equality before the law
2012 (Eighteenth)	5	Rights when overseas, civic quality, political participation, morality

The term did not appear in any CCP national congress reports until the 1987 one given by then pro-reform general secretary Zhao Ziyang, in which the term debuted as the bearer of legal rights and legal consciousness (Zhao 1987). This could be seen as a reaffirmation of the new statement of *gongmin* as a legal status with rights in the 1982 Constitution. The term, however, was missing in the 1992 report, which came in the aftermath of the 1989 pro-democracy movements in which the term was employed by protesters in their demands for legal civil and political rights.

After a decade-long dormancy, *gongmin* reappeared in the 1997 report delivered by Jiang Zemin, serving as the carrier of the 'four-have' of having ideal (*lixiang*), morality (*daode*), knowledge (*wenhua*) and discipline (*jilü*) (Jiang 1997). The 'four-have' was originally proposed by Deng Xiaoping in the early 1980s as the requirement for Chinese people in socialist modernization. The association of *gongmin* with the requirement implied that more than as a legal term used in the constitution and laws, the term began to be incorporated into the political language of the CCP for ideological propaganda. Jiang Zemin also delivered the 2002 report in which the term was not attached to the 'four-have', but instead brought back to the narrative of legal rights, directly associated with morality, a component of the 'four-have', and newly linked to the subject of political participation (Jiang 2002).

The 2007 and 2012 reports were delivered by Hu Jintao. In the 2007 report the term continued to be used in association with legal rights and political participation, and, not found in former reports, was used to reiterate the constitutional statement of equality before the law. Furthermore, in place of the association with morality in the 2002 report, the term appeared in the call for citizenship awareness education which, as the report stated, aimed to develop 'socialist democracy, rule of law, liberty, equity, fairness and justice' (Hu 2007). Turning away from the socialist-style slogan of the 'four-have' and morality in the 1997 and 2002 reports, the 2007 report saw the term being attached to education, a more general topic, and to terms and concepts commonly found in the political discourses of Western democracies. There is no immediate or systematic explanation of those terms and concepts in the report. But the modifier 'socialist' indicates that the CCP retains the ideological authority to define them. Nevertheless, it is 'the first time' that *gongmin* is attached to education (*jiaoyu*) and citizenship awareness education, whatever it is meant to be, is 'lifted…to such a high level' (Tu 2011, p. 431). This unprecedented terminological connection between *gongmin* and education could be seen in a positive light as the official sanction to discussions about citizenship education (*gongmin jiaoyu*) in China. Yet the expression of citizenship awareness education is not necessarily a favourite of the CCP. In the 2012 report (the latest one at the time of writing this book), the expression was removed, and *gongmin* was reattached to morality as in the 2002 report (Hu 2012). While the association with political participation remained, connection to equality before the law was lost. Also, for the first time the term was used as the bearer of both rights that the party-state vowed to protect overseas and civic quality (*wenming suzhi*).

Putting the above observations under the analytical lens of the three-dimensional Western perspective of citizenship, it is suggested that the term *gongmin* in the CCP congress reports are often, though not always, in association with rights and moral responsibilities in the content dimension and political participation in the depth dimension. In other words, these three elements in Western citizenship seem to be of primary focus in the party-state's account of *gongmin*. How are citizenship rights, morality and political participation considered by the party-state and addressed at the policy level in contemporary China? In what follows I shall examine each of the three aspects in turn.

Rights

Some legal citizenship rights were stated in the first constitution of the PRC in 1954, but primarily limited to real property rights and inheritance rights with the state retaining the right to property confiscation and nationalization. The list of legal rights was considerably expanded in the 1982 Constitution and its amendments. Its latest 2004 version covers most of citizenship legal rights, from civil, political, social to cultural, which are commonly recognized in Western democracies and international law. A key feature of the CCP regime's contemporary policy on rights is its introduction of human rights into the legal citizenship rights discourse.

With the realization that 'the issue of human rights cannot be avoided in international settings' and hence shifting from its former position of having 'always shied away from any discussion about human rights' (Yu 1995, p. 94), the CCP regime started to take an active position on the rights issue in the 1990s, carrying out actions including international engagement, official review, constitutional amendment, national planning and public promotion. Specifically, first, it gave positive responses to international human rights treaties. The most significant was that it successively signed the International Covenant on Economic, Social and Cultural Rights in 1997 and the International Covenant on Civil and Political Rights in 1998. The former was ratified at the state level in 2001 with reservation to Article 8 on freedom of association and trade union rights, while the latter remains unratified up to present. Second, since its publication of the White Paper on Human Rights in China in 1991, which is the first official statement on human rights and also the first government white paper, the regime has, at the time of writing, reviewed the issue ten times in the form of white paper under the title of Progress in China's Human Rights (1995, 1996, 1998, 2000, 2003, 2004, 2009, 2012, 2013 and 2014), plus a white paper in 2000 summarizing the developments of human rights in the first half century of the PRC. Third, the regime's engaging attitude towards human rights culminated in the latest constitutional amendment in 2004, in which respect and protection for human rights are unprecedentedly incorporated as a principle into Article 33 as shown in the preceding section. Fourth, the regime has also introduced national projects to support its position on human rights. It published its first national plan on human rights in 2009 titled National Human Rights Action Plan of China (2009–2010). The two-year plan detailed specific schemes for developing and protecting citizens' rights, covering almost all aspects of rights and taking into account of diverse minority groups. With its self-evaluation that all the aims set in the 2009 plan had been successfully achieved, the government launched another similar plan in 2012 to be followed till 2015. Fifth, the party-state has also created some—but limited, especially when compared with the variety of official campaigns for citizenship morality which will be detailed soon—approaches to outreaching the public for its policy on rights. For example, in 2014 it declared 4 December, the day in 1982 that the current Constitution was promulgated, as Constitution Day, with the expressed purpose of promoting among the public the awareness of rule of law and legal rights and obligations.

Economic development is arguably the primary drive behind the regime's shift in the stance on human rights. The two international covenants were signed in the last years of China's decade-long negotiation for the membership, which was finally gained in 2001, of the World Trade Organization (WTO), whose standing for open and free trade demands the protection of trade-related human rights such as property rights and labour rights. Here lies what Wang (2016) called the 'coordinated compliance of international trade and human rights' (p. 83). While conventional instrumentalist arguments hold that the CCP's compliance with international trade regimes represented by the WTO case gives the international community leverage to push the Chinese government to comply with human rights, Wang (2016) argued that the benefits of such compliance are two-way, as it could also contribute to the international trade and eventually economic development in China, a key legitimacy ground of the CCP regime.

Compliance does not necessarily mean full submission. Wang (2016) also pointed out that the compliance of international human rights standards by the Chinese authorities is often an endeavour of 'selective adaption' depending upon local interpretation, acceptance and complementarity (pp. 79–80). In a more specific manner, Li (2007) listed three elements in the interpretation of human rights in Chinese official documents and announcements that show 'a strong combination of cultural relativism and developmentalism' (p. 149):

> Human rights for Chinese people are primarily social and economic rights rather than civil and political rights, and the right to subsistence is the most basic right;
> China is still a developing country, so development, stability and national independence are the most important rights; China should implement UHRR [United Nations' Universal Human Rights Regime] according to its specific cultural, historical and political conditions; and
> The issue of human rights is a domestic one concerning sovereignty, and other countries should not interfere in this area. (p. 149)

Human rights so interpreted is hierarchized and conditioned, carrying the undertone that civil and political rights and individual interests can be sacrificed for social and economic rights and state interests at the discretion of the party-state and in the name of state sovereignty. Furthermore, while compliance with international trade institutions does push the CCP regime to improve the capacity of its legal system, the issue of the absence of an independent judiciary, which is in effect subordinate to political wills, lingers on (Wang 2016). The absence places citizens in an unsecured position, as they are unable to claim, negotiate and exercise their legal rights free of the fear of political intervention and repression.

Morality

The expression of *gongmin* as the bearer of ideal, morality, knowledge and discipline (the so-called 'four-have') in the CCP's 1997 congress report marked the start of the appeal to *gongmin* for morality in official discourses. Following the 1997 report and paving the way for the 2002 report which singled out morality to be attached to *gongmin*, the CCP specially issued in 2001 the Guideline for Improving Citizens' Morality (*Gongmin daode jianshe shishi gangyao*) (CCP Central Committee 2001), an influential reference which continues to guide official narratives and policies about civic morality. The guideline prominently places the Maoist cliché of 'to serve the people' (*wei renmin fuwu*) as the core and collectivism as the principle of citizens' morality. Covering from domestic life to work and social life, the guideline lists ten virtues as the basic ethical code of conduct for *gongmin*, including patriotism (*aiguo*), law-abidingness (*shoufa*), courtesy (*mingli*), integrity and honesty (*chengxin*), solidarity (*tuanjie*), friendliness (*youshan*), diligence and frugality (*qinjian*), self-empowerment (*ziqiang*), professional dedication (*jingye*), and devotion (*fengxian*). Side by side with the intact 'four-have', the guideline also sets out loving home country, people (*renmin*), work, science and socialism as the basic requirement of morality, which, known as the 'five-love', is mentioned as an encouragement yet not in association with *gongmin* in Article 24 of the latest version of the constitution.

There have been a variety of concerted efforts by the authorities to uphold the guideline. A follow-up document was issued by the CCP in 2003 to provide practical advices for the promotion of the guideline. That document designated 20 September, the day in 2001 that the guideline was issued, as Citizens' Morality Promotion Day since 2003 (CCP Central Committee 2003). Adding to the party-state's push for morality is a national forum on citizens' morality held in every March since 2004, together with wave after wave of morality campaigns across the country, including the biennial nationwide selection of moral paragons since 2007.

It is not hard to discern that the citizenship morality defined and promoted in the guideline firmly clings to socialism, collectivism and patriotism, all of which are key themes in the party-state's ideological propaganda in earlier years. As far as citizenship is concerned, what distinguishes the guideline from earlier propaganda language is that those socialist, collectivist and patriotist virtues are attached to and aimed at *gongmin*, legal citizens who are, unlike *renmin*, neither the holder of state power nor necessarily the upholder of socialism, according to the current constitution. There could be two intentions behind this new attachment. One is to tighten the ideological control on legal citizens who are not constitutionally bound to socialist ideology; and the other intention is to use the legal and politically neutral term of *gongmin* to promote socialist morality at a time that socialism is no longer a solid legitimacy ground for the CCP and blatant ideological propaganda has lost attention from the public.

Paralleling socialist ideology, traditional Chinese values are also taken advantage of in the party-state's narrative construct of citizenship morality in the guideline. The evidence is the incorporation of traditional virtues such as courtesy, integrity and honesty in the proposed basic ethical code of conduct, and the call for the combination of traditional virtues and contemporary spirits. Indeed, recent years have witnessed a surge of official promotion of traditional Chinese values, a move running counter to the party-state's outright rejection of Chinese tradition in the Cultural Revolution. But according to Ai's (2015) study on the political use of tradition in contemporary China, upholding traditions for the party-state is 'useful as a way to fill up the vacuum left in the ideological system…to promote China's "cultural soft power" internationally and to combat the influence of Western liberalism on China' (p. 215). Also, the definition of tradition in contemporary party-state discourses is observed by Ai (2015) to be 'broad', ranging from Confucianism to Maoism, and 'vague', subject to the 'invention' by the party-state which self-poises as the 'legitimate custodian' of Chinese tradition (pp. 216–7). This insight deepens our understanding of the mixture of traditional values and socialist ideology in the guideline, which manifests the party-state's stance on citizenship in terms of morality.

Political Participation

Political participation is the third primary focus in the party-state's account of *gongmin* if measured by our Western analytical lens. While the CCP has a history of mobilizing the public to meet its political aims, an ample example of which is the

Cultural Revolution, it has been keeping the public away from participating in the form of universal suffrage in state affairs. Notwithstanding, as introduced at the start of this book, the party-state's increased dependence on performance for ruling legitimacy pushes it not only to allow and even encourage citizens to take part in governance for a robust market economy but also to meet political demands from citizens. The party-state's response to the push is primarily formulated with the rhetoric of 'enhancing *gongmin*'s orderly political participation' (*kuoda gongmin youxu de zhengzhi canyu*), which repeatedly appeared in 2002, 2007 and 2012 national congress reports of the CCP.

The People's Congress (PC) and the Chinese People's Political Consultative Conference (CPPCC) at five administrative levels, from village (no CPPCC at this level), county, municipal, provincial to national, are proclaimed by the party-state as two main institutional avenues for collective participation in the political system. The former has the legislative power while the latter does not. Laws made by the National People's Congress (NPC) and its standing committee possess the highest authority. The party-state did approve and widen direct elections by citizens for PC representatives at the village and county levels in recent decades—representatives beyond those two levels are in principle indirectly elected by representatives at a lower level. Yet, it is widely observed that the PC membership at any level is in fact 'determined by CCP leaders', resulting in that local PCs are 'not independent of control by the local CCP organs' (Zang 2011, p. 173). For the CPPCC, members are elites from different social sectors that are chosen through the mechanism of recommendation and under the direction of the CCP.

The CCP's predominant power in the two institutions, together with the elitist nature of the CPPCC, means that they are not universally accessible to ordinary citizens. O'Brien (1990) concluded in his study of the NPC that, on one hand, the CCP recognized 'the need to obtain information, advice and support from key sectors of the population' and, consequently, 'the political system exhibited increasing inclusiveness for much of the 1980s'; on the other hand that recognition 'did not diminish the party's commitment to suppress dissent and maintain political power', and the political system remained 'illiberal and authoritarian' as it 'did not guarantee equal rights for all citizens' (p. 177). Without systemic political reform in place or in sight, what observed by O'Brien arguably remains unchanged in the early twenty-first century.

In addition to the above two established avenues supposedly designed for collective political participation but actually confined to certain groups of citizens, there have been institutional developments on local self-governance in villages and cities. In 1998 the Chinese government enacted the PRC Organic Law of Villager Committees, mandating direct village elections nationwide. The law gives villagers the power not only to nominate candidates and vote for the members and chairpersons of villager committee—these posts have considerable power from the distribution of village land to mediation of local civil disputes, but also to run for office in their own village without the condition of being a CCP member. Schubert and Ahlers (2012) favourably commented that 'the overall balance sheet of village elections more than a decade after the implementation of the 1998 Organic Law can be called positive', while acknowledging that 'the configuration of political power in the villages are not altered' (p. 22). Indeed, the autonomy in local governance tolerated by the CCP does not necessarily serve as evidence of democratization in the authoritarian regime, as whoever is elected, the leadership of the CCP remains unchallengeable. Moreover, the autonomy available to local citizens and embodied in choice and contestation for office does not necessarily hurt but could instead strengthen the CCP regime. Based on their survey of village voters and the finding that 'even when competition is structured to the benefit of party members, the perception of competition as choice between candidates is sufficient to engage voters and increase their perception that the electoral process is fair', Landry et al. (2010) suggested that 'contested elections in authoritarian regimes may simultaneously strengthen demand for accountability and loyalty to the regime' (p. 763).

As the urban counterpart to villager committees, community resident committees were officially promoted, following a nationwide campaign of 'community building' (*shequ jianshe*), as a new model of local self-governance in cities in 2000. Under the management of committee members elected by residents in the community, the committee is designed to carry out a broad range of functions, from welfare service provision to morality promotion and to connection of the CCP to the grassroots. With such functions community resident committees are supposed to take over the role played by the now-dismantled socialist work unit system in providing welfare services to urban residents and to meet the governance challenges in the face of the increasingly floating and heterogeneous urban population driven by the influx of rural migrants (Bray 2006). The urban governance through community resident committees, similar to their counterpart in villages, seems to be able to win general support from local citizens. Based on their survey of citizens governed by such committees in Beijing, Chen et al. (2007) reported that the self-governance system was widely embraced. Nevertheless, their study also exposed the limits of the committee model. For instance, it 'lacks appeal' to citizens who hold strong belief in democracy and doubt its efficacy, given that the committees are 'largely dominated' by local CCP organizations and the government; and it earns 'less faith' from citizens residing in new housing areas than from those in traditional housing complexes, partly because its failure to protect the interests, such as property rights, of new homeowners (p. 521).

Another evidence of the party-state's confidence in leading while engaging with citizens is that it has also shown efforts to open the door for ordinary citizens to monitor the government. Following the first ever statement in the 2007 CCP national congress report to protect the right of people (not *gongmin* but *renmin*) to information, participation, expression and monitoring regarding governmental affairs (*zhiqingquan, canyuquan, biaodaquan, jianduquan*), the Chinese government implemented the Regulations of the PRC on Open Government Information in 2008. The regulation is supposed to guide government organs to meet the needs of citizens (the regulation used *gongmin*) to access to government information, monitor government and demand transparency and accountability in governance. Unsurprisingly, barriers exist in practice, one of which is the pretext of 'state secrets' (*guojia jimi*). For example, when a research team in the Research and

Support Centre for Public Participation at Peking University required, in the name of citizen (*gongmin*), governmental departments to release information about office expenses per official in 2012, the Central Bank of China declined on the basis of state secrets.[2] Under the same pretext, the Ministry of Environmental Protection refused Beijing-based lawyer Dong Zhengwei's request for the release of information about the nationwide survey of soil pollution in 2013.[3] These cases illustrate that on one hand relevant legislations and regulations are in place and the party-state keep vowing to protect political rights and encouraging citizens to get involved in governance; on the other hand, the extent to which citizens are allowed to monitor government and engage in governmental affairs in practice is subject to the will of the authorities.

It is fair to say that the legislative foundation for Chinese citizens to take part in political affairs has been enhanced by the introduction of relevant laws and regulations since the 1990s. The enhancement can be seen as a strategy by the CCP regime to solidify its legitimacy increasingly based on governance performance and meeting social demands. The avenues of political participation opened up, however, are far from universally accessible or obstacle-free in practice. Moreover, those changes seem to work well for the benefits of the regime. The competitive local elections for local officials allows the regime to transfer accountability from central to local and increase loyalty to the central; and the regime can win the support of social elites by incorporating them into the political system through such institutions as the PC and the CPPCC. In addition, there have been very few officially organized and nationwide campaigns for citizenship political participation, as opposed to some for rights and various more for morality.

Citizenship-Related Education

By analyzing the CCP national congress reports, the last section identified that three elements of Western citizenship—morality, rights and political participation—are of primary focus in the party-state's account of *gongmin*. The party-state's policies on the three elements, together with its public pedagogical measures for them, were then discussed in turn. This section continues to review citizenship-related education in contemporary China with the focus on school education for further disclosing the party-state's stance on citizenship. But first of all, it is necessary to clarify the difference between the phrases of citizenship education and citizenship-related education used in this book.

[2]See the news report 'Nine ministries responded to citizens' request and publicized office expense per capital' (in Chinese), *Legal Daily Newspaper*, 2 November 2012, http://epaper.legaldaily.com.cn/fzrb/content/20121102/Articel06005GN.htm (accessed 16 November 2016).

[3]See the news report 'The Ministry of Environmental Protection refuses to make public for the reason of state secret' (in Chinese), *Legal Daily Newspaper*, 25 February 2013, http://epaper.legaldaily.com.cn/fzrb/content/20130225/Articel06001GN.htm (accessed 16 November 2016).

There is no formal curriculum subject title containing the term *gongmin* in schools, particularly at the compulsory level. As a recently surfaced term in the Chinese official language, *gongmin jiaoyu* or citizenship education, if defined in the broadest sense of citizenship concerning the relationship between individual and community, is conducted under the CCP regime primarily through political education, ideological education and moral education, which are 'interrelated' and 'actually three-in-one in connotation' (Lee and Ho 2008, p. 139). Indeed, political and moral elements are parts of Western citizenship and can be found in school citizenship education in the West. For instance, when citizenship education was introduced as a formal subject in England in 2001, it contained the three strands of political literacy, social and moral responsibilities and community involvement. Also, by the 'introduction' of the aforementioned Guideline for Improving Citizens' Morality (Li et al. 2004, p. 458; Tse 2011, p. 174), the term *gongmin* is now part of the official language in education. But simply equating the long established political, ideological and moral education with *gongmin jiaoyu* or citizenship education would both obscure the fact that there is no formal subject title containing the term *gongmin*, and, more substantially, risk losing the legal element, which is not necessarily contained in political, ideological and moral education but is a starting point shared between China and the wider world for discussion and comparison on citizenship and citizenship education.[4] It is thus arguably more appropriate to refer to the existing political, ideological and moral education as, simply following W. O. Lee and Ho (2008), ideopolitical-moral education or, from the perspective of citizenship, citizenship-related education.

Law (2011) helpfully summarized four measures taken by the party-state to harness ideopolitical-moral education since the 1990s. First, the party-state has enshrined socialism as the political cause of education in all national laws for education—most of which were enacted in the 1990s—and by so doing legalized and secured, to use Law's (2011, p. 107) words, the 'political bottom line' of any educational changes. Second, the regime started in the early 2000s the ongoing curriculum revisions and amendments on primary and secondary ideopolitical-moral education as attempts to accommodate social transitions and follow evolving socialist doctrines put forward by the CCP. Third, as a more flexible way to echo official policies and address unanticipated issues, what Law (2011) called 'ad hoc political education campaigns' have been also undertaken by the party-state, such as the campaign in the early 2000s for the study of national ethical code of conduct soon after the publication of the Guideline for Improving Citizens' Morality, and the intensified campaign for

[4]Lately in April 2016 the Ministry of Education commanded that the ideopolitical-moral education textbooks for Grades 1 and 7 would be renamed as Morality and Rule of Law (*Daode yu fazhi*) since 2016. This is a sign of institutional approval of the legal element in the ideopolitical-moral education by the authorities. But the approval is arguably not wholehearted. The curriculum is so far not correspondingly updated; and there is no change on the textbook names or curricula for other grades, which remain as Moral Character and Life (*Pinde yu shenghuo*) for Grade 2, Moral Character and Society (*Pinde yu shehui*) for Grades 3–6, Thought and Moral Character (*Sixiang pinde*) for Grades 8–9, and Though and Politics (*Sixiang zhengzhi*) for Grades 10–12.

education in ethnic solidarity in the late 2000s amid unrest among ethnic minorities. Fourth, the party-state has also made efforts to 'strengthen…student work on campus' in order to 'promote its political doctrines and develop party work outside the formal curriculum' (Law 2011, p. 126). That has been done primarily through active recruitment of student members into the CCP as well as into its youth-targeted organs set up in primary and secondary schools.

Neither political education nor political penetration into schools is new under the CCP regime—both were exemplified during the Cultural Revolution (Kwong 1988). The contemporary feature of ideopolitical-moral education is arguably the changes brought about by the curriculum reform within the legalized political bottom line of socialism. By analyzing official documents and educational policies between 1990 and 2002, Lee and Ho (2008) identified the changes since the mid-1990s in the policy and curriculum of moral education, which long involved ideology and politics as well as morality. According to them, personal moral values such as psychological qualities 'tended to outweigh' political values such as patriotism and socialism; social values such as family and occupational ethics 'became increasingly apparent'; and there was 'a clear rise of the mention of "global outlook"' (p. 146). Their case study on moral education policymaking in Guangdong Province demonstrated the above tendencies and, furthermore, that local government, academics, teachers and the public were given more autonomy by the party-state in the reform. They concluded that ideopolitical-moral education in the period featured 'depoliticization' and 'decentralization', having passed from the period of political orientation to the period of paralleling political and moral orientations, and finally to the period of moral orientation (p. 152).

In accordance with the observation by Lee and Ho (2008) of increased emphasis on personal and social values, Lu and Gao (2004) concluded their study of moral education curriculum reform at the primary level that the curriculum has become 'child centred', focusing on morality in children's lives and using 'everyday life events as source materials for textbooks' (p. 495). Similar findings were reported by Tse (2011) in his comparison of the 1997 and 2005 versions of moral education textbooks at the lower secondary level, both used nationwide and published before and after the curriculum reform by the most authoritative textbook publishing house the People's Education Press. Tse (2011) found that 'while collectivism and socialism are still endorsed as the guiding principles [like the old textbooks], there is a salient recognition of self or individual [in the new ones which]…were designed with closer connection to the real life of society and the students' (p. 167). The changes of content and approach in moral education textbooks are succinctly described by Wang and Tan (2014) as 'from ideopolitical indoctrination to real-life narration' (p. 195).

The recognition of self is expressed in terms of not only morality but also rights as the outcome of curriculum reform. Tse (2011) also reported in the textbook comparison study that, while the priority of national or collective interests over personal ones and the expectation of active contribution to the country expressed in the 1997 textbooks remain in the new ones, the notion of human rights is now 'frequently mentioned'; and participation in governance is narrated as both responsibilities fulfilment and rights exercise (p. 167). Also, the 2005 textbooks were found to give a response to the emerged global perspective at the policy and curriculum level identified by Lee and Ho (2008). Alongside the persistent emphasis on national culture, traditions and identity, the new textbooks, as Tse (2011) observed, cover more on cultural diversity and global issues and require mutual respect and global-mindedness. Tse (2011) concluded that moral education textbooks 'have been gradually shifting' from the previous 'narrow and limited focus on ideological-political indoctrination…towards a relaxed notion of citizenship, with a growing emphasis on individual rights and global elements' (p. 177).

The increased appreciation for the global perspective and human rights in the reformed ideopolitical-moral education is arguably limited. Taught in the subject expressly for morality, rights are structurally placed in a subordinate position to morality. In addition, full and open teaching and learning of rights are effectively not allowed, given the political bottom line of socialism and the unchallengeable rule of the party-state. The restriction by the interest of the party-state also applies to the newly highlighted global perspective. One point similarly revealed by Pan's (2014) and Law's (2014) respective investigations of how international event—the former looking at the 2008 Beijing Olympic Games and the latter the 2010 Shanghai World Exposition—is used in local and global citizenship education is that, promoting national pride and national identity is at the heart of citizenship-related education in China. From the perspective of population governance, Greenhalgh (2010) pointed out that cultivating independent persons with global awareness is in essence part of the party-state's project on the population, which is treated no longer as a burden but human capital for the rise of China to a global power.

The characteristics of contemporary citizenship-related education can be encapsulated as the recognition of individual citizen confined under socialism, collectivism and patriotism. What further constrains the recognition is the party-state's self-claimed paternalistic role which is indoctrinated through citizenship-related education (Fairbrother 2014). In short, the recognition is subject to political and ideological purposes. In this sense, whatever the essentially ideopolitical-moral education is called, either long established moral, ideological and political education or the new name of citizenship consciousness education recently emerged in the official discourse, they are just 'different terms but similar purposes' which are 'to initiate students into a set of sociopolitical ideas, skills, values, and behaviours that…[the CCP] deems acceptable' (Law 2006, pp. 606–7).

The changes, as well as continuities, in citizenship-related education unravelled above come as no surprise, for they are in full accordance with the party-state's stance on rights, morality, and political participation elaborated earlier. Given the absolute control of state power claimed by the CCP and the authoritarian nature of the CCP regime, it is logically and realistically hard to expect that the party-state would allow a free citizenship discourse in society or meet claims challenging its authority by and in the name of citizens. But at the same time, contemporary Chinese society is not necessarily in a passive relationship to the state, because meeting needs in society have become part of the regime's legitimacy ground, as introduced at the beginning of the book. The next section will discuss further and illustrate the contemporary state-society dynamics, and by doing so connect the state perspective we have focused on so far to the social one to be unveiled in the following chapters.

The State-Society Dynamics

The dynamics between the party-state and the society in policymaking and governance is indeed part of the background against which this book is written. It is in the sense of there being space for both sides to act and react that I call it a dynamic relationship. Given that there is little direct political challenge from society against the party-state, which actually enjoys popular support on the whole (Teets et al. 2010; Wright 2010), the contemporary Chinese state-society relation is not necessarily deadlocked, but has space for the party-state to rule on the legitimacy ground of socialist ideology and governance performance on one hand, and for social forces to exert influences on policymaking and governance on the other hand.

One key feature of governance under the CCP regime since its launch of the economic reform in 1978 is decentralization. Zheng (2010) outlined two stages of decentralization in China: from central to local governments between 1978 and the mid-1990s, and from state to society since the late 1990s. According to Zheng (2010), in the first stage the regime devolved economic and political powers from the central to local governments, giving the latter the authority in economic and other local affairs and developing an 'interdependent' relation between the two government levels in the sense of mutual influence on decision-making (p. 36). With the 'dynamism' gained in the first stage (Zheng 2010, p. 35), in the second stage of decentralization the regime, on one hand, recentralized crucial economic and political powers through a series of reforms from taxation to personnel selection, and on the other hand passed certain powers from state to society through economic corporatization and privatization, limited political democratization (such as the aforementioned village elections), and the approval of NGOs.

It should be noted that the increased autonomy in society as the consequence of the state-initiated decentralization does not mean that a Chinese civil society is created, if civil society is defined, following Taylor (1995), as society 'where there are free associations that are not under tutelage of state power' in a minimal or negative sense, not to mention civil society in a stronger or positive sense that 'as a whole can structure itself…through such free associations' and 'can significantly determine or inflect the course of state policy' (p. 208). What the decentralization brought about is closer to what Frolic (1997) called 'state-led civil society', which 'is created by the state, principally to help it govern, but also to co-opt and socialize potentially politically active elements in the population' (p. 56).

This book examines the meaning of *gongmin* in contemporary Chinese society through newspaper content analysis and investigation of the perceptions of university students and migrant workers in Guangdong Province. I shall highlight in turn the characteristics of Guangdong Province, the media sector and the two social groups of university students and migrant workers in contemporary China to illustrate the contemporary state-society dynamics. The source of data used in this book is also explained.

Guangdong Province

Guangdong Province is located in the southern end of mainland China, geographically far from Beijing and sharing a border with Hong Kong. According to the 2010 China Census, it has a population of about 100 million, standing out as the most populous province. With 'considerably shallower' social roots of the CCP in it (Goodman 1997, p. 6), the province has a tradition of political diversity and individualism, earning 'some reputation as a crucible of democratic and liberal politics' before 1949 (Goodman and Feng 1994, p. 182). All of Liang Qiqiao, Sun Yat-sen and Kang Youwei mentioned in the first section of this chapter as key contributors to the Chinese discourse of citizenship at the beginning of the twentieth century had origins in the province. But that liberal political tradition, according to Goodman and Feng (1994), seems to be 'surrendered' under the CCP regime, particularly after the 1980s (p. 182). This might not be a bewildering development, given that the province has been given greater local powers, albeit driven by economic purposes, than other regions by the central government since the start of the economic reform.

In his study on Guangdong Province under reform, Vogel (1989) pointed out that although Guangdong Province was, like other provinces, subject to 'enough leverage' in the hands of the central government vital to the success of reform at the regional level, from appointment of regional heads to technical help, the province was granted 'special freedom and support' and 'more leeway than other localities', primarily due to its connections to the outside world perceived by the central government as economic opportunities (p. 81). The provincial government thus enjoyed 'significantly increased' authority in 'agricultural, industrial, transport, commercial, educational, cultural, technical, and public health activities' (Vogel 1989, p. 85) in the first stage of nationwide decentralization from central to local governments between 1978 and the mid-1990s identified by Zheng (2010). More recently, Guangdong is one of the few provinces that pioneer in transferring administrative authority from provincial government to social organizations, though which play no more than 'a supportive, subsidiary role' (Gao and Tyson 2017, p. 14). Positioned at the forefront in the economic reform, Guangdong Province became an engine for China's economy in the past decades (Di Tommaso et al. 2013).

Accompanying the economic success, there was, as Vogel (1989) reported, concern by the provincial authorities that the unleashed desire for and the pursuit of personal gains in the market might undermine morality, the commitment to the public good in particular, in the society. Probably out of such concern the

Guangdong Propaganda Department instructed the publication in 1995 of the booklet New Three Character Classic (*Xin sanzijing*). With a name echoing the Three Character Classic—a traditional child-oriented reading summarizing Chinese history and Confucian tenets in three-characters rhymed lines—and the content dominantly promoting traditional, personal and social values, the booklet not only became a national hit with about 40 million copies sold nationwide, but also fuelled a boom of similar publications outside the province (Lee and Ho 2005). The particular case illustrates that alongside its economic influence, Guangdong Province is also a region for other localities to look at for what and how to address the social consequences of the ongoing economic reform.

The Media

The media sector experienced dramatic changes under the state-society decentralization. With the removal of state subsidies, the growing financial independence and the deregulation in terms of personnel and management, China's media, from television and radio to newspaper and magazine, has been dramatically commercialized since the 1990s, becoming much more responsive to the interests of readers as consumers in order to make profits through sales and advertising (Li and Liu 2009; Scotton and Hachten 2010; Shirk 2011; Stockmann 2013). Take the example of newspapers, the number of which increased more than ten times under the CCP regime to about 1900 at the beginning of the 2010s (Zhou 2015). With the finding that daily newspapers in main cities also covered negative stories about the economic reform reported in Western media outlets, Smith (2002) suggested that city-level newspapers are now more able than before to bypass official propaganda to carry interesting and controversial pieces to cater to readers. Observing newspapers in the contemporary Chinese context, Guo (2010) discussed that a salient change in newspapers is that they have started to represent the economic and social sectors that gain increased influence in society.

Neither of the two studies above ignored the persistent media control and censorship by the party-state. The state still has the final say on what is included and excluded in newspapers, as reminded by Smith (2002); and newspapers, as Guo (2010) commented, are indeed put on a 'dual-track system' (p. 50), operating as enterprises to earn revenue and survive in the market on one hand, and still being part of the party-state's ideological propaganda mechanism on the other hand. This circumstance is succinctly summarized by Hachten (2010) in the way that 'a mix of Party logic and market logic…is the defining feature of media in China today' (p. 21). The control from the top may face countermeasures at the bottom. Tong (2009) revealingly reported how the journalists in her study used self-censorship to bypass political taboos in order to publish news pieces on highly politically sensitive topics.

Nevertheless, the commercialization has dynamized the Chinese media once in an essentially passive relation to the party-state. Indeed, the impact of the commercialization has been the focus in the recent literature on Chinese media (McCormick 2003). There are arguments that the party-state is losing control over the commercialized and diversified media (e.g. Lynch 1999). But this kind of argument, as McCormick (2003) traced, is contested by a more cautious evaluation that the party-state, in fact, manages to keep its control over the media in an increasingly indirect and diffuse way. Furthermore, there are also studies contending that the media commercialization is not a threat to but plays into the hands of the party-state for its authoritarian rule (Lin 2012; Stockmann 2013). In her study covering a wide range of stakeholders and an extensive number of Chinese newspapers, Stockmann (2013) concluded that commercialization gives credibility to media sources in the eye of readers and, by so doing, stabilizes the authoritarian rule of the party-state, which finely balances between tolerating freedom for the media to respond to market needs and controlling media content.

The dynamics brought about by the commercialization of newspapers, televisions and radios, or what Latham (2007) called 'orderly media' in the sense that they are still controllable and predictable for the party-state, is paralleling with the surge and spread of telecommunications or 'disorderly media', such as messages via mobile phone and the Internet, which are comparatively individualized, contingent and unpredictable. Latham (2007) argued that disorderly media challenges the hierarchical sender-recipient relation and the durability of information assumed in the traditional propaganda model of Chinese media, by providing an alternative model in which not only can citizens per consumers be independent decision-makers but also information becomes disposable. He suggested that this alternative model deepens, and hence needs to be 'incorporated' into, our understanding of orderly media, because the everyday consumption of orderly media in contemporary China 'involves a swathe of disorderly media practices (Latham 2007, p. 309).

Guangdong Province has been notable in the media commercialization. It is the home to the first newspaper group in China—the form used by the regime to integrate newspaper resources and increase market competitiveness—established in 1996. It is also not lacking of newspapers increasingly giving voice to society despite under lesser or stricter yet persistent state censorship. *Southern Metropolis Daily* (*Nanfang dushibao*), wherein the use of *gongmin* is analyzed in this book, is one of such newspapers. Established in 1997 at the peak of the growth of the newspaper industry, the newspaper is described by Goldman (2005) as an 'outspoken' (p. 187) newspaper under the Southern Newspaper Group which is 'daring' (p. 225) to express public opinion even if contradicting the state. The newspaper falls into what Stockmann (2013) categorized nonofficial newspapers, which, as opposed to party-state official newspapers, not only feature less party-state involvement and more financially independent and reader-oriented but are also observed to be more credible in the eyes of readers (Gang and Bandurski 2011; Stockmann 2013). Indeed, with the largest circulation among daily newspapers in Guangdong Province, the newspaper has earned the reputation of independent reporting (Tong 2009). In addition, it exceptionally and expressly takes on the role of raising citizenship consciousness in China.[5]

The newspaper allows us to glimpse the public opinion, seen as the collective discourse, of *gongmin* in society, though from a critical perspective what it reflects is hardly all voices but the dominant ones in it, because of the unequal contribution by social groups of varied prestige and position to the formation of public opinion (Blumer 1948). Given the persistent state censorship, the newspaper alone cannot show the extent to which it deviates from the official stance in the media sector. For reference and comparison purpose the use of *gongmin* in *People's Daily* (*Renmin ribao*), the mouthpiece newspaper of the party-state, is also analyzed in this book.

University Students

The party-state's higher education policy has also gone through significant reforms under the decentralization since the 1990s. Similar to the media sector, universities fully relied on state funding until the beginning of the 1990s. Since then the party-state has significantly reduced its financial support, propelling higher education institutions (HEIs) to seek after other funding resources including charging students tuition fees which were free before (Ding et al. 2011). With the remaining state funding as leverage, and through projects of building world-class, or Westernized as some may criticize, universities, including the Project 211 which intends to develop one hundred high-quality HEIs for the twenty-first century, the party-state introduced and accelerated internal competition among universities (Mok 2002). Driven by the intention to increase effectiveness and global competitiveness and to create more education opportunities, the party-state has also considerably transferred the provision and administration of higher education to local governments to allow universities to better meet local needs, reconstructed universities through institutional mergers and cooperation, and opened the door for, and indeed encouraged, not merely domestic social and private sectors to fund and run HEIs but also foreign institutions to cooperate with local ones to provide transnational higher education (Mok 2002, 2005; Ong and Chan 2016). Once again, these developments do not mean that the party-state control over HEIs has vanished. Mok (2005) suggested that what changed is the governance model from 'the interventionist state model' to 'the deregulated state model' in the administration and to 'the accelerationist state model' in the marketization and involvement of social forces, alongside 'considerable extent of control' by the party-state (pp. 78–9). This observation echoes our earlier discussion on the contemporary characteristics of Chinese media.

---

[5]'To raise citizenship awareness' (*qimeng gongmin yishi*) is mentioned in the introduction to the newspaper on its official website (http://nd.oeeee.com/incfiles/guanyunandou/200712/t20071229_632591.htm, accessed 14 April 2017).

The state-led acceleration in higher education resulted in the surge of numbers of institutions and students (Shi 2015), though that happened primarily in non-prestigious and especially private kinds of institutions (Ross et al. 2010, p. 306). In the decade of 2004–2014, the number of regular HEIs (*putong gaoxiao*) increased from 1731 to 2529, in which the number of privately run HEIs (*minban gaoxiao*) tripled from 226 to 728 (National Bureau of Statistics of China 2005, 2015). In terms of the number of students, the total gross enrolment rate covering all forms of higher education rose dramatically from 3.5% in 1991 to 37.5% in 2014; and the total number of university students experienced a nearly ten-fold increase in the period to over 35 million (Li 2009, p. 386; Ministry of Education of the PRC 2015). The radical expansion has made Chinese higher education, using then Vice Minister of Education Wu Qidi's words, 'the largest system of higher education in the world' (Wu 2008, p. 9). It is, as Stone (2011) commented, 'irrefutable that Chinese higher education has moved from elite education to mass education' (p. 73).

Facing the expanded number of university students, the party-state has reconfigured its relation with the students. According to Ross et al. (2010), the party-state has detached itself from direct student management, and instead established a tripartite state-university-student relationship. In this relationship, universities are given authority over student management on one hand and subject to regulations and laws on university governance imposed by the party-state on the other hand, while students are given more legal guarantees by the party-state to protect their rights in universities. The activated role in student management gives universities space to compete for, and satisfy the needs of, students.

On the part of students, who now are normally required to pay tuition fees and have to compete by themselves in the job market upon graduation, the payment of tuition and relevant fees, which keep rising particularly in private institutions, could be a considerable financial cost, contributing to the inequality in access to higher education which is widely seen in society as a public service sector. There have been social demands for the party-state to step in again to address the educational inequality and, as a response, official commitments to allocating more resources to higher education and financially supporting students from disadvantaged backgrounds and underdeveloped regions (Mok 2012). Such commitments, however, as Mok (2012) expected, do not amount to the reversal of the marketization of higher education, but imply 'a combination of state and market effects' in future Chinese higher education development (p. 237).

In short, as part of the economic reform, Chinese higher education has been dramatically decentralized and marketized in recent decades, while Chinese university students have expanded in number, and been placed in a consumer-like relationship with universities and an indirect but responsive relationship with the party-state which provides legal protection for students subject to university management regulations. It is important to note that what remains unchanged is the party-state's ideopolitical control over university students, an act unsurprising in socialist China yet at odds with the party-state's ambition for world-class universities which are supposed to preserve rather than stifle open and free thinking. The ideopolitical-moral education discussed earlier is also carried out at the university level, through either formal subjects or on-campus student work. Also, the party-state periodically issues guidelines for universities to strengthen ideopolitical work on students, and constantly monitor students' minds through such as the annual nationwide survey on the ideopolitical attitudes among university students commissioned by the Ministry of Education since 1991, soon after the student-led 1989 pro-democracy movements.

The two universities whose students were investigated in Study II of this book are both public universities listed in the aforementioned prestigious Project 211. With their main campuses in Guangzhou, the capital of Guangdong Province, both have experienced campus expansion and cooperation with private colleges in recent years. Both are multi-disciplinary universities, covering undergraduate and graduate education, and being attended by not only mainland Chinese students but also students from Hong Kong and Macao, probably due to university orientation and reputation and geographical and cultural proximity.

Migrant Workers

A consequence of the planned-to-market economic reform was the industrial restructuring, which shifted the main ownership pattern of industrial enterprise from state-owned and state-controlled to private, foreign-owned and joint-venture. This shift altered the makeup of workers. Paralleling the sharp decline of the percentage of state-owned enterprise workers in industrial workers (from nearly 70% in 1990 to about 36% in 2003) was the rapid rise of migrant workers, who have already constituted more than half of the industrial workforce and more than one third of the service sector workforce (Lee 2007, pp. 40, 6). In contemporary Chinese context the term of migrant worker used here refers in general to people of rural origin migrating to and working in cities and towns, especially those in economically developed areas, against the background of the release of immense peasant labour in villages as a result of agricultural decollectivization, and the increased employment opportunities created in the opening up and expansion of private, foreign and joint-venture enterprises under the economic reform. Official data reported that there were about 277 million of rural migrant workers in 2015 nationwide (National Bureau of Statistics of China 2016).

Migrant workers, often short of education and economic and social resources, are a social group belonging to what Wright (2010) called 'the vast lower tier of China's onion dome-shaped socioeconomic hierarchy' (p. 85). They suffer what Lee (2007) observed 'double subordination' (p. 199), as workers by the market and as migrants by the state. The market exposes workers to be exploited for profits, while the state not only fails to effectively exercise its legal power to protect them from workplace grievances (typically unpaid wages, disciplinary violence, and lack of industrial injury compensation) but also deprives them as rural migrants living in cities of social welfare enjoyed by urban inhabitants through the household registration (*hukou*) system. The system dichotomously separates citizens, normally according to the household registration status (HRS) of parents, into rural and urban, the statuses of which entitle citizens to unequal social rights, such as education and healthcare, due to uneven urban-rural developments. While the statuses are officially transferable, 'hundreds of millions' of rural migrants moved but did not transfer to the urban status (Young 2013, p. 1), because of limited transfer quotas and stringent transfer eligibilities particularly in big cities where are often the popular migration destinations. Although policies intended to address the inequalities behind the statuses are observed particularly in towns and small cities in recent years and there are even official proposals to abandon the statuses per se, the urban status remains the major barrier in rights attainment, leading to the rights disparity between rural migrants and local residents in cities (Wu and Wang 2014). Unequal official status often gives rise to social exclusion. Without the urban status, while living in cities, rural migrants become the 'floating population' in cities (Solinger 1999) and are often seen as 'strangers' by urban citizens (Zhang 2001).

Ironically, migrant workers' socioeconomic disadvantages coexist with their increased economic and political significances in contemporary China. Given the growing contribution of the private sector to employment, tax revenue and GDP, Wright (2010) predicted that private sector workers, of which 'an extremely high proportion' is rural migrants, are 'both large and critical to China's continued economic growth', and their 'political proclivities are likely to shape China's future trajectory' (p. 116). Perhaps because of these significances, migrant workers are now officially recognized as part of the working class by the CCP, which states itself as the representative of the working class in the constitution. Then chairman of the All-China Federation of Trade Unions, the exclusive official trade union representative, unprecedentedly declared at its fourteenth congress in 2003 that migrant workers are new members of the working class in China (Wang 2003). But this political recognition does not mean that migrant workers would gain the social superiority once enjoyed by state-owned enterprise workers. Lee (2007) gave a helpful comparison of these two types of workers in relation to the party-state. She argued that in contrast to the socialist social contract used by the party-state to secure the benefits of state-owned enterprise workers for their political acquiescence in pre-reform years and still deplorable by them in reform-era protests, it is the legal contract—in other words, laws and regulations—that the party-state uses to regulate migrant workers. Together with our discussion earlier in this section, it becomes clear that the party-state similarly employs the legal approach to reconfiguring its relationship with the media sector, university students and migrant workers in contemporary China.

The economic success of Guangdong Province made it one of the most popular destinations for migrant workers from other places of China. The four privately owned factories whose workers were surveyed in Study II of this book—two garment factories, one cosmetic factory and one plastic product factory—were located in Shantou, a coastal city on the east end of the province. Although not the most popular destination in the province for migrant workers, the city as one of the four Special Economic Zones designated at the beginning of economic reform also attracts migrant workers, particularly those from rural areas of geographical proximity to the city, either outside or inside the province. At the time of the investigation, most of the workers in the four factories were migrants.

A Note on Students and Workers

Before closing this section on the state-society dynamics and this chapter on citizenship in the party-state perspective and moving forward to the meaning of citizenship in society, the focus of the second part of this book, it is worthy of noting the social distinction, the potential coalition, and the historical connection between university students and migrant workers in the Chinese context.

The above respective overviews of universities students and migrant workers in relation to the party-state, set against the background of economic reform, make clear two points. First, university students equipped with education as cultural capital, which is convertible from and to economic and social capital (Bourdieu 1986), and thus more able to compete for higher positions in the social echelon are distinguishable from migrant workers who are often lacked of those kinds of capital and therefore less able for social competition and largely stuck at the bottom of the socioeconomic ladder. Such social distinction or distance implies different social power, enabling the study of the two groups' perceptions in this book to explore the variation of the meaning of citizenship produced and interpreted at the individual level in society.

Second, despite their social distance, both university students and migrant workers are now similarly governed by the party-state through the legal approach. If the two groups can speak and communicate in the language of citizenship or *gongmin* bearing legal connotation, they could act as a joint social force in citizenship negotiation with the authorities. The possibility of their joint contribution to citizenship does not come out of blue but is well suggested by the past. Both students and workers were active citizens in political struggles in modern Chinese history. Similar with students often seen as the protagonist in modern political movements, workers, as Perry (2002) observed, also engaged both as labourers and citizens 'prominently in a series of political confrontations that have changed the face of modern China' (p. 133). Furthermore, there was a worker–intellectual nexus in China in early modern political uprisings and beyond. Evidence can be found from the May Fourth Movement against imperialism and for a new culture in 1919, to the June Fourth Movement against corruption and for democracy in 1989. The examination of the meaning of citizenship in society, to which we are turning, can be seen as a search for the possibility of such student–worker coalition in the contemporary Chinese context.

References

Ai, J. (2015). *Politics and traditional culture: The political use of traditions in contemporary China*. Singapore: World Scientific.

Blumer, H. (1948). Public opinion and public opinion polling. *American Sociological Review, 13* (5), 542–549.

Bourdieu, P. (1986). The forms of capital. In J. Richardson (Ed.), *Handbook of theory and research for the sociology of education* (pp. 241–258). New York: Greenwood.

Bray, D. (2006). Building 'community': New strategies of governance in urban China. *Economy and Society, 35*(4), 530–549. doi:10.1080/03085140600960799.

CCP Central Committee. (2001). *Guideline for improving citizens' morality* (in Chinese). http://www.people.com.cn/GB/shizheng/16/20011024/589496.html. Accessed May 9, 2016.

CCP Central Committee. (2003). *On further improving citizens' morality* (in Chinese). http://www.gov.cn/test/2005-06/27/content_9957.htm. Accessed May 9, 2016.

Chan, C., Ngok, K., & Phillips, D. (2008). *Social policy in China: Development and well-being*. Bristol: The Policy Press.

Chen, J., Lu, C., & Yang, Y. (2007). Popular support for grassroots self-government in urban China: Findings from a Beijing survey. *Modern China, 33*(4), 505–528. doi:10.1177/0097700407303966.

Culp, R. (2007). Synthesizing citizenship in modern China. *History Compass, 5*(6), 1833–1861. doi:10.1111/j.1478-0542.2007.00478.x.

Di Tommaso, M. R., Rubini, L., & Barbieri, E. (2013). *Southern China: Industry, development and industrial policy*. Oxon: Routledge.

Ding, X., Li, F., & Sun, Y. (2011). Thirty years of reforming China's higher education funding mechanism. In W. J. Morgan & B. Wu (Eds.), *Higher education reform in China: Beyond the expansion* (pp. 81–92). Oxon: Routledge.

Fairbrother, G. P. (2014). The Chinese paternalistic state and moral education. In K. J. Kennedy, G. P. Fairbrother, & Z. Zhao (Eds.), *Citizenship education in China: Preparing citizens for the "Chinese Century"* (pp. 11–26). New York: Routledge.

Feng, A. (2006). Contested notions of citizenship and citizenship education: The Chinese case. In G. Alred, M. Byram, & M. Fleming (Eds.), *Education for intercultural citizenship: Concepts and comparisons* (pp. 86–105). Clevedon, England: Multilingual Matters.

Fielder, C. (2016). Taking steps toward an understanding of "civil society with Chinese characteristics": An exploration through the eyes of Chinese faith-based organizations. In S. N. Romaniuk & M. Marlin (Eds.), *Democracy and civil society in a global era* (pp. 169–187). New York: Routledge.

Frolic, B. M. (1997). State-led civil society. In T. Brook & B. M. Frolic (Eds.), *Civil society in China* (pp. 46–67). New York: M. E. Sharpe.

Gang, Q., & Bandurski, D. (2011). China's emerging public sphere: The impact of media commercialization, professionalism, and the Internet in an era of transition. In S. L. Shirk (Ed.), *Changing media, changing China* (pp. 38–76). New York: Oxford University Press.

Gao, H., & Tyson, A. (2017). Administrative reform and the transfer of authority to social organizations in China. *The China Quarterly*, 1–20, doi:10.1017/S030574101700087X.

Goldman, M. (2005). *From comrade to citizen: The struggle of political rights in China*. Cambridge, MA: Harvard University Press.

Goldman, M., & Perry, E. J. (2002). Introduction: Political citizenship in modern China. In M. Goldman & E. J. Perry (Eds.), *Changing meanings of citizenship in modern China* (pp. 1–19). Cambridge, MA: Harvard University Press.

Goodman, D. S. G. (1997). China in reform: The view from the provinces. In D. S. G. Goodman (Ed.), *China's provinces in reform: Class, community and political culutre* (pp. 1–20). London: Routledge.

Goodman, D. S. G., & Feng, C. (1994). Guangdong: Greater Hong Kong and the new regionalist future. In D. S. G. Goodman & G. Segal (Eds.), *China deconstructs: Politics, trade and regionalism* (pp. 177–201). London: Routledge.

Greenhalgh, S. (2010). *Cultivating global citizens: Population in the rise of China*. Cambridge, MA: Harvard University Press.

Guo, K. (2010). Newspapers: Changing roles. In J. F. Scotton & W. A. Hachten (Eds.), *New media for a new China* (pp. 43–60). Oxford: Wiley-Blackwell.

Hachten, W. A. (2010). Development and theory of the media. In J. F. Scotton & W. A. Hachten (Eds.), *New media for a new China* (pp. 19–27). Oxford: Wiley-Blackwell.

Harris, P. (2002). The origins of modern citizenship in China. *Asia Pacific Viewpoint, 43*(2), 181–203.

Hu, J. (2007). *Report to the Seventeenth National Congress of the Communist Party of China* (in Chinese). http://cpc.people.com.cn/GB/64162/64168/106155/106156/6430009.html. Accessed November 26, 2016.

Hu, J. (2012). *Report to the Eighteen National Congress of the Communist Party of China* (in Chinese). http://www.xj.xinhuanet.com/2012-11/19/c_113722546.htm. Accessed November 26, 2016.

Isaka, Y. (1994). Kōmin. *Nihon Daihyakka Zensho (Nipponika)* (in Japanese) (electronic ed.). Tokyo: Shogakukan.

Jiang, Z. (1997). *Report to the Fifteen National Congress of the Communist Party of China* (in Chinese). http://cpc.people.com.cn/GB/64162/64168/64568/65445/4526285.html. Accessed April 28, 2016.

Jiang, Z. (2002). *Report to the Sixteen National Congress of the Communist Party of China* (in Chinese). http://cpc.people.com.cn/GB/64162/64168/64569/65444/4429125.html. Accessed April 28, 2016.

Kwong, J. (1988). *Cultural revolution in China's schools: May 1966–April 1969*. Stanford, California: Hoover Institution Press.

Landry, P. F., Davis, D., & Shiru, W. (2010). Elections in rural China: Competition without parties. *Comparative Political Studies, 43*(6), 763–790. doi:10.1177/0010414009359392.

Latham, K. (2007). Sms, communication, and citizenship in China's information society. *Critical Asian Studies, 39*(2), 295–314. doi:10.1080/14672710701339493.

Law, W. W. (2006). Citizenship, citizenship education, and the state in China in a global age. *Cambridge Journal of Education, 36*(4), 597–628. doi:10.1080/03057640601049322.

Law, W. W. (2011). *Citizenship and citizenship education in a global age: Politics, policies, and practices in China*. New York: Peter Lang Publishing.

Law, W. W. (2014). Globalisation, citizenship education, and international events: 2010 Shanghai World Exposition education in China. In K. J. Kennedy, G. P. Fairbrother, & Z. Zhao (Eds.), *Citizenship education in China: Preparing citizens for the "Chinese Century"* (pp. 100–127). New York: Routledge.

Lee, C. K. (2007). *Against the law: Labour Protests in China's rustbelt and sunbelt*. Berkeley: University of California Press.

Lee, W. O., & Ho, C. H. (2005). Ideopolitical shifts and changes in moral education policy in China. *Journal of Moral Education, 34*(4), 413–431. doi:10.1080/03057240500410160.

Lee, W. O., & Ho, C. H. (2008). Citizenship education in China: Changing concepts, approaches and policies in the changing political, economic and social context. In J. Arthur, I. Davies, & C. Hahn (Eds.), *The SAGE handbook of education for citizenship and democracy* (pp. 139–157). London: Sage.

Li, B., & Wu, Y. (1999). The conception of citizenship in People's Republic of China. In A. Davidson & K. Keekly (Eds.), *Globalization and citizenship in the Asia-Pacific* (pp. 157–168). Hampshire: Macmillan Press.

Li, J. (2007). Human rights vs state interests in China: Case studies. *New Zealand Journal of Asian Studies, 9*(2), 147–168.

Li, J. (2009). Fostering citizenship in China's move from elite to mass higher education: An analysis of students' political socialization and civic participation. *International Journal of Educational Development, 29*(4), 382–398. doi:10.1016/j.ijedudev.2008.10.001.

Li, L., & Liu, L. (2009). 30 years' reform of China's mass media. *Asia Europe Journal, 7*(3–4), 405–415. doi:10.1007/s10308-009-0237-z.

Li, P., Zhong, M., Lin, B., & Zhang, H. (2004). Deyu as moral education in modern China: Ideological functions and transformations. *Journal of Moral Education, 33*(4), 449–464. doi:10.1080/0305724042000315581.

Lin, F. (2012). Information differentiation, commercialization and legal reform: The rise of a three-dimensional state-media regime in China. *Journalism Studies, 13*(3), 418–432. doi:10.1080/1461670X.2011.616402.

Lu, J., & Gao, D. (2004). New directions in the moral education curriculum in Chinese primary schools. *Journal of Moral Education, 33*(4), 495–510. doi:10.1080/0305724042000315617.

Lynch, D. C. (1999). *After the propaganda state: Media, politics, and "thought work" in reformed China*. Stanford, CA: Stanford University Press.

McCormick, B. L. (2003). Recent trends in Mainland China's media: Political implications of commercialization. *Issues and Studies, 39*(1), 175–215.

Min, T. (1989). *National polity and local power: The transformation of late imperial China*. Cambridge: Harvard University Press.

Ministry of Education of the PRC. (2015). *Overview of education in China: Developments in 2014* (in Chinese). http://www.moe.gov.cn/jyb_sjzl/s5990/201511/t20151125_220958.html. Accessed June 7, 2016.

Mizoguchi, Y. (1995). *Chugoku no kō to shi [The Concepts of Gong and Si in China]*. Tokyo: Kenbun Shuppan.

Mok, K. H. (2002). Decentralization and changing governance of higher education in post-Mao China. *Public Administration and Development, 22*(3), 261–273.

Mok, K. H. (2005). Globalization and educational restructuring: University merging and changing governance in China. *Higher Education, 50*(1), 57–88.

Mok, K. H. (2012). Bringing the state back in: Restoring the role of the state in Chinese higher education. *European Journal of Education, 47*(2), 228–41.

Nathan, A. J. (1985). *Chinese democracy*. Berkeley: University of California Press.

National Bureau of Statistics of China. (2005). *China statistics yearbook* (in Chinese). http://www.stats.gov.cn/tjsj/ndsj/2005/indexch.htm. Accessed June 7, 2016.

National Bureau of Statistics of China. (2015). *China statistics yearbook* (in Chinese). http://www.stats.gov.cn/tjsj/ndsj/2015/indexch.htm. Accessed June 7, 2016.

National Bureau of Statistics of China. (2016). *Statistical Communiqué of the People's Republic of China on the 2015 National Economic and Social Development*. http://www.stats.gov.cn/english/PressRelease/201602/t20160229_1324019.html. Accessed June 14, 2016.

Ni, S., Cheng, L., & Sin, K. K. (2010). Who are Chinese citizens? A legislative language inquiry. *International Journal for the Semiotics of Law - Revue internationale de Sémiotique juridique, 23*(4), 475–494. doi:10.1007/s11196-010-9167-8.

O'Brien, K. J. (1990). *Reform without liberalization: China's National People's Congress and the politics of institutional change*. New York: Cambridge University Press.

Ong, K. C., & Chan, D. K. K. (2016). Transnational higher education and challenges for university governance in China. In K. H. Mok & K. M. Yu (Eds.), *Internationalization of higher education in East Asia: Trends of student mobility and impact on education governance* (pp. 115–137). Abingdon and New York: Routledge.

Pan, S. (2014). Multileveled citizenship education in Beijing: Liberation with limitation. In K. J. Kennedy, G. P. Fairbrother, & Z. Zhao (Eds.), *Citizenship education in China: Preparing citizens for the "Chinese Century"* (pp. 128–143). New York: Routledge.

Perry, E. J. (2002). From Paris to the Paris of the East—and back: Workers as citizens in modern Shanghai. In M. Goldman & E. J. Perry (Eds.), *Changing meanings of Citizenship in modern China* (pp. 133–156). Cambridge, MA: Harvard University Press.

Ross, H., Zhang, R., & Zhao, W. (2010). The reconfiguration of state-university-student relationships in post/socialist China. In I. Silova (Ed.), *Post-Socialism is not dead: (Re)reading the global in comparative education* (pp. 299–328). Emerald: Bingley.

Saito, T. (2009). Kang Youwei in Tokyo and Shigenobu Okuma (in Japanese). *Journal of Liberal Arts of Waseda University, 126,* 47–78.

Schubert, G., & Ahlers, A. L. (2012). *Participation and empowerment at the grassroots: Chinese village elections in perspective*. Lanham, MD: Lexington Books.

Scotton, J. F., & Hachten, W. A. (Eds.). (2010). *New media for a new China*. Oxford: Wiley-Blackwell.

Shi, X. (2015). The path towards mass higher education in China. In J. C. Shin, G. A. Postiglione, & F. Huang (Eds.), *Mass higher education development in East Asia: Strategy, quality, and challenges* (pp. 63–88). Dordrecht: Springer.

Shirk, S. L. (Ed.). (2011). *Changing media, changing China*. New York: Oxford University Press.

Smith, C. J. (2002). From "leading the masses" to "serving the consumers"? Newspaper reporting in contemporary urban china. *Environment and Planning A, 34,* 1635–1660. doi:10.1068/a3563.

Solinger, D. J. (1999). *Contesting citizenship in urban China: Peasant migrants, the state, and the logic of the market*. California: University of California Press.

Stockmann, D. (2013). *Media commercialization and authoritarian rule in China*. Cambridge: Cambridge University Press.

Stone, L. (2011). Preparing for the twenty-first century: Liberal education and undergraduate educational reform at Sun Yat-sen university. In J. Ryan (Ed.), *China's higher education reform and internationalisation* (pp. 69–86). Oxon: Routledge.

Taylor, C. (1995). *Philosophical arguments*. Cambridge, MA: Harvard University Press.

Teets, J. C., Rosen, S., & Gries, P. H. (2010). Introduction: Political change, contestation, and pluralization in China today. In P. H. Gries & S. Rosen (Eds.), *Chinese politics: State, society and the market* (pp. 1–21). Oxon: Routledge.

Tong, J. (2009). Press self-censorship in China: A case study in the transformation of discourse. *Discourse & Society, 20*(5), 593–612. doi:10.1177/0957926509106412.

Tse, T. K.-C. (2011). Creating good citizens in China: Comparing Grade 7–9 school textbooks, 1997–2005. *Journal of Moral Education, 40*(2), 161–180. doi:10.1080/03057240.2011.568098.

Tu, Y. (2011). Citizenship with Chinese characteristics? An investigation into Chinese university students' civic perceptions and civic participation. *Frontiers of Education in China, 6*(3), 426–448. doi:10.1007/s11516-011-0140-4.

Vogel, E. F. (1989). *One step ahead in China: Guangdong under reform*. Cambridge, MA: Harvard University Press.

Wang, C. (2016). Coordinated compliance and private approach of international engagement in China's human rights. In T. C. Chen & D. Chen (Eds.), *International engagement in China's human rights* (pp. 79–97). New York: Routledge.

Wang, X., & Tan, C. (2014). From ideopolitical indoctrination to real-life narration: Reform of textbooks for moral and citizenship education in China. In K. J. Kennedy, G. P. Fairbrother, & Z. Zhao (Eds.), *Citizenship education in China: Preparing citizens for the "Chinese Century"* (pp. 195–207). New York: Routledge.

Wang, Z. (2003). *Report to the Fourteenth Congress of All-China Federation of Trade Unions* (in Chinese). http://www.shzgh.org/renda/node5902/node5911/node6582/userobject1ai1165448.html. Accessed May 29, 2017.

Wang, Z. (2012). *Never forget national humiliation: Historical memory in Chinese politics and foreign relations*. New York: Columbia University Press.

Whyte, M. K. (Ed.). (2010). *One country, two societies: Rural-urban inequality in contemporary China*. Cambridge, MA: Harvard University Press.

Wright, T. (2010). *Accepting authoritarianism: State-society relations in China's reform era*. California: Stanford University Press.

Wu, Q. (2008). Opening address. In J. Y. Lin & B. Pleskovic (Eds.), *Higher education and development: Annual World Bank conference on development economics—Regional 2008* (pp. 9–11). Washington, D.C: The World Bank.

Wu, W., & Wang, G. (2014). Together but unequal: Citizenship rights for migrants and locals in urban China. *Urban Affairs Review, 50*(6), 781–805. doi:10.1177/1078087413518172.

Young, J. (2013). *China's Hukou System: Markets, migrants and institutional change*. London: Palgrave Macmillan.

Yu, H. (1995). On human rights and their guarantee by law. In M. Davis (Ed.), *Human rights and Chinese values: Legal, philosophical, and political perspectives* (pp. 93–115). Hong Kong: Oxford University Press.

Yu, X. (2002). Citizenship, ideology, and the PRC Constitution. In M. Goldman & E. J. Perry (Eds.), *Changing meanings of citizenship in modern China* (pp. 288–307). Cambridge, MA: Harvard University Press.

Zang, X. (2011). Government and changing state-society relations. In X. Zang (Ed.), *Understanding Chinese society* (pp. 170–182). Oxon: Routledge.

Zarrow, P. G. (1997). Introduction: Citizenship in China and the West. In J. A. Fogel & P. G. Zarrow (Eds.), *Imagining the people: Chinese intellectuals and the concept of citizenship, 1890–1920* (pp. 3–38). New York: M. E. Sharpe.

Zhang, L. (2001). *Strangers in the city: Reconfigurations of space, power and social networks within China's floating population*. California: Stanford University Press.

Zhao, Z. (1987). *Report to the Thirteen National Congress of the Communist Party of China* (in Chinese). http://cpc.people.com.cn/GB/64162/64168/64566/65447/4526368.html. Accessed April 28, 2016.

Zheng, Y. (2010). China and democracy: Not a contradiction in terms. In J. Wong & Z. Bo (Eds.), *China's reform in global perspective* (pp. 13–53). Singapore: World Scientific.

Zhou, S. (2015). China: Media system. In W. Donsbach (Ed.), *The concise encyclopedia of communication*. Oxford: Wiley-Blackwell.

Part II
The Meaning of *Gongmin* in Society

Chapter 4
Gongmin as Identity

Each of this and the next two chapters will unveil the meaning of *gongmin* in contemporary Chinese society in one of the three dimensions of the Western lens of citizenship, i.e. the extent dimension about identity, the content dimension about rights and responsibilities and the depth dimension about participation. It should be noted that the separation of discussion does not mean that the three dimensions are deemed irrelevant to each other in the meaning of *gongmin*. Rather, in light of the evolution of citizenship conception in the West that, for instance, participation often starts from rights and responsibilities while identity is shaped through participation and for rights, there could be similar connections between the three dimensions of the social meaning of the Chinese term *gongmin*. The connections are indeed identified in the chapters. In a similar structure, each of the three chapters will first review what have already be studied by existing research about the particular dimension of citizenship in society with particular attention to the two social groups of university students and migrant workers targeted in this book, then present the empirical findings of the two sub-studies of this book and at last discuss the implications of the findings for contemporary Chinese society.

Citizenship-Related Identities in Society

The term *gongmin*, the designation of passport holder in the Chinese constitution, connotes a legal status. There are empirical studies reporting the spreading identification with that legal status in society, notably among socioeconomically disadvantaged groups such as migrant workers and peasants, amid the party-state's ongoing attempts to regulate its relation with the society in legal terms as discussed in the preceding chapter. The legal reform gave birth to a range of worker-related laws, among which the Labour Law enacted in 1995 'has proven pivotal in labour contentions as it accords, on paper at least, all labourers the same contractual status and rights regardless of social origin and ownership sector' (Lee 2007, p. 197).

S. Chen, *The Meaning of Citizenship in Contemporary Chinese Society*,
Governance and Citizenship in Asia, https://doi.org/10.1007/978-981-10-6323-7_4

Against this backdrop, Lee (2007) reported, based on fieldwork in Guangdong Province, that migrant workers 'enthusiastically embrace the regime's project of legal reform' by adopting the legalistic language of the party-state; and citizenship has become 'the most empowering identity' among the insurgent identities forged by them to articulate workplace grievances and demand legal rights (p. 27). However, migrant workers' citizen identity is reportedly empowered by laws on one hand and often disillusioned in practice on the other hand. Citizenship, as Lee (2007) revealed, often turned to be little more than 'an empty slogan and status' for migrant labours (p. 27), especially when they could not protect their legal rights by appealing to the status under 'the illiberal legal system… beholden to local government and business interests' (p. 199).

There is evidence that peasants also adopt the official legalistic language in their own social and cultural struggles. For the rural legal activists fighting to regain control over expropriated farmlands in the study of Brandtstadter (2011), engaging the law was the means both to articulate the citizenship status against legal injustice and to retain the identity of peasant whose culture is often portrayed through education and propaganda as backward and subject to be transcended in the party-state's development project in the name of modernization. This predominantly economic development project also affects the identification of ethnic minorities. Wu (2014) reported that the ethnic identity of the ethnic minorities in his study was reinforced by both of the commodification of ethnicity, such as ethnic tourism in ethnic regions for economic purposes, and the wage discrimination against ethnic minority migrant workers in cities. Not only is ethnic identity affected by the market, it also suffers because of state policy. For the Tibetan students reported by Yi (2006), their ethnic and cultural identity was at stake as they were caught in the dilemma created by education policy of attending either mainstream schools, a course often securing better social mobility and economic opportunity, or ethnic minority schools for daily cultural practice, language in particular, which is unavailable in, or perhaps more accurately, intentionally excluded from, mainstream schools.

There are also empirical studies examining the self, local, national and global identification among Chinese young people. A salient self-identity has been reported in recent years. Both the Beijing and the Shanghai secondary school students in Pan's (2011) and Law and Ng's (2009) respective studies were found to perceive their self-identity as the most important among the self, local, national and global identities. Similarly, Liu (2008) observed that 'with little reference to the socialist-collectivist values', only-child university students adopted 'an individualized approach [in life planning], displaying a form of the self consistent with the autonomous, self-authoring and individualistic neoliberal subject' (p. 193). Pan (2011) reasoned the outstanding self-identity as an outcome of the emerged recognition of the self in the recently reformed citizenship-related education, while Liu (2008) saw it as the internalization of neoliberal personhood under the neoliberal market economy. Drawing upon these two arguments, it seems that the recent education reform serves neoliberal purposes, which is indeed a tendency observable across the globe (Turner and Yolcu 2014). What is distinct in the Chinese case is that, as Liu (2008) reminded us, the Chinese neoliberal move is blended with the socialist ideology. She discussed that while the saliently self-conscious young people in her study made 'scanty reference' to collective values, it does not necessarily lead to the total loss of official ideology or their unconcern about those values (p. 209).

As to local identity, on one hand, Law and Ng (2009) found in the above-mentioned study that Shanghai students identified with both their city and the nation strongly. They reasoned it as a result of both the central control of the party-state and the attempts by the local government to promote collective identity among its citizens. On the other hand, Pan (2011) reported that Beijing students expressed little distinction between national and local identities probably due to the special status of Beijing as the capital and the resulting blur of national and local relationship in the view of the students. These two studies imply that specific societal contexts contribute to local identity formation in society. This association is supported by Goodman's (2002) study of the social effects of the official promotion of provincial identity, primarily to mobilize social resources for economic purposes, in Shanxi Province during the 1990s. That study reported, based on interviews with local business people, that the official appeal to provincialism or localism seemed to 'have had a significant impact' on their local identification, though often not at the intended provincial level but 'at more local levels in cities, towns and villages, and especially at the county level' (p. 857). Goodman (2002) reasoned that the greater official push and more favourable social effects in the case, compared with similar official endeavours often ending up in internal conflicts in other provinces, could be due to the strong local culture within the province and the relatively homogenous population of the particular province. This reasoning similarly implies the influence of local societal contexts on citizens' local identity formation.

Although the Beijing students in Pan's (2011) study saw little distinction between local and national identities, their identification with the latter was still 'more significant' (p. 294). Chinese young people's strong national identification has been repeatedly confirmed by empirical studies. Chinese university students are found to be 'on average, patriotic and nationalistic' (Fairbrother 2003, p. 618), having 'a strong sense of patriotism' and 'loyalty to the nation' along with conformity with official discourse, high concern for social justice and desire to social contribution (Tu 2011, p. 442) and 'sharing their positive affective orientation towards Chinese nationality' regardless of demographic backgrounds including gender, rural/urban origin, discipline, parental education level and family income (Li 2009, p. 389). In a more nuanced study by Sinkkonen (2013) which distinguished between patriotism as a feeling of proud and emotional attachment to a country and nationalism as a superior view and uncritical support of a country, Chinese university students with CCP membership and of rural background were found to be more patriotic and nationalistic than those not. But nationalism among Chinese young people might not be built on the belief in the superiority of the country, as Fong (2004) exposed. Using the term 'filial nationalism' to describe the nationalistic sentiment of the Chinese teenagers in her study, she discussed that Chinese teenagers viewed the nation not as themselves but as their parents, assigning themselves the filial duty to contribute to China considered backward and inferior in their imagined global community, as like bringing their parents out of poverty. He (2015) commented that this nation-as-parent analogy is a reflection of 'the strong association of patriotic loyalty and familial metaphors in school curricula and propaganda' (p. 319). Through her own study of nationalism among overseas Chinese students, He (2015) revealed the similarities between the language used by the students and the official discourse on patriotism, suggesting the success of the latter in 'tapping a widespread willingness among students' to identify with its narrative of China (p. 315). Similarly, Pan (2011) reasoned in the case of Beijing students that 'the nation state and schools serve as powerful generators of national identity among students' (p. 301).

As to the identification with the global community among Chinese young people, Pan's (2011) study detected the cognitive but not affective orientation towards global identity among secondary students. She discussed that such global identity was 'a conceptualized relationship between self and world' without direct and personal global experiences (p. 302). This finding, together with the strong national identity mentioned above, challenges, as Pan (2011) noticed, the not unpopular theoretical temptation to expect the decline of national citizenship in the wave of global citizenship. Another evidence for that challenge can be found in my study about overseas Chinese students' understanding of global citizenship (Chen 2011). In that study, while the global citizen identity was not accepted by the majority of the students, for those accepting the identity, a national affiliation, that is, global citizen identity not independent from but built upon national citizen identity, was detected. These empirical findings echo our discussion in Chap. 3 of the increased appreciation for the global perspective in the seemingly multileveled Chinese citizenship-related education which nonetheless places the promotion of national pride and national identity at the heart.

The review of existing empirical research above gives us some ideas of the contemporary development in Chinese society of a range of identities theoretically relevant to citizenship viewed through our Western analytical lens. In most, if not all, of the existing scholarship, however, there is little, if any, explicit attention paid to the connotative link between those identities and the term *gongmin* as identity and the implication of such link for Chinese citizenship. In the following sections of this chapter, the link is examined in three aspects: the criteria for the identity of 'Chinese *gongmin*'; the identity of *gongmin* vis-à-vis state and society and *gongmin* as multileveled identity. The examination is based on the empirical results of Study II in this book which investigated the perceptions of university students and migrant workers regarding *gongmin* by survey and interview. The extent dimension about identity was not covered by Study I, the other sub-study of this book which examined through content analysis the meaning of *gongmin* in newspapers. The reason is that it was impossible to either identify whom the term *gongmin* was referred to or measure it in the three aspects in most of the collected newspaper articles.

The Identity of 'Chinese *Gongmin*'

The modern equation of state and nation complicated the answer to the question of who is a citizen in modern discourse by associating citizenship as legal membership of the state with national membership based on alleged cultural and ethnic homogeneities such as common homeland, common culture (typically language) and common descent. But as elaborated in Chap. 2, contemporary challenges posed by postmodernization and globalization have brought the modern association into question. Does such association exist in the meaning of *gongmin* understood by contemporary Chinese citizens? In the questionnaire used in Study II, I explored this question by investigating the attitude towards the five statements that Chinese *gongmin* are people (a) living in China, (b) born in China, (c) of Chinese descent, (d) holding Chinese passport and (e) speaking *putonghua* (or Mandarin, the official Chinese language). With the results shown in Fig. 4.1 and Table 4.1,[1] in what follows I shall explain the key findings about the five statements in turn.

(1) *As legal identity*

The finding in this respect was that both students and workers similarly considered Chinese *gongmin* first and foremost as a legal identity. In response to the five statements, student respondents (58.2%) defined Chinese *gongmin* more than anything else on the basis of holding passport, a proof of the legal membership of the state (Fig. 4.1). This was also one of the two criteria equally embraced by most of the worker respondents (53.1%). No statistically significant difference was found between the two groups over this legal understanding (Table 4.1). In addition, it was confirmed by Chi-square tests that the attitude was commonly shared—as no significant association (defined strictly as $p < 0.001$ in this book) was found—among respondents in each group, regardless of all of the four targeted demographic backgrounds of age, gender, educational level and the location of primary school attended (treated as a HRS indicator in this book).[2]

Respondents' understanding of 'Chinese *gongmin*' in legal terms was also confirmed in the interview data. Student and worker interviewees similarly tended to mention words such as law and nationality when asked to describe what came into mind when they heard the term *gongmin*. In describing 'Chinese *gongmin*', almost every student interviewee first and foremost referred to people possessing Chinese nationality, which was also mentioned by many worker interviewees, though not as immediately as student interviewees and often following a self-blame on lack of education and after a moment of recalling what they learned in moral education particularly in lower secondary schools, where many workers said they encountered the term *gongmin* for the first time. Both quantitative and qualitative

[1]In this book the percentage of disagreement is the sum of percentages of strongly disagreement and disagreement, and percentage of agreement the sum of percentages of strongly agreement and agreement, in the survey results.

[2]An explanation of the demographic variables in the questionnaire is in the Appendix.

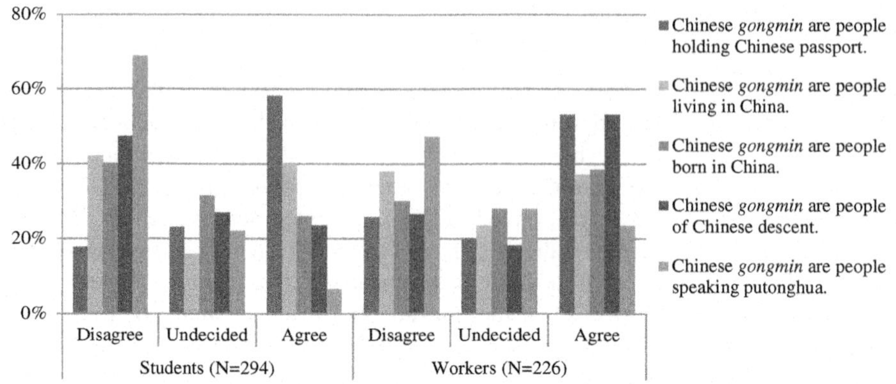

Fig. 4.1 Attitudes towards five statements about 'Chinese *gongmin*'

Table 4.1 Chi-square test result of attitudes towards five statements about 'Chinese *gongmin*' by student/worker group

Student/Worker Group		Pearson Chi-square	df	*p*-value	Cramer's *V*	*N* of valid cases
Chinese *gongmin* are people	Holding Chinese passport	5.039	2	0.081	0.099	514
	Living in China	4.526	2	0.104	0.094	512
	Born in China	10.725	2	0.005	0.146	505
	Of Chinese descent	49.416	2	0.000*	0.312	508
	Speaking *putonghua*	38.389	2	0.000*	0.274	510

*$p < 0.001$

results indicated a strong legal connotation in both student and worker respondents' understanding of 'Chinese *gongmin*'. This is not a surprising finding, given the legal use of the term in Chinese constitution and laws, a source for public pedagogy, and in citizenship-related education in schools, as reflected in the interviewees' explanations. Such strong approval by both groups, however, was not found in their perceptions of the other four criteria of residence, birthplace, ethnicity and language for 'Chinese *gongmin*', probably because of the predominant understanding of the term in legal sense.

(2) *As residential identity*

Student respondents' response was equally divided on the statement that Chinese *gongmin* are people living in China (40.1% agreed and 42.2% disagreed). So was the response of worker respondents (37.2% agreed and 38.1% disagreed). Such

Table 4.2 Result for the pairwise comparisons using the LSD method for worker respondents' attitude about 'Chinese *gongmin*' based on residence by educational level

Comparison	Pearson Chi-square	df	*p*-value	Cramer's *V*
Primary school or below versus Lower secondary school	4.510	2	0.105	0.166
Primary school or below versus Upper secondary school or above	34.224	2	0.000*	0.566
Lower secondary school versus Upper secondary school or above	25.243	2	0.000*	0.388

*$p < 0.001$

divided response on whether 'Chinese *gongmin*' can be defined by residence in China or not was statistically similar between the two groups (Table 4.1). In other words, the idea of defining 'Chinese *gongmin*' as residential identity was controversial for both groups.

Such controversy was shared within the student group, but was not within the worker group, given that while this divisive attitude was not statistically affected by the four demographic variables for student respondents, it was significantly associated with educational level for worker respondents [X^2 (4, N = 219) = 38.875, $p = 0.000$, Cramer's $V = .298$]. Follow-up tests using the LSD method specified the relationship between the attitude of worker respondents and their educational levels by detecting two significant pairwise differences (Table 4.2). The differences indicated that workers with the educational level of upper secondary school or above were 3.14 times more likely than those with primary school or below educational level to disagree to the statement (Table 4.3). Put it simple, for migrant workers, the more educated, the more likely to discard the statement. The finding in this respect can be summarized as there being divided opinion over 'Chinese *gongmin*' as residential identity, a controversy shared by students and workers and affected by educational level in the case of workers.

(3) *As birthplace identity*

The eligibility for legal Chinese citizenship currently follows the jus sanguinis principle other than the jus soli principle except for some uncommon occasions. It means that by law birthplace is not the eligibility for legal 'Chinese *gongmin*' in most cases. Despite the irrelevance in law, 'Chinese *gongmin*' was found to be acceptable as a birthplace identity by a majority of worker respondents (38.5%), noticeably more than student respondents (25.9%), although the gap was statistically not significant (Table 4.1). By contrast, a majority of student respondents (40.1%) disagreed with the statement that Chinese *gongmin* are people born in China. In other words, students and workers had a split view on Chinese *gongmin* as birthplace identity.

The reason behind student respondents' negative attitude towards the idea that being born in China is the criterion for Chinese *gongmin* was, as revealed in the interviews, typically their exclusion from 'Chinese *gongmin*' of people born in

Table 4.3 Worker respondents' attitude towards 'Chinese *gongmin*' based on residence by educational level

		Chinese *gongmin* are people living in China		
		Disagree	Undecided	Agree
Primary school or below	Count	11	9	31
	Expected count	19.6	11.9	19.6
	% within educational level	21.6%	17.6%	60.8%
	Adjusted residual	−2.8	−1.1	3.8
Lower secondary school	Count	35	29	48
	Expected count	43.0	26.1	43.0
	% within educational level	31.3%	25.9%	42.9%
	Adjusted residual	−2.2	0.9	1.4
Upper secondary school or above	Count	38	13	5
	Expected count	21.5	13.0	21.5
	% within educational level	67.9%	23.2%	8.9%
	Adjusted residual	5.3	0.0	−5.2

China but holding foreign legal citizenship. This kind of people seemed to be accepted as, at least was not expressly excluded from, 'Chinese *gongmin*' by worker interviewees who held a positive attitude toward the idea. Student interviewees' explanation confirmed their predominant understanding of *gongmin*, either Chinese or of other countries, in legal sense.

(4) *As ethnic and cultural identity*

But if students strictly followed the legal definition of *gongmin*, they would approve 'Chinese *gongmin*' based on ethnicity, given the just sanguinis principle adopted by Chinese law. This was not the case. A majority of student respondents (47.3%) did not see Chinese descent as necessary for Chinese *gongmin*; by contrast, worker respondents designated Chinese *gongmin* to people of Chinese descent as prevailingly as to people holding Chinese passport (53.1%). At the same time, both student and worker respondents disagreed the most (69.0 and 47.3%), and agreed the least (6.5 and 23.5%), to the statement that Chinese *gongmin* are people speaking Mandarin, an illustrator of official Chinese culture, among the five statements. The two groups' attitudes towards both statements were significantly different, indeed the only two among all the five statements (Table 4.1). It meant that among the five criteria for 'Chinese *gongmin*', ethnicity and culture were the only two of which students and workers held significantly different perception. By comparing the adjusted residuals in Table 4.4, the differences can be identified as workers were more likely to accept, while students were more likely to oppose, 'Chinese *gongmin*' as an ethnic and a cultural identity.

Table 4.4 Respondents' attitudes towards two statements about 'Chinese *gongmin*' significantly associated with student/worker group

Group		Disagree	Undecided	Agree
		Chinese *gongmin* are people of Chinese descent		
Students	Count	139	79	69
	Expected count	112.4	67.8	106.8
	% within group	48.4%	27.5%	24.0%
	Adjusted residual	4.9	2.4	−7.0
Workers	Count	60	41	120
	Expected count	86.6	52.2	82.2
	% within group	27.1%	18.6%	54.3%
	Adjusted residual	−4.9	−2.4	7.0
		Chinese *gongmin* are people speaking *putonghua*		
Students	Count	203	65	19
	Expected count	174.5	72.0	40.5
	% within group	70.7%	22.6%	6.6%
	Adjusted residual	5.2	−1.4	−5.5
Workers	Count	107	63	53
	Expected count	135.5	56.0	31.5
	% within group	48.0%	28.3%	23.8%
	Adjusted residual	−5.2	1.4	5.5

Table 4.5 Result for the pairwise comparisons using the LSD method for workers' attitude about 'Chinese *gongmin*' based on language by educational level

Comparison	Pearson Chi-square	df	*p*-value	Cramer's *V*
Primary school or below versus Lower secondary school	13.267	2	0.001	0.285
Primary school or below versus Upper secondary school or above	31.866	2	0.000*	0.551
Lower secondary school versus Upper secondary school or above	11.586	2	0.003	0.105

*$p < 0.001$

Education was found once again to affect workers' understanding. This time was on their perception on 'Chinese *gongmin*' as cultural identity [X^2 (4, N = 219) = 33.403, $p = 0.000$, Cramer's $V = .276$]. Specifically, workers with upper secondary school or above education background were about 3.98 times more likely than those with primary or lower one to reject 'Chinese *gongmin*' as a cultural identity (Tables 4.5 and 4.6). This tendency was similar with that of the effect of educational level on 'Chinese *gongmin*' as residential identity. Bringing

Table 4.6 Worker respondents' attitude towards 'Chinese *gongmin*' based on language by educational level

		Chinese *gongmin* are people speaking *putonghua*		
		Disagree	Undecided	Agree
Primary school or below	Count	9	20	20
	Expected count	23.3	13.9	11.9
	% within educational level	18.4%	40.8%	40.8%
	Adjusted residual	−4.6	2.2	3.1
Lower secondary school	Count	54	36	24
	Expected count	54.1	32.3	27.6
	% within educational level	47.4%	31.6%	21.1%
	Adjusted residual	0.0	1.1	−1.1
Upper secondary school or above	Count	41	6	9
	Expected count	26.6	15.9	13.6
	% within educational level	73.2%	10.7%	16.1%
	Adjusted residual	4.5	−3.4	−1.6

together the two cases, it seemed that workers with higher educational level perceived less 'Chinese *gongmin*' as identity based on residence and culture. Can we generalize the effect of education beyond workers? Because student respondents, who had higher educational level than worker respondents on average, also held a split view over the residential identity, we cannot generalize the finding as higher education level leading to more likely rejection of 'Chinese *gongmin*' as residential identity. But such interpretation is possible in the case of cultural identity, given students' general disapproval of it for 'Chinese *gongmin*'.

There were student interviewees expressly opposing Chinese ethnicity and language as criteria for 'Chinese *gongmin*'. One student interviewee explained her understanding of the term in this way:

> I don't think language or ethnicity is the criterion of being a Chinese *gongmin*. Broadly speaking, I think you are Chinese *gongmin* as long as you are legally living here. Wait … I think you should live here for certain number of years. One year? Ten years, perhaps? I don't know. (S2)

The explanation above suggested that while students predominantly understood 'Chinese *gongmin*' in legal terms, it does not necessarily follow that they would accept the current official jus sanguinis principle for the legal status. Also, the quotation illustrated the controversy around 'Chinese *gongmin*' as residential identity in the understanding of students. There were also worker interviewees defining 'Chinese *gongmin*' based on ethnicity. For example, two worker interviewees similarly commented in the following way:

> I think Chinese *gongmin* are Chinese people, people with yellow skin and black eyes. (W6)
>
> Chinese *gongmin* are people having Chinese roots. (W8)

The first quotation revealed that at least for that worker interviewee, the ethnicity based on which 'Chinese *gongmin*' was defined was highly likely the Han majority, or at least not ethnic minorities with a physical appearance different from 'yellow skin' and 'black eyes'. It was not hard to find evidence from the interview data to support the quantitative finding that 'Chinese *gongmin*' was more often defined in terms of ethnicity and culture by workers as opposed to students. But it is also important to note that views running counter to the quantitative tendency were also recorded in the interviews. For instance, one student interviewee (S1) saw Chinese descent as the prerequisite for 'Chinese *gongmin*', while one worker respondent (W11) regarded 'Chinese *gongmin*' as a legal and a residential identity, irrespective of ethnicity or culture.

Gongmin Vis-à-Vis State and Society

The last section has shown the two social groups' perception of 'Chinese *gongmin*' which, in a nutshell, is predominantly a legal identity and controversially a residential identity for both groups, while more likely to be an identity based on birthplace and particularly on ethnicity and culture for workers as opposed to students. Similarities and differences were also found in their perception of the relationship of *gongmin* with state and society, the second aspect in the identity dimension of *gongmin*.

Citizen in modern Western discourse is the entity owning the sovereignty of the state and enjoying the universally equal status and rights guaranteed and protected by the state. In Western citizenship, the liberal tradition emphasizes the independence of individual citizens, while the civic republican tradition celebrates citizens as community members. Notwithstanding their distinct reasons for citizenship participation, both traditions recognize citizens' participatory role in the state affairs. Based on these ideas in Western citizenship conception, the *gongmin*–state and *gongmin*–society relations in the meaning of *gongmin* were measured through four statements, two for each relation, in the questionnaire, the attitudes towards which by student and worker respondents are shown in Fig. 4.2. None of the four demographic variables was found to significantly influence student or worker respondents' attitudes towards the four statements, meaning that the attitudes were consistent within each of the two groups.

(1) *The* gongmin*-state relation*

A comparison of worker respondents' attitudes towards the subordinate and the active role of *gongmin* in relation to the state suggested a clear gap between the two (61.9 and 41.6%, respectively), with a close-to-majority proportion (40.7%) of workers being undecided on the latter (Fig. 4.2). It indicated that workers placed

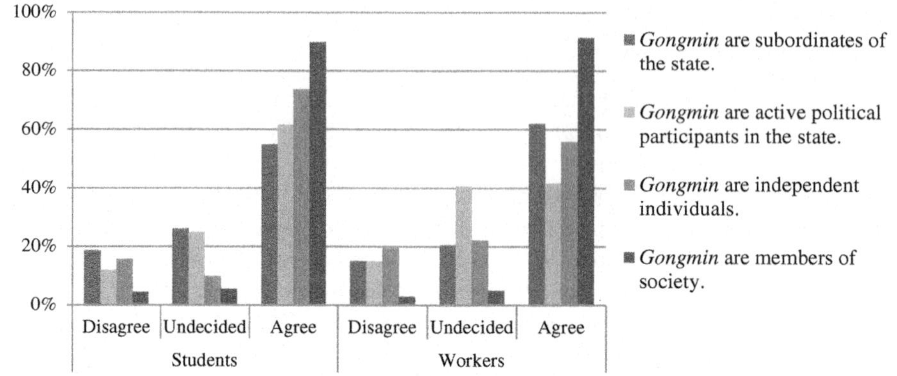

Fig. 4.2 Attitudes towards four statements about *gongmin* in relation to state and society

gongmin in a subordinate position in the face of the state, while not explicitly opposed against *gongmin* playing an active role in it. For the reason behind the subordination, one illustrative comment was that 'the state exists first and then *gongmin* comes along; no state, no *gongmin* and [in such case] people may fall to be slaves of other states' (W4). It seemed that it was based on the consideration of the protection of *gongmin* by the state from other supposedly hostile states that the worker interviewee assigned a subordinate role to *gongmin*. This reasoning corresponded to the paternalistic role self-claimed by the party-state and to the state propaganda of nationalism which necessarily contains constructed hostile others. The party-state's paternalistic role was also reflected in the comment by another worker interviewee, for whom *gongmin* was not entirely subordinate to the state but could have an active role for personal sake:

> The state for us is like the family. We as *gongmin* are part of the family and should follow its guide and do what is good for it… But if the family doesn't consider my interest, I would speak out and guard my interest. (W9)

While for workers *gongmin* was largely subordinate to the state, the students' understanding of *gongmin*-state relation was more complex. There were more student respondents accepting the active role than the subordinate role of *gongmin* vis-à-vis the state (61.6% compared with 54.8%). But the margin was narrow, especially when compared with either the agreement gap in the case of workers or the agreement gap between the two *gongmin*–society statements by the students themselves. It seemed that the term *gongmin* carried a dual role, both subordinate and active, vis-à-vis the state in the students' perception. Such view might be a result of the recently reformed citizenship-related education featuring increased recognition of self and intact state-centeredness. Notwithstanding the dual-role understanding, students were still about 1.47 times more likely than workers to perceive *gongmin* as an active entity vis-à-vis the state (Tables 4.7 and 4.8). The finding in this respect could be summed up in the way that while workers viewed *gongmin* largely in subordinate relation to the state, students assigned it a more

Table 4.7 Chi-square test result of attitudes towards four statements about *gongmin* in relation to state and society by student/worker group

Student/Worker Group	Pearson Chi-square	df	*p*-value	Cramer's *V*	*N* of valid cases
Gongmin are subordinates of the state	3.592	2	0.166	0.084	511
Gongmin are active political participants in the state	20.754	2	0.000*	0.202	509
Gongmin are independent individuals	19.829	2	0.000*	0.197	511
Gongmin are members of society	1.188	2	0.552	0.048	516

*$p < 0.001$

Table 4.8 Respondents' attitudes towards two statements about *gongmin* in relation to state and society significantly associated with student/worker group

Group		Disagree	Undecided	Agree
		Gongmin are active political participants in the state		
Students	Count	35	73	181
	Expected count	39.2	93.7	156.1
	% within group	12.1%	25.3%	62.6%
	Adjusted residual	−1.1	−4.0	4.5
Workers	Count	34	92	94
	Expected count	29.8	71.3	118.9
	% within group	15.5%	41.8%	42.7%
	Adjusted residual	1.1	4.0	−4.5
		Gongmin are independent individuals		
Students	Count	46	29	216
	Expected count	51.3	45.0	194.8
	% within group	15.8%	10.0%	74.2%
	Adjusted residual	−1.2	−4.0	4.0
Workers	Count	44	50	126
	Expected count	38.7	34.0	147.2
	% within group	20.0%	22.7%	57.3%
	Adjusted residual	1.2	4.0	−4.0

active role alongside a subordinate one. The finding suggested that the two possible relations of *gongmin* to the state, i.e. subordinate and active, are not necessarily exclusive to each other in the understanding of individual citizens. Such non-exclusiveness was also found in the perception about *gongmin*–society relation.

(2) *The* gongmin*–society relation*

Figure 4.2 shows that about 90% of student and worker respondents agreed that *gongmin* are members of society, considerably higher than the two groups' degree of agreement on the statement that *gongmin* is independent individuals, though which was also embraced by a majority of the respondents (73.5 and 55.8%, respectively). It indicated that *gongmin* was profoundly a collective identity in society for both students and workers without statistical difference (Table 4.7). This finding is not a surprise, given its consistency with what has long been taught in citizenship-related education and the connotations of publicity and collectivity etymologically associated with the characters of *gong* and *min* in the term *gongmin*.

But the two group held a significantly different view on *gongmin* as an individual identity, in the way that students were more likely to embrace it, while workers were more likely to be uncertain about it (Tables 4.7 and 4.8). In other words, the two groups shared a collectivistic understanding of the identity of *gongmin* on one hand, while students nevertheless also held a more individualistic understanding of the identity than workers on the other hand. This again could be associated with the increased recognition of self in the recently reformed citizenship-related education.

Gongmin as Multileveled Identity

This section turns to the third aspect in the dimension of identity. Modern citizenship is a state-centred concept, so is the modern citizen identity. Among the challenges against the state-centeredness driven by contemporary postmodernization and globalization, there have been advocates that citizenship should be understood as a multi-layered construct extendable from the national to the local and global levels. To what extent is such extension accepted by Chinese citizens? Does the term *gongmin* have the connotative capacity for such extension in contemporary Chinese society? The third aspect about *gongmin* as identity explored these two questions through students' and workers' attitudes towards three statements on the survey (Fig. 4.3). The two groups were found to hold similar attitudes (Table 4.9). Let us have a close look at their acceptance of *gongmin* as identity at the local, national and global levels in turn.

(1) *As local identity*

It was interesting to find that while both student and worker respondents were all living in the Guangdong Province when the research was conducted, not all (62.9 and 49.1%, respectively) accepted the identity of Guangdong *gongmin* (Fig. 4.3). A further analysis of the data found that the acceptance was significantly associated with the background variable of whether the primary school attended by respondent was in or out of the province in both cases of students [X^2 (2, N = 271) = 35.620, $p = 0.000$, Cramer's $V = 0.363$] and workers [X^2 (2, N = 214) = 44.897,

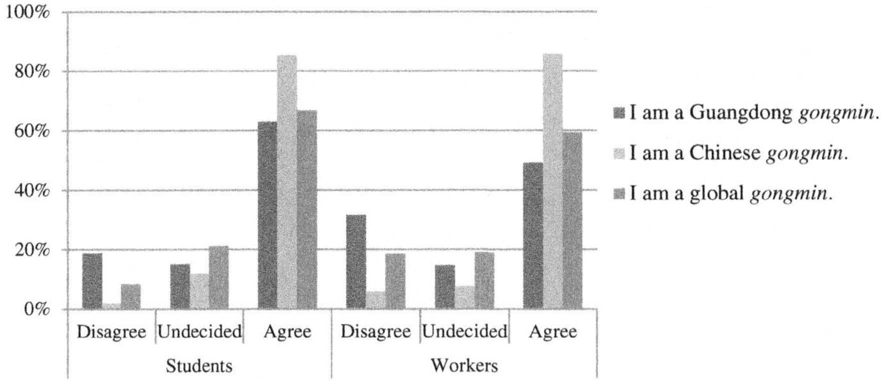

Fig. 4.3 Attitudes towards three statements about *gongmin* as multileveled identity

$p = 0.000$, Cramer's $V = 0.458$]. The data indicated that the identity was about 1.98 and 2.73 times more likely to be accepted by students and workers who attended primary school in Guangdong Province, respectively, than those did not (Table 4.10). In other words, whether receiving primary education in the locality or not was a significant factor in their acceptance of the local identity of *gongmin* despite the fact that they were living in the place at the time. In other words, the fact of living did not lead to local identification.

Given that in the Chinese education system where one receives primary education is determined, in principle, by the official HRS, the result suggested the HRS to be a more substantial factor in the acceptance, which was indeed expressed by interviewees. There were student and worker interviewees similarly reasoning their acceptance or rejection of the identity of Guangdong *gongmin* on the basis of their HRS was or was not in the province. Although not pointed out explicitly by the interviewees, the fact that the HRS determines the place where citizens are entitled to enjoy and excise their citizenship rights, economic and social rights in particular, might contribute to the determining effect of the HRS on the acceptance of *gongmin* as local identity.

It was also found in the interviews that there were students and workers declining the identity of Guangdong *gongmin* for other reasons, as one student interviewee explained:

> Guangdong is not a country. It sounds strange to speak of Guangdong *gongmin*…*Gongmin* is a legal term in association with the nation-state … never heard of *gongmin* used at the local or global level. (S10)

The explanation was another testament to the predominant understanding of *gongmin* in legal terms by the two groups. It seemed that the predominance of legal understanding of the term could hinder its use as identity in non-legal local context.

Table 4.9 Chi-square test result of attitudes towards three statements about *gongmin* as multileveled identity by student/worker group

Student/Worker group	Pearson Chi-square	df	*p*-value	Cramer's *V*	*N* of valid cases
I am a Guangdong *gongmin*	12.807	2	0.002	0.160	499
I am a Chinese *gongmin*	7.276	2	0.026	0.119	516
I am a global *gongmin*	11.426	2	0.003	0.151	502

$^{*}p < 0.001$

Table 4.10 Attitude towards the statement about *gongmin* as a local identity by primary school location (PSL)

		I am a Guangdong *gongmin*		
		Disagree	Undecided	Agree
Students				
In Guangdong Province	Count	30	37	162
	Expected count	43.9	35.5	149.6
	% within PSL	13.1%	16.2%	70.7%
	Adjusted residual	−5.9	0.7	4.4
Out of Guangdong Province	Count	22	5	15
	Expected count	8.1	6.5	27.4
	% within PSL	52.4%	11.9%	35.7%
	Adjusted residual	5.9	−0.7	−4.4
Workers				
In Guangdong Province	Count	21	11	84
	Expected count	38.5	17.9	59.6
	% within PSL	18.1%	9.5%	72.4%
	Adjusted residual	−5.1	−2.6	6.7
Out of Guangdong Province	Count	50	22	26
	Expected count	32.5	15.1	50.4
	% within PSL	51.0%	22.4%	26.5%
	Adjusted residual	5.1	2.6	−6.7

(2) *As national identity*

Given the predominantly legal understanding of *gongmin* by both groups, it was not surprising to find that the identity of Chinese *gongmin* was accepted by about 85% of student and worker respondents (Fig. 4.3), considerably surpassing the degrees of agreement on the other two statements and, in other words, triumphing over *gongmin* as a local or a global identity. Such strong identification with *gongmin* at the national level was shared by the two groups (Table 4.9), suggesting the strong capacity of *gongmin* to be pronounced as national identity for students and workers.

Student and worker interviewees' reasons for their acceptance of Chinese *gongmin* were largely consistent with the finding of 'Chinese *gongmin*' explained earlier. Students often committed to the identity because of the possession of the Chinese nationality, while workers tended to claim the identity more for the reason that they were ethnic Chinese. Inconsistency was nevertheless detected. There were some student interviewees also referring to being born in China as their reason of acceptance, although the student respondents in general, as reported above, dismissed 'Chinese *gongmin*' as an identity defined by birthplace. In addition, interestingly, there was one worker interviewee denying being a Chinese *gongmin* on the basis that only 'successful' people, such as people of high educational level and people with business success, are eligible for the identity (W2). This particular understanding, albeit uncommon among the interviewees, revealed that for some people the term *gongmin* might be even perceived as a privileged status rather than an equal one shared by citizens in the state.

(3) *As global identity*

Alongside students' and workers' conditional acceptance of *gongmin* at the local level and their strong acceptance of it at the national level was their wide acceptance of it at the global level, given that a majority of student and worker respondents (66.7 and 59.3%, respectively) similarly perceived themselves as global *gongmin* both in and between groups (Fig. 4.3 and Table 4.9).

Student and worker interviewees had similar reasons for the acceptance. Some reasoned that they were global *gongmin* because of being human beings on the earth and members of the global village, while some justified their acceptance on the grounds that China was part of the world and they were members of China, so they were global as well as Chinese *gongmin*. The global identity using the term *gongmin* seemed to be understood and accepted either with the implication of universality or in relation to nationality, the latter of which corresponded with the strong acceptance of *gongmin* as national identity.

Social Implications

The last section presented and explained the three aspects of *gongmin* as identity in Chinese society based on the findings from the investigation in Study II of university students' and migrant workers' perceptions. Unaffected by age or gender, the two groups shared some perceptions regarding *gongmin* as identity. The most salient were their approval of 'Chinese *gongmin*' as legal identity and *gongmin* as collective social identity and their acceptance of the identity of *gongmin* at the national and global levels. Also, for both groups, the acceptance of *gongmin* as local identity seemed to be conditional, while 'Chinese *gongmin*' as residential identity turned out to be controversial. Differences of perception were nevertheless not hard to find. 'Chinese *gongmin*' defined in terms of ethnicity and culture was likely to be embraced by workers but opposed by students. At the same time, not only was the identity of *gongmin* more individualistic in the eyes of students as opposed to workers but the position of *gongmin* vis-à-vis the state was perceived both active and subordinate by students while largely subordinate by workers. The perceptual similarities and differences in the three aspects of *gongmin* as identity bear implications for citizenship in Chinese society.

First, the finding of the strong acceptance of 'Chinese *gongmin*' perceived first and foremost as legal identity adds evidence to the observation of the increased identification with the legal status of *gongmin* in Chinese society. It not merely confirms the salient awareness of legal citizen identity among migrant workers reported by Lee (2007), but complements that the awareness is similarly shared by university students. This suggests that despite their social distinction, the two groups as ordinary citizens are capable to communicate in the language of citizenship, at the very least under their shared legal understanding of and identification with 'Chinese *gongmin*'. This might not be a surprising finding if we consider it as an outcome of the official use of the term *gongmin* in legal narratives and the party-state's recent attempts to regulate state–society relation in legal terms. What is less anticipatable from the finding, however, is whether the two groups and other ordinary citizens would actually express the legal identity in citizenship practice, or see it as an identity too powerless to claim as in the case of the migrant workers studied by Lee (2007). Nevertheless, the sharing recognition of *gongmin* as legal identity raises the prospect of university students and migrant workers acting as a joint social force in citizenship negotiation with the party-state.

The identity of 'Chinese *gongmin*' might be understood in ethnic and cultural as well as legal senses in Chinese society, as evidenced by the migrant workers' perception. Reflecting the official eligibility for legal Chinese citizenship which, following the jus sanguinis principle, is based primarily on Chinese ethnicity, the existence of such understanding in society risks leaving open for the authorities to manoeuvre what is counted as 'Chinese ethnicity', 'Chinese culture' and 'Chinese *gongmin*' in a state consisting of diverse ethnic groups and cultures. At a time that the identities of ethnic and cultural minorities are not celebrated but tend to be marginalized in official narratives and policies, as witnessed in the struggles of the peasants reported by Brandtstadter (2011) and the Tibetan students by Yi (2006), the blur of the legally defined identity of 'Chinese *gongmin*' on one hand and ethnicity and culture on the other hand may alienate ethnic and cultural minorities from that legal identity. Such alienation may in turn bar the minorities from communication and collaboration with other citizens under the identity of legal citizen, and hence weaken the mobilizing power of the legal identity of *gongmin* in Chinese society. Given the existence of the ethnic understanding of 'Chinese *gongmin*' which implies that the identity is ascribed according to inborn Chinese ethnicity, it is not hard to understand the controversy among students and workers over the idea of 'Chinese *gongmin*' as residential identity acquirable through the act of living in the country. The controversy could nonetheless be viewed in positive light as a sign that 'Chinese *gongmin*' understood in the acquirable and hence less exclusive sense is not impossible to achieve in contemporary Chinese society.

Second, the findings of *gongmin*-society relation have implications for the existing observation of the salient awareness of self among Chinese young people (Law and Ng 2009; Liu 2008; Pan 2011). University students' more individualistic understanding of *gongmin*, as opposed to migrant workers averagely a decade older in the sample, might be a result of young people's salient self-identity. The self-identity, however, does not necessarily impede them from forging a collective identification through the term *gongmin* with other social groups, because university students did share their endorsement of *gongmin* as members of society with migrant workers. For the term *gongmin*, it might not be an effective term for young people to express their awareness of self, or in other words, to convey the self-identity of young people, given the more collectivistic than individualistic understanding of the term by university students.

Turning to the *gongmin*–state relationship, the nation-as-parent analogy deployed by the party-state (He 2015) and expressed by the Chinese young people in Fong's (2004) study is observed in this study. Workers' understanding of *gongmin* as subordinate to the state seems to fall in line with the party-state propaganda, as illustrated by the quoted words from a worker interviewee. Though not expressly pointed out by workers, the particular understanding might also be derived from their experience as rural migrants living in city where the authorities, albeit often failing to do so, are their first and last resort to appeal to for rights protection. For university students, the coexisting active and subordinate roles of *gongmin* in the state in their understanding might be a result of the recent citizenship-related education featuring increased recognition of self on one hand and intact state orientation on the other hand. At a more substantial level, the awareness of the active role of *gongmin* by students could attribute to the social group's possession of cultural capital translatable to social mobility and political influence. In short, there seems to be perceptual difference in society concerning the *gongmin*-state relationship, probably due to varied sociopolitical resources and experience, as in the case of students and workers. If this is the case, then the prospect of joint negotiation in the name of legal citizen by socio-politically distinct social groups with the state would be limited even though they commonly embrace that identity.

Third, the strong acceptance of *gongmin* as national identity by students and workers not just confirms the strong national identification in Chinese society reported in existing literature (Fairbrother 2004; Fong 2004; Li 2009; Pan 2011; Sinkkonen 2013; Tu 2011), but also complements that, first, the identification may be derived from legal or/and ethnic reasons, and second, the national identity can be well expressed via the term *gongmin*. Also, the strong acceptance suggests that the term is most accepted and pronounceable at the national level among the multiple levels from local to global. This does not come as a surprise if we recall the use of the term in the state discourse elaborated in Chap. 3. The conditional embracement of *gongmin* at the local level suggests that living in one place does not automatically lead to identification with the locality, which seems to depend upon the official HRS in this study. In light of the implications given by existing studies (Goodman 2002; Law and Ng 2009; Pan 2011) that local societal contexts affect local identity formation in society, efforts such as making favourable policy and providing social and cultural support in Guangdong could contribute to the development of the identity of Guangdong *gongmin* among citizens living in it regardless of backgrounds.

The general adoption of the identity of *gongmin* at the global level by students and workers seems to echo the detected global awareness among secondary school students in the study of Pan (2011), yet run counter to the modest acceptance of *gongmin* at the global level among overseas Chinese students in my previous study (Chen 2011). Given the reasons behind the adoption explained by the students and workers, which were either derived from the physical connection to the earth or depended upon the national belongingness similarly found in Chen's (2011) study, such adoption might be little more than an imagination of the relationship between self and world without direct and personal affective attachment to the global community, as was the case in Pan's (2011) study. Nevertheless, the adoption, albeit likely to be vague and dependent, shows positively that *gongmin* as identity is not constrained at the national level but extendable to be expressed and embraced at the global level in Chinese society.

References

Brandtstadter, S. (2011). The law cuts both ways: Rural legal activism and citizenship struggles in neosocialist China. *Economy and Society, 40*(2), 266–288. doi:10.1080/03085147.2011.548944.

Chen, S. (2011). Developing global citizenship: The effect of studying abroad. *International Journal of Development Education and Global Learning, 3*(3), 45–64.

Fairbrother, G. P. (2003). The effects of political education and critical thinking on Hong Kong and Mainland Chinese university students' national attitudes. *British Journal of Sociology of Education, 24*(5), 605–620. doi:10.1080/0142569032000127161.

Fairbrother, G. P. (2004). Patriotic education in a Chinese middle school. In W. O. Lee, D. L. Grossman, K. J. Kennedy, & G. P. Fairbrother (Eds.), *Citizenship education in Asia and the Pacific: Concepts and issues* (pp. 157–174). Hong Kong: Comparative Education Research Centre, The University of Hong Kong.

Fong, V. (2004). Filial nationalism among Chinese teenagers with global identities. *American Ethnologist, 31*(4), 631–648.

Goodman, D. S. G. (2002). Structuring local identity: Nation, province and county in Shanxi during the 1990s. *The China Quarterly, 172,* 837–862. doi:10.1017/S0009443902000529.

He, R. (2015). Identifying with a "rising China"? Overseas Chinese student nationalism. In E. Vickers & K. Kumar (Eds.), *Constructing modern Asian citizenship* (pp. 314–340). Oxon: Routledge.

Law, W. W., & Ng, H. M. (2009). Globalization and multileveled citizenship education: A tale of two Chinese cities, Hong Kong and Shanghai. *Teachers College Record, 111*(4), 851–892.

Lee, C. K. (2007). *Against the law: Labour protests in China's rustbelt and sunbelt.* Berkeley: University of California Press.

Li, J. (2009). Fostering citizenship in China's move from elite to mass higher education: An analysis of students' political socialization and civic participation. *International Journal of Educational Development, 29*(4), 382–398. doi:10.1016/j.ijedudev.2008.10.001.

Liu, F. (2008). Constructing the autonomous middle-class self in today's China: The case of young-adult only-children university students. *Journal of Youth Studies, 11*(2), 193–212. doi:10.1080/13676260701800746.

Pan, S. (2011). Multileveled citizenship and citizenship education: Experiences of students in China's Beijing. *Citizenship Studies, 15*(2), 283–306. doi:10.1080/13621025.2011.549730.

Sinkkonen, E. (2013). Nationalism, patriotism and foreign policy attitudes among Chinese university students. *The China Quarterly, 216,* 1045–1063. doi:10.1017/S0305741013001094.

Tu, Y. (2011). Citizenship with Chinese characteristics? An investigation into Chinese university students' civic perceptions and civic participation. *Frontiers of Education in China, 6*(3), 426–448. doi:10.1007/s11516-011-0140-4.

Turner, D. A., & Yolcu, H. (Eds.). (2014). *Neo-liberal educational reforms: A Critical analysis.* New York: Routledge.

Wu, J. (2014). The rise of ethnicity under China's market reforms. *International Journal of Urban and Regional Research, 38*(3), 967–984. doi:10.1111/j.1468-2427.2012.01179.x.

Yi, L. (2006). Choosing between ethnic and Chinese citizenship: The educational trajectories of Tibetan minority children in northwestern China. In V. L. Fong & R. Murphy (Eds.), *Chinese citizenship: Views from the margins* (pp. 41–67). Oxon: Routledge.

Chapter 5
Rights and Responsibilities of *Gongmin*

The last chapter detailed the extent dimension about identity in the meaning of *gongmin* in Chinese society. This chapter proceeds to the second dimension about content, exploring rights and responsibilities bound with the term at the collective or macro level (Study I) and at the individual or micro level (Study II) in society. Following a similar structure as in the previous chapter, I shall at first give a review of citizenship rights and responsibilities in Chinese society with particular attention to migrant workers and university students, before detailing the findings of the two sub-studies in turn. The chapter will conclude with a discussion of the social implications of the findings.

Citizenship Rights and Responsibilities in Society

Recent years have witnessed an expanded body of research reporting the increase of rights consciousness in Chinese society against the backdrop of increased numbers of popular protests and legal claims by Chinese citizens. For example, grounded on her detailed research on ordinary Chinese citizens' political struggles in the late twentieth century featuring waves of demands for freedom of speech and association and for a system of checks and balances, Goldman (2005) concluded that a major change in the period was 'a growing sense of rights consciousness, particularly of political rights… [which] gradually spread to the population in general—workers, peasants, the growing middle class, and religious believers' (p. 2).

The rise of rights consciousness in the case of workers is recorded in detail by Lee (2007) in her wide-ranging and careful observation of protests by workers at the threshold of the twenty-first century. She discussed that workers, either laid-off workers from state-owned enterprises deprived of formerly enjoyed social security benefits or peasant-turned migrant workers in cities suffering various workplace grievances, commonly 'make strong claims based on the law and workers' legal rights' even though not placing much confidence on the part of law enforcement

S. Chen, *The Meaning of Citizenship in Contemporary Chinese Society*,
Governance and Citizenship in Asia, https://doi.org/10.1007/978-981-10-6323-7_5

(p. 202). Drawing upon protests by villagers in rural China against grievances from cadre misconduct to tax burdens, O'Brien and Li (2006) coined the term 'rightful resistance' to describe those protests often with claims framed in reference to legal rights stated in law, and discussed it as a reflection of 'the rising rights consciousness and a growing fluency in "rights talk"' among citizens in rural China (p. 127). This kind of rights-based resistance, as Kelly (2006) complemented, is also employed by other social groups, such as urban homeowners and company investors, in their own struggles for rights, property rights in particular.

As the growth of rights consciousness in Chinese society becomes a common observation, the nature of such rights consciousness in contemporary Chinese popular protests is increasingly lucubrated. Perry (2008) explored the nature through Chinese conceptions of rights in the ethical discourses of philosophers, political leaders, and protestors. She argued that distinct from Anglo-American conceptions of human rights and civil society, which 'ipso facto imply a liberal critique of overweening state power', rights in the Chinese context 'are seen more as state-authorized channels to enhance national unity and prosperity than as naturally endowed protections against state intrusion'; and accordingly, 'popular demands for the exercise of political rights are perhaps better seen as an affirmation of—rather than an affront to—state power' (pp. 46–7). On the grounds of the absence of direct challenge against state authorities in contemporary Chinese rights-based protests, she suggested that the consciousness behind the protests is 'rules consciousness' rather than 'rights consciousness' (p. 47). This suggestion is questioned by Li (2010) through the case of rural citizens. He at first conceptually clarified rule consciousness and rights consciousness, the former targeting local rule-enforcement authorities with 'no challenge to the legitimacy of existing rules, no demand for rule change or new rules, and no demand for participation in rule-making', while the latter targeting central rule-making authorities with the challenges and demands absent in the former (p. 50). Drawing upon his analysis of claims made by villagers, he argued that 'ordinary Chinese people do have rules consciousness, but it is problematic to conclude that they only have rules consciousness and no rights consciousness' (p. 65).

If challenging existing rules is a defining characteristic of rights consciousness understood by Perry (2008) and Li (2010), then it can also be found in the case of workers. In her study on strikes by Chinese workers, Chan (2011) differentiated between rights-based protests which claim wages no more than the legal minimum (equal to rules consciousness) and interest-based protests which demand wages higher than the legal standards (equal to rights consciousness). While concluding that Chinese labour disputes around the beginning of the current century tended to be rights-based rather than interest-based, she highlighted a protest in Guangdong Province in 2010 which demanded and realized a higher wage rise than the officially proposed one, recognizing it as 'the first publicized interest-based strike in China in recent times' (p. 50).

Lorentzen and Scoggins (2015) provided another approach to understanding the nature of the heightened rights consciousness in contemporary Chinese society. Defining rights consciousness broadly as 'a greater willingness by an aggrieved individual or group to make a claim for redress on the basis of a "right"' (pp. 639–40), they clarified three interactive factors behind rights-conscious behaviour: (1) changing values, which could result in behaviour challenging the status quo of the state (similar with aforementioned rights consciousness); (2) changing government rights-granting policy, behaviour driven by which is no more than recognition of rules set by the state (similar to aforementioned rules consciousness); and (3) changing shared expectations about how the society would respond to the behaviour, be it challenging or following official rules. The three factors, according to Lorentzen and Scoggins (2015), can overlap and be interrelated in practice, in the way that there could be more than one factor behind a particular rights-conscious behaviour and that one factor might promote another. This relational account helpfully connects and correlates rights consciousness and rules consciousness by and large understood separately by Perry (2008) and Li (2010).

The review above makes clear that, first, rights consciousness can be defined in the narrow sense as necessarily comprising the element of challenging existing rules and in the broad sense as covering all claims made on the basis of rights; and second, there is empirical evidence of the rise of rights consciousness understood in either the narrow or the broad sense. This book uses the term in the broad sense if not otherwise noted.

The rise of rights consciousness, however, does not necessarily mean that the consciousness is commonly shared in society or that all rights are equally weighted at all times. For instance, Wong (2012) observed that migrant workers are a heterogenous group in which those born in the 1980s and the 1990s are 'likely to be more knowledgeable, determined and skilled in asserting their rights as citizens' (p. 890). For consciousness about different rights, the results of a national survey about citizenship attitudes conducted by a team at Peking University in 2008 suggested that Chinese citizens are concerned with civil (the rights to survival and privacy) and social (the right to work) rights more than political rights such as the right to political participation (Shen 2009). From the cultural perspective, Bell (2006) argued that influenced by Chinese traditional values, 'the Chinese may be more willing to sacrifice a civil or political liberty in cases of conflict with a social or economic right' (p. 61). It is empirically and culturally suggested that political rights are deemed less important in Chinese society.

Rights and responsibilities are often perceived as two opposite—in the sense of one existing at the expense of the other—but necessary sides of the same coin of citizenship in Western conception. In the Chinese discourse, the two might be less antagonistic and could even be integrated. Focusing on the idea of freedom, Fung (2006) discussed that while often seen exclusively as a right in the West, freedom in modern Chinese thought means not just personal liberty grounded on right but also liberty of service to society grounded on social responsibility. In other words, the responsibility of social contribution as an autonomous moral agent is the extension to, rather than at the expense of, the right to personal liberty. Neither entirely unique nor unfound in the West as Fung (2006) importantly pointed out, the Chinese understanding of freedom illustrates that rights and responsibilities are not necessarily antagonistic elements of citizenship in the Chinese context.

There has been a general concern by the public and the authorities since the 1990s that the Chinese society is experiencing 'moral decline', particularly the decline of family and social ethics including the commitment to public good. The reasons for such decline are contested, but similarly formulated in relation to either the market or the party-state. As summarized by Ding (2001, p. 102), some see the decline as 'a negative side-effect of the market economy', blaming free competition and materialization for the unrestrained selfishness and the collapsed collectivism, while some contend that the so-called moral decline is in effect the 'necessary and inevitable' value change from collectivism to individualism, which is a positive response to the market economy and a necessary step towards democratic politics. Also, there are some such as Link (1993) who view the moral decline as the moral vacuum left by the failure of communism, and some such as intellectual He Qinglian who argue that rather than the market economy, the reason for the perceived moral decline is that 'the totalitarian practices employed during the process of primitive accumulation undermined any sense of social regulation and fairness' (cited in Goldman 2005, p. 124). Whether a decline or not, if moral values are changed in society, so would be the list of citizenship responsibilities in the public perception which is not necessarily shared among citizens of different backgrounds. For instance, in the study by Li (2009) on the political socialization and civic participation of Chinese university students, female students and students growing up in rural areas are found to be more willing than male students and students from urban areas to take the social responsibility of active contribution to the common good.

In the context of rising rights consciousness and changing moral values in society, to what extent are rights, from civil to political, social and cultural, and responsibilities, both legal and moral, expressed in relation to the term *gongmin* in society? This question is investigated in this book at both collective/macro (Study I) and individual/micro (Study II) social levels. In what follows I shall present and explain the findings of the two sub-studies in turn.

At the Collective Level

Considering newspapers as a window onto the meaning of *gongmin* in society at the collective/macro level, Study I examined, through content analysis, the use of the term in *Southern Metropolis Daily*, an influential nonofficial newspaper in Guangdong Province, with reference to the term appearing in *People's Daily*, the mouthpiece of the party-state. There are three key findings regarding the meaning of *gongmin* at the collective social level, including the discrepancy between state and society, the primacy of civil and political rights, and the weak connotation of responsibilities.

Table 5.1 Percentage of articles involving *gongmin* in semantic connection with rights and responsibilities in the two newspapers

%	Rights	Responsibilities
Southern Metropolis Daily (n = 2257)	37.0	8.2
People's Daily (n = 2744)	27.0	18.5

(1) *The discrepancy between state and society*

It was found that the meaning of *gongmin* in the nonofficial newspaper was significantly distinct from that in the official newspaper. Table 5.1 shows the percentage of articles involving *gongmin* in positive semantic connection with rights and responsibilities in all the articles containing the term in the two newspapers. Similarly in both newspapers, there were more articles containing *gongmin* in connection with rights than articles in which *gongmin* was connected with responsibilities (37.0 vs. 8.2% and 27.0 vs. 18.5%), But the nonofficial newspaper, as opposed to the official one, was found to have more articles with *gongmin*-rights connection (37.0 vs. 27.0%) but fewer articles with *gongmin*-responsibilities connection (8.2 vs. 18.5%). These differences between the two newspapers were statistically significant (Table 5.2). The data suggested that the term was about 1.37 times more likely to be connected with rights in the nonofficial newspaper when compared with the official one. By contrast, the probability of *gongmin* in connection with responsibilities was about 2.26 times more likely to appear in the latter than in the former. In other words, there was a discrepancy in the meaning of *gongmin* between state and society, in the way that the term had the stronger connotation of responsibilities in official discourses while stronger connotation of rights in macro social discourses. Was the strong connotation equally shared by different rights in the latter? The second finding gives an answer to this question.

(2) *The primacy of civil and political rights*

The degrees of semantic connection between *gongmin* and specific rights varied in both newspapers, which similarly showed more concern for civil and political rights than on social and cultural rights (Fig. 5.1). Nevertheless, the term was still significantly more likely to be connected to political rights in the nonofficial newspaper than in the official one (Table 5.3). This suggested that the strong connotation of rights in the macro social meaning of *gongmin* was primarily about civil and political rights, the latter of which had a significantly weaker connotation in official discourses.

Table 5.2 Chi-square test result of articles involving *gongmin* in connection with rights and responsibilities by newspaper (N = 5001)

Newspaper	Pearson Chi-square	df	p-value	Phi
Rights	57.334	1	0.000*	0.107
Responsibilities	110.413	1	0.000*	−0.149

*$p < 0.001$

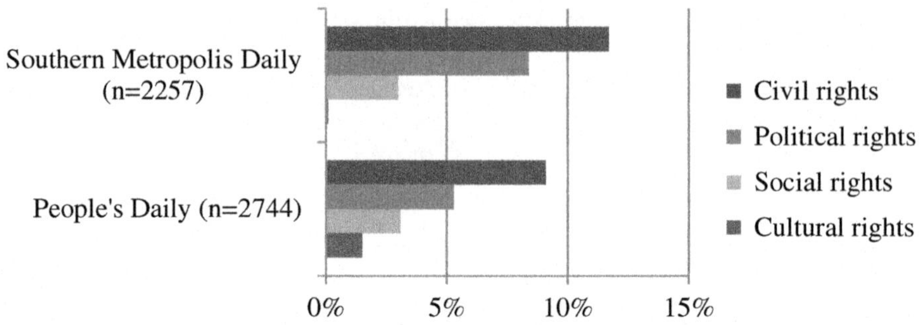

Fig. 5.1 Percentage of articles involving *gongmin* in semantic connection with four kinds of rights in the two newspapers. *Source* Chen (2013)

Table 5.3 Chi-square test result of articles involving *gongmin* in semantic connection with specific rights and responsibilities by newspaper (N = 5001)

Newspaper		Pearson Chi-square	df	*p*-value	Phi
Rights	Civil	8.692	1	0.003	0.042
	Political	18.968	1	0.000*	0.062
	Social	0.036	1	0.849	−0.003
	Cultural	34.839	1	0.000*	−0.083
Responsibilities	Moral	109.264	1	0.000*	−0.148
	Legal	68.964	1	0.000*	−0.117

*$p < 0.001$

The other significant difference found in terms of rights between the two newspapers was that the official one was more likely than the nonofficial one to use the term *gongmin* in reference to cultural rights (Table 5.3). However, the analysis of the contents in which the Chinese term *wenhua quanli* (literally cultural rights) was used in the newspapers suggested that it might not bear the same meaning of cultural rights as in Western citizenship conception. The term was, particularly in the official newspaper, less about rights to minority cultures, as might be expected in Western discourse, but more about rights to access to media, such as music and movies, or to culture related public facilities, such as museums. These rights would largely fall into the category of social rights in Western conception.

(3) *The weak connotation of responsibilities*

Turning to responsibilities, there were considerably less articles expressing *gongmin* in connection with responsibilities than with rights in the nonofficial newspaper (8.2 vs. 37.0%, Table 5.1). The proportions of the two categories of responsibilities were similarly low (Fig. 5.2), indicating that the term *gongmin* carried the weak connotation of responsibilities, either legal or moral, in collective social discourses. This was significantly distinct from official discourses in which both legal and

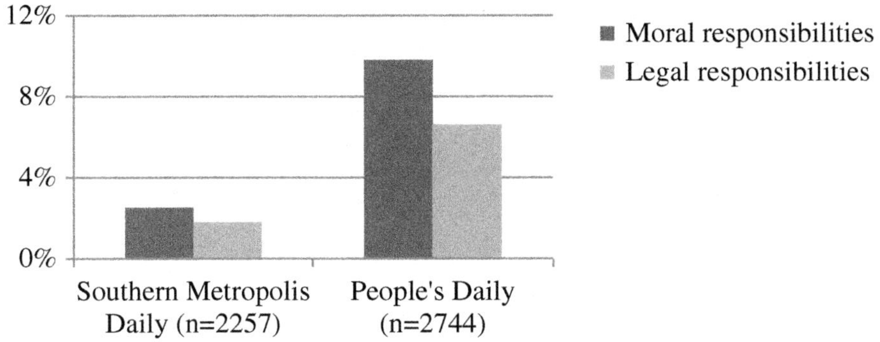

Fig. 5.2 Percentage of articles involving *gongmin* in semantic connection with two kinds of responsibilities in the two newspapers. *Source* Chen (2013)

moral responsibilities connotations of the term were comparatively stronger (Table 5.3).

From the perspective that there is a power imbalance between social sectors and actors in the formation of the collective meaning of *gongmin* in society, what shown above is the meaning upheld by dominant social powers. But dominance does not necessarily mean exclusiveness. Is the collective discourse faithfully followed by social groups of diffident positions and powers? Furthermore, from the educational perspective, the collective discourse of *gongmin* approached in this study through the mass media has the public pedagogical function for the understanding of *gongmin* by individual citizens at the micro social level, though orderly media like newspapers nowadays may have disorderly features that consumers act as independent decision-makers and information becomes disposable (Latham 2007). Is that function effective in the Chinese context? Answers to these questions lie in the findings of Study II to which we turn below.

At the Individual Level

To explore the micro-level social meaning of *gongmin*, Study II investigated university students' and migrant workers' perceptions of the term through a survey and in-depth interviews. In the survey respondents were asked to give their attitude towards a list of specific rights and responsibilities that *gongmin* should have. Figure 5.3 shows the degree of agreement by the two groups on the specific must-have rights and responsibilities for *gongmin*.

Student and worker respondents' attitudes towards these rights and responsibilities were not significantly affected by any of the four demographic variables, except that gender proved to be a factor in workers' attitude towards conscription as a must-have responsibility for *gongmin* [X^2 (1, N = 208) = 18.751, p = 0.000, Phi = 0.300] in the way that male workers were likely to be positive while female

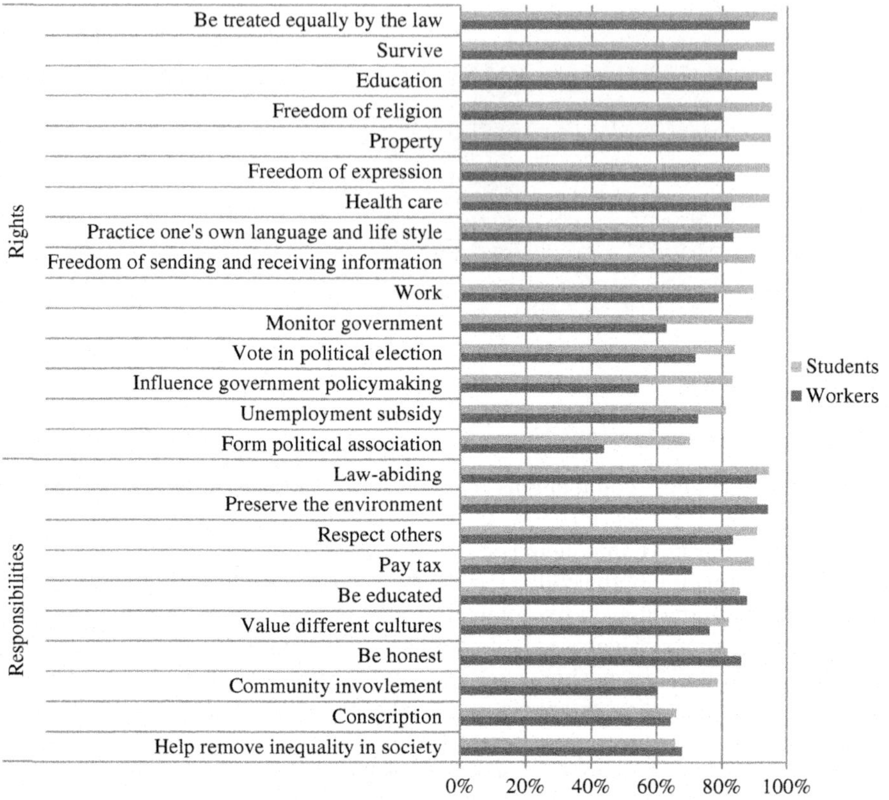

Fig. 5.3 Degree of agreement (including strongly agree and agree) by students and workers on rights and responsibilities that *gongmin* should have

workers were likely to hold an undecided attitude (Table 5.4). No interview data were available to explain the difference. Given that conscription is historically a practice with men rather than women at the centre, the different understanding between female and male workers on the particular responsibility might not be a

Table 5.4 Worker respondents' attitude towards the responsibility of conscription by gender

Workers: responsibility of conscription		Undecided	Agree
Gender			
Female	Count	53	76
	Expected count	39.1	89.9
	% within group	41.1%	58.9%
	Adjusted residual	4.3	−4.3
Male	Count	10	69
	Expected count	23.9	55.1
	% within group	12.7%	87.3%
	Adjusted residual	−4.3	4.3

surprise. In spite of the difference, the result indicated a general perceptual similarity among respondents within each group. Such similarity, however, was found neither among different rights and responsibilities nor between students and workers.

(1) *Rights*

Political rights were found to enjoy the least certainty of necessity among different kinds of rights in both students' and workers' understandings of *gongmin*. Figure 5.3 indicates that all of the specific rights listed in the questionnaire covering civil, political, social and cultural rights were considered to be necessary for *gongmin* by more than half of student and worker respondents, respectively, except the right to form political association, a political right, by worker respondents (43.8%). Indeed, a comparison of the degrees of agreement between the listed rights suggested that political rights, which were illustrated by the rights to monitor government, to vote in elections, to influence government policymaking and to form political association, were among the least necessary rights for student and particularly worker respondents. It seemed that compared with their general consent to civil, social and cultural rights, students and workers were similarly less certain about whether *gongmin* should have political rights.

The interview data revealed that students' and workers' reasons for their lukewarm attitude towards political rights tended to be different. On one hand, for students it was in relation to their lack of opportunity to touch these rights in daily life practice. One student interviewee (S2), who said she had never voted in political election, explained her undecided attitude toward the statement that *gongmin* should have the right to form political association in this way: 'I have never seen people around me form political association… I have little idea about it in practical life'. In addition, when talking about *gongmin*'s must-have rights, student interviewees' tendency to refer to civil and social rights implied their less concern on political rights for *gongmin*.

On the other hand, it was less the lack of political rights exercise but more the disillusion generated in individual political experience that led some worker interviewees to be sceptical of the necessity of political rights for *gongmin*. Some worker interviewees mentioned their experience of voting in village elections. One (W6) described with a laugh the dark side of the elections as he was once offered cash bribes by election candidates for a vote, while another one (W11) felt that the act of voting 'is hard to make real difference'. Such experience of unfairness and feeling of uselessness seemed to lead some workers to question the function and consequently doubt about the necessity of political rights for *gongmin*. Also, there were some worker interviewees blaming their lack of education and knowledge for their undecided attitude towards *gongmin*'s political rights. The interview data suggested that sociopolitical experience and resources, which have been discussed to have an impact on individual citizens' understandings of *gongmin*-state relationship in Chap. 4, also helped shape the content of rights in the meaning of *gongmin* at the individual level.

While sharing with workers the lesser certainty on political rights, students did overall have a more affirmative attitude towards rights than workers. The two groups had significantly different attitudes towards two third of the listed rights (Table 5.5), in the way that, as suggested by the adjusted residuals in Table 5.6, students were more likely to agree the necessity of those rights for *gongmin* while workers were more likely to have an undecided attitude towards most of them and

Table 5.5 Chi-square test result of respondents' attitudes towards listed must-have rights and responsibilities for *gongmin* by student/worker group

Student/Worker group	Pearson Chi-square	df	*p*-value	Cramer's *V*	*N* of valid cases
Rights					
Be treated equally by the law	17.672	2	0.000*	0.185	519
Survive	19.368	2	0.000*	0.194	516
Education	6.886#	2	0.032	0.115	519
Freedom of religion	29.235	2	0.000*	0.238	517
Property	15.424	2	0.000*	0.173	517
Freedom of expression	19.543	2	0.000*	0.194	520
Health care	25.040#	2	0.000*	0.219	520
Practice one's own language and life style	8.494	2	0.014	0.128	519
Freedom of sending and receiving information	17.648	2	0.000*	0.185	513
Work	14.737#	2	0.001	0.169	517
Monitor government	50.059	2	0.000*	0.312	515
Vote in political election	14.811	2	0.001	0.169	518
Influence government policymaking	47.868	2	0.000*	0.304	517
Unemployment subsidy	5.712	2	0.057	0.105	517
Form political association	37.159	2	0.000*	0.268	516
Responsibilities					
Law-abiding	6.831	2	0.033	0.115	520
Preserve the environment	2.590	2	0.274	0.071	518
Respect others	6.705	2	0.035	0.114	518
Pay tax	31.862	2	0.000*	0.248	520
Be educated	0.994	2	0.608	0.044	520
Value different cultures	6.495	2	0.039	0.112	519
Be honest	4.017	2	0.134	0.088	517
Community involvement	35.403	2	0.000*	0.262	516
Conscription	2.522	2	0.283	0.070	514
Help remove inequality in society	2.506	2	0.286	0.070	517

*$p < 0.001$
#1 cell has expected count less than 5

Table 5.6 Respondents' attitudes towards specific rights and responsibilities of *gongmin* significantly associated with student/worker group

		Disagree	Undecided	Agree
Right to be treated equally by the law				
Students	Count	6	3	285
	Expected count	6.8	12.5	274.7
	% within group	2.0%	1.0%	96.9%
	Adjusted residual	−0.5	−4.2	3.7
Workers	Count	6	19	200
	Expected count	5.2	9.5	210.3
	% within group	2.7%	8.4%	88.9%
	Adjusted residual	0.5	4.2	−3.7
Right to survive				
Students	Count	6	5	282
	Expected count	10.2	14.2	268.6
	% within group	2.0%	1.7%	96.2%
	Adjusted residual	−2.0	3.8	4.3
Workers	Count	12	20	191
	Expected count	7.8	10.8	204.4
	% within group	5.4%	9.0%	85.7%
	Adjusted residual	2.0	−3.8	−4.3
Right to freedom of religion				
Students	Count	6	8	280
	Expected count	8.5	23.9	261.6
	% within group	2.0%	2.7%	95.2%
	Adjusted residual	−1.3	−5.2	5.2
Workers	Count	9	34	180
	Expected count	6.5	18.1	198.4
	% within group	4.0%	15.2%	80.7%
	Adjusted residual	1.3	5.2	−5.2
Right to property				
Students	Count	7	7	279
	Expected count	9.6	16.4	266.9
	% within group	2.4%	2.4%	95.2%
	Adjusted residual	−1.3	−3.6	3.8
Workers	Count	10	22	192
	Expected count	7.4	12.6	204.1
	% within group	4.5%	9.8%	85.7%
	Adjusted residual	1.3	3.6	−3.8

(continued)

Table 5.6 (continued)

		Disagree	Undecided	Agree
Right to health care				
Students	Count	6	10	278
	Expected count	5.1	26.0	262.9
	% within group	2.0%	3.4%	94.6%
	Adjusted residual	0.6	−5.0	4.3
Workers	Count	3	36	187
	Expected count	3.9	20.0	202.1
	% within group	1.3%	15.9%	82.7%
	Adjusted residual	−0.6	5.0	−4.3
Right to freedom of expression				
Students	Count	9	7	278
	Expected count	11.3	18.7	264.0
	% within group	3.1%	2.4%	94.6%
	Adjusted residual	−1.1	−4.2	4.1
Workers	Count	11	26	189
	Expected count	8.7	14.3	203.0
	% within group	4.9%	11.5%	83.6%
	Adjusted residual	1.1	4.2	−4.1
Right to freedom of sending and receiving information				
Students	Count	8	16	265
	Expected count	17.5	22.0	249.6
	% within group	2.8%	5.5%	91.7%
	Adjusted residual	−3.5	−2.0	4.0
Workers	Count	23	23	178
	Expected count	13.5	17.0	193.4
	% within group	10.3%	10.3%	79.5%
	Adjusted residual	3.5	2.0	−4.0
Right to monitor government				
Students	Count	12	19	263
	Expected count	17.1	45.7	231.2
	% within group	4.1%	6.5%	89.5%
	Adjusted residual	−1.9	−6.6	6.9
Workers	Count	18	61	142
	Expected count	12.9	34.3	173.8
	% within group	8.1%	27.6%	64.3%
	Adjusted residual	1.9	6.6	−6.9

(continued)

Table 5.6 (continued)

		Disagree	Undecided	Agree
Right to influence government policymaking				
Students	Count	10	40	244
	Expected count	18.8	66.5	208.7
	% within group	3.4%	13.6%	83.0%
	Adjusted residual	−3.2	−5.6	6.9
Workers	Count	23	77	123
	Expected count	14.2	50.5	158.3
	% within group	10.3%	34.5%	55.2%
	Adjusted residual	3.2	5.6	−6.9
Right to form political association				
Students	Count	28	59	206
	Expected count	32.4	87.4	173.2
	% within group	9.6%	20.1%	70.3%
	Adjusted residual	−1.2	−5.5	5.9
Workers	Count	29	95	99
	Expected count	24.6	66.6	131.8
	% within group	13.0%	42.6%	44.4%
	Adjusted residual	1.2	5.5	−5.9
Responsibility of community involvement				
Students	Count	21	42	231
	Expected count	15.4	69.5	209.1
	% within group	7.1%	14.3%	78.6%
	Adjusted residual	2.2	−5.8	4.3
Workers	Count	6	80	136
	Expected count	11.6	52.5	157.9
	% within group	2.7%	36.0%	61.3%
	Adjusted residual	−2.2	5.8	−4.3
Responsibility of paying tax				
Students	Count	7	23	264
	Expected count	9.0	45.2	239.7
	% within group	2.4%	7.8%	89.8%
	Adjusted residual	−1.0	−5.5	5.5
Workers	Count	9	57	160
	Expected count	7.0	34.8	184.3
	% within group	4.0%	25.2%	70.8%
	Adjusted residual	1.0	5.5	−5.5

even a negative attitude towards two of them (the right to freedom of sending and receiving information and the right to influence government policymaking). This echoes and corroborates the finding in Chap. 4 that workers viewed *gongmin* largely in subordinate relation to the state while students assigned it a more active role.

In addition, it is interesting to find that unlike civil, social and political rights upon which students expressed their approval more clearly than workers, the two groups commonly agreed (both over 80% without a significant difference) upon the necessity of the right to practice one's own language and life style. This suggested that they shared an affirmative attitude towards the need of cultural rights for *gongmin*. But for workers, cultural rights seemed not without restraint. When asked about *gongmin*'s right to freedom of religion, a cultural as well as civil right, one worker interviewee (W1) reasoned his objection to the right on the grounds that 'some religions would disseminate information harmful to the state'. Such explanation conveyed the idea of putting the state first, reflecting, once again, workers' subordinate understanding of *gongmin* in relation to the state.

(2) *Responsibilities*

Rights and responsibilities, two sides of the same coin in Western citizenship conception, did not always receive the same level of necessity in individual citizens' understanding of *gongmin*. The result of averaging the degrees of agreement on the listed rights and responsibilities indicated that students assigned more necessity on rights than on responsibilities while workers held a reverse attitude with a narrower gap (Table 5.7). It seemed that students were more aware of *gongmin*'s rights than responsibilities, as opposed to the higher consciousness of responsibilities over rights, or in relative terms, a balanced understanding of the two aspects, by workers.

Whether with higher or lower awareness, students' and workers' understanding of responsibilities for *gongmin* was found to be similarly influenced by their concern about personal interest. While each of all the listed responsibilities was deemed as necessary for *gongmin* by more than half of student and worker respondents, respectively, the responsibility of helping remove inequality in society, an illustration of social and moral responsibility, was one of the responsibilities agreed least by both student and worker respondents (Fig. 5.3). One student interviewee explained her disagreement on the necessity of the particular responsibility for *gongmin* in this way:

> I don't want to say helping remove inequality in society is *gongmin*'s responsibility… I don't think I would help actively if the act would hurt me, no matter in physical or other form, even though I wanted to. You can't ask someone to sacrifice for others nowadays. (S11)

Table 5.7 Average degree of agreement (including strongly agree and agree) by students and workers on *gongmin*'s must-have rights and responsibilities

%	Rights	Responsibilities
Students	89.7	82.5
Workers	76.0	78.1

Worker interviewees similarly expressed their concern about personal interest and reluctance to sacrifice it when talking about *gongmin*'s responsibilities. This might appear at odds with the finding in the preceding chapter of *gongmin* as identity that the two groups similarly perceived *gongmin* more as members of society than as independent individuals. Not necessarily contradicting with each other, the two findings could accommodate in the way that while the two groups saw *gongmin* more as a collective than as an individual identity in society, they did not expect *gongmin* to commit to the collective good at the cost of individual interest. We may call this the logic of ranking without replacing. Such accommodation deepens our understanding of *gongmin* as identity in society that citizens' embracement of *gongmin* as a collective identity does not necessarily lead to their willingness of self-sacrifice for collective or public good in the name of *gongmin*.

The two responsibilities towards which students and workers had significant different attitude were taxpaying and community involvement, the latter of which was agreed least by worker respondents (Table 5.5). Workers were less likely than students to view the two responsibilities as necessary for *gongmin* (Table 5.6). One reason that workers kept the legal responsibility of taxpaying at a distance was that, as revealed in the interviews, it was considered by some as a responsibility that should be laid only on wealthy *gongmin*, whom they stressed that they were not. Together with the finding in the previous chapter that there was worker considering 'Chinese *gongmin*' as a status for 'successful' people only, it seemed that there existed among workers the perception of *gongmin* as a privileged status entailing certain non-universal responsibilities. With regard to the responsibility of community involvement, some worker interviewees' reference to their tight working schedule and lack of community activities implied that for workers community involvement might be an unrealistic burden that *gongmin* should bear. It seemed that the scope of responsibilities, either legal or moral, in workers' understanding of *gongmin* was bounded by their self-perceived socioeconomic circumstances such as income and leisure time. The migrant worker case implied that socioeconomic conditions could be another factor in determining the content of responsibilities in the meaning of *gongmin* in society.

Social Implications

The findings presented in the last section unveil the similarities and variations in the meaning of *gongmin* regarding rights and responsibilities in society. The discrepancy between official and collective social discourses, in the way of the *gongmin*-responsibilities semantic connection more salient in the former as opposed to the *gongmin*-rights connection stronger in the latter, suggests that the content dimension in the social meaning of *gongmin* has latitude, if limited, to deviate and distance itself from the official stance. This can be seen as a testament to the dynamized Chinese state–society relation. The observed autonomy enjoyed by the society provides the context in which we explore the social implications of other findings.

The found broad similarity of attitude towards *gongmin*'s must-have rights and responsibilities within each of the social groups of students and workers regardless of age, gender, educational level, and rural/urban background (except the responsibility of conscription influenced by gender) appears to be not consistent with previous reports that young and educated migrant workers are more likely to assert their rights as citizens (Wong 2012) and that female university students and those from rural areas are more willing than male students and those from urban areas to take the responsibility of social contribution (Li 2009). One possible interpretation to the seeming conflict could be that the effects of the four tested demographic backgrounds on individual citizen's perception of citizenship rights and responsibilities are contingent and changeable. This needs to be tested with more empirical studies. But if the interpretation is correct, it means that those demographic differences are not insurmountable obstacles to developing social consensus on what rights and responsibilities are necessary for *gongmin*.

While consensus may be achievable, there are nevertheless variations, and even distinctions, in the understanding in contemporary society, either between collective and individual levels or at the individual level. One striking distinction about the rights of *gongmin* between the two social levels is the considerably greater concern over *gongmin*'s civil and political rights than over social and cultural rights in collective social discourses on one hand, and the uncertainty over the necessity of political rights for *gongmin* in contrast with the affirmed necessity of civil, social and cultural rights in individual perceptions on the other hand. In other words, the collective concern over political rights in society is not followed by individual university students and particularly migrant workers living in it. This finding gives an immediate complement to the previous report (Lee 2007) of the increased consciousness of citizenship rights among migrant workers that the rights in their citizenship consciousness are unlikely political ones.

The concern over *gongmin*'s political rights at the collective social level, if following Lorentzen and Scoggins's (2015) classification of factors behind rights-conscious behaviour, could be driven by government policies, social values, or/and shared expectations. The first factor is highly likely, given the heightened official rhetoric and increased policies about citizenship rights and political participation. The latter two are also possible, in light of Goldman's (2005) record of the spread of political rights consciousness in the population to the extent that an alternative political party was unprecedentedly created by citizens and unsurprisingly crushed by the party-state in the late 1990s. This has two implications for the distinction between the two social levels. First, if the collective consciousness is driven by government policies, then the distinction implies that policies about political rights fail to effectively reach such social groups as university students, who attributed their lesser concern over *gongmin*'s political rights to the lack of relevant experience, and migrant workers, who expressed their disillusion generated in political practice for their uncertainty on political rights. Second, if the collective consciousness of political rights is derived from social values and shared expectations, then the distinction implies that the social groups of university students and particularly migrant workers are unlikely among the leading forces in shaping such values and expectations in contemporary Chinese society.

Another noticeable distinction between the two social levels regarding *gongmin*'s rights is the relatively low attention to social and cultural rights at the collective level on one hand, and the general affirmation at the individual level on cultural rights, illustrated by the right to practice one's own language and life style, and social rights, illustrated by the rights to education, health care, and, albeit to a lesser degree, unemployment subsidy, on the other hand. The low attention at the collective level might be resulted from, in the light of Lorentzen and Scoggins (2015) again, the absence of either relevant government policy or such collective social values and expectations. For social rights, it is fair to say that there are official efforts on the development of social citizenship rights, such as the nationwide realization of 9-year free compulsory education in 2008. But cultural rights are far less supported by government policy, an epitome of which is the difficulty to practice ethnic culture in mainstream schools facing the Tibetan students reported by Yi (2006). Notwithstanding the low attention at the collective level, the general affirmation at the individual level is a positive sign that the awareness of social and cultural rights as necessary for *gongmin*, if not ready to become collective social value and expectation, is detectable in society, at least among the migrant workers and especially the university students in this study.

In addition to the above two distinctions between the two social levels, the degrees of attachment of rights to *gongmin* also vary at the individual level, as suggested by the finding that students tended to hold a more affirmative attitude towards rights when compared with workers. Despite the variations and distinctions above, there is one feature apparently shared between the two levels in the social meaning of *gongmin*. That is the strong attachment of civil rights, the only one among the four examined kinds of rights able to reach such consensus.

The above comparison of rights between the two social levels gives two implications for our understanding of rights consciousness in Chinese society. First, it exposes the complexities in the priority order of different rights in the Chinese context which is often oversimplified by previous studies, such as the empirical report of Chinese citizens' priority of civil and social rights over political rights (Shen 2009) and the cultural account of the significance of social and economic rights over civil and political rights (Bell 2006). Second, it suggests that rights consciousness in Chinese society, which one might prefer to distinguish from rules consciousness, is a topic requiring more nuanced treatment with regard to specific rights by specific social groups at different social levels.

Rights and responsibilities, the two aspects in the content dimension of citizenship, seem not to always have equal weight in the social meaning of *gongmin*. On one hand rights tend to triumph over responsibilities not merely in the collective social discourse but in university students' understanding of *gongmin*; on the other hand a fairly balanced view of the two aspects, even to the extent that responsibilities slightly outweigh rights, is also possible at the individual level as in the case of migrant workers. Given the convergence and divergence of meaning of *gongmin* between the two social levels in terms of rights and responsibilities, it can be discussed, as answer to the questions at the end of the last section, that the collective discourse is not faithfully followed by individual citizens, and its public pedagogical function cannot be said effective. If the cultural observation by Fung (2006)—that rights and responsibilities are concepts not necessarily antagonistic but possibly integrated in the Chinese context—holds water, then it is not unreasonable to argue that the strong rights connotations are not to blame for the relatively weak responsibilities connotations existing at the two social levels in the meaning of *gongmin*, and, furthermore, that rights consciousness and practice are possible to the drive for responsibilities ones in Chinese society. This preliminary argument requires more future empirical research on the conceptual and practical relationship between citizenship rights and responsibilities in Chinese society.

The found unwillingness to sacrifice personal interest for the collective good, an attitude shared by students and workers in their perception of *gongmin*'s responsibilities, on the surface appears to support the popular 'moral decline' claim that individualism prevails over collectivism in contemporary Chinese society. But the revealed logic behind the unwillingness—that is, ranking *gongmin* as a collective over an individual identity without replacing individual for collective interest—gives important insights for that claim. What is in decline is absolute collectivism requiring the sacrifice of the individual for the collective, rather than the consciousness of collectivity which remains strong in society; and what is on the rise is the awareness of personal interest, rather than the kind of individualism at the expense of the collective.

In addition to changed moral values, socioeconomic conditions are probably another factor in the content of responsibilities in individual citizens' understanding of *gongmin*. Similarly, individual sociopolitical experience and resources seem to help shape the understanding of *gongmin*'s rights in society. Are the influences of socioeconomic and sociopolitical conditions inevitable or surmountable? If inevitable, does it mean that it would be hard to reach a social consensus on what rights and responsibilities *gongmin* should have, given the socioeconomic and sociopolitical differences between social groups? Or in the language of power, does it mean that difference of social powers necessarily leads to different understandings of *gongmin*? If surmountable, how can it be done? These join the list of questions and issues opened up by the findings of the social meaning of *gongmin* in the content dimension unveiled in this chapter.

References

Bell, D. A. (2006). *Beyond liberal democracy: Political thinking for an East Asian context*. Princeton, NJ: Princeton University Press.

Chan, A. (2011). Strikes in China's export industries in comprarative perspective. *The China Journal, 65,* 27–51.

Chen, S. (2013). The discrepancy of meaning of citizenship between the state and society in China: Implications for citizenship education and policymaking. *Education, Citizenship and Social Justice, 8*(3), 263–275. doi:10.1177/1746197913497660.

Ding, Y. (2001). *Chinese democracy after Tiananmen*. Vancouver: UBC Press.

Fung, E. S. K. (2006). The idea of freedom in modern China revisited: Plural conceptions and dual responsibilities. *Modern China, 32*(4), 453–482. doi:10.2307/20062650.

Goldman, M. (2005). *From comrade to Citizen: The struggle of political rights in China*. Cambridge, MA: Harvard University Press.

Kelly, D. (2006). Citizen movements and China's public intellectuals in the Hu-Wen era. *Pacific Affairs, 79*(2), 183–204.

Latham, K. (2007). Sms, communication, and citizenship in China's information society. *Critical Asian Studies, 39*(2), 295–314. doi:10.1080/14672710701339493.

Lee, C. K. (2007). *Against the law: Labour protests in China's rustbelt and sunbelt*. Berkeley: University of California Press.

Li, J. (2009). Fostering citizenship in China's move from elite to mass higher education: An analysis of students' political socialization and civic participation. *International Journal of Educational Development, 29*(4), 382–398. doi:10.1016/j.ijedudev.2008.10.001.

Li, L. (2010). Rights consciousness and rule consciousness in contemporary China. *The China Journal, 64,* 47–68.

Link, P. (1993). China's 'core' problem. In W. Tu (Ed.), *China in transformation* (pp. 189–206). Cambridge, MA: Harvard University Press.

Lorentzen, P., & Scoggins, S. (2015). Understanding China's rising rights consciousness. *The China Quarterly, 223,* 638–657. doi:10.1017/S0305741015000776.

O'Brien, K. J., & Li, L. (2006). *Rightful resistance in rural China*. New York: Cambridge University Press.

Perry, E. J. (2008). Chinese conceptions of "rights": From Mencius to Mao—and now. *Perspectives on Politics, 6*(1). doi:10.1017/s1537592708080055.

Shen, M. (2009). *Attitudes towards citizenship in China: Data report of a national survey 2008*. Beijing: Social Sciences Academic Press.

Wong, L. (2012). Chinese migrant workers: Rights attainment deficits, rights consciousness and personal strategies. *The China Quarterly, 208,* 870–892. doi:10.1017/s0305741011001044.

Yi, L. (2006). Choosing between ethnic and Chinese citizenship: The educational trajectories of Tibetan minority children in northwestern China. In V. L. Fong & R. Murphy (Eds.), *Chinese citizenship: Views from the margins* (pp. 41–67). Oxon: Routledge.

Chapter 6
Gongmin and Participation

The last two chapters have unveiled the meaning of *gongmin* in the dimensions of extent and content respectively. This chapter moves on to the third and last dimension, presenting the meaning in the depth dimension about participation at the two social levels before discussing its social implications. But first of all, I shall draw upon available research to highlight some features of citizenship participation in contemporary Chinese society.

Citizenship Participation in Society

There are two kinds of citizenship participation considered in this book: political participation that has the intent or effect of influencing the making or implementation of public policies; and civic, or nonpolitical or social, participation that is voluntary activity in community primarily about solving problems and helping others (Zukin et al. 2006). I shall review the perception and practice about the two kinds in society, with particular attention to migrant workers and university students, as a window onto contemporary Chinese citizenship participation.

Political participation is often the means to, and sometimes the goal of, rights which, as shown in the preceding chapter, contemporary Chinese citizens are aware of. Indeed, one feature of the political landscape in the late twentieth-century Chinese society was intellectuals both inside and outside the establishment expressing political views and taking political actions to directly challenge and push the boundaries of policies for political engagement as a right accessible to all ordinary citizens (Goldman 2005). Petitions and protests for other than political rights, whether in law or not, are also political participation given their impact on government policies. Chinese society has also witnessed a 'dramatic rise of' and 'routinized' social protests since the 1990s (Chen 2014, pp. 3–4), typically by migrant workers for social rights, villagers for land rights, homeowners for property rights, and urban citizens for environmental rights. Given the challenges posed to the

S. Chen, *The Meaning of Citizenship in Contemporary Chinese Society*,
Governance and Citizenship in Asia, https://doi.org/10.1007/978-981-10-6323-7_6

authorities, most, if not all, of such political participations are, unsurprisingly, without official sanctions and subject to suppressions by the authoritarian party-state.

On the contrary, what the party-state allows, and indeed puts in efforts to develop, is political participation through institutionalized official channels, which is encapsulated in the official expression of 'enhancing *gongmin*'s orderly political participation'. The widespread community resident committees in urban areas and the villager committees in rural areas are two key institutions for citizenship political participation at the grassroots, as introduced in Chap. 3. Available literature shows that participation in these institutions varies among citizens, depending upon a range of factors. For example, Xu et al. (2010) showed evidence, based on data from a nationwide survey, that the act of voting in the committees in rural and urban areas is similarly facilitated by a sense of community, measured by knowledge of neighbours, and neighbouring, measured by expectation of mutual help in neighbourhood. That study also found that male, older, married rural citizens and urban citizens with higher self-perceived socioeconomic status are more likely to vote in the committees. Focusing on the urban community resident committees, which have the dual role of carrying out welfare provisions handed down from the top and taking the initiative to address local needs and concerns, Xu (2007) reported in her empirical study on community participation in Beijing that although participation in official service provisions was common, particularly among older residents benefiting from the provisions, participation in the process of decision-making was not favoured by most of the studied citizens. She reasoned that the disfavour was because Chinese citizens' post-Cultural Revolution traumatic political apathy and disinclination to collective action, and the absence of encouragement from the authorities for ordinary citizens to participate in community decision-making.

Migrant workers are reported in the literature, as Palmer et al. (2011) observed, as a social group neither participating nor having the motivation to participate in the urban communities where they live and work or the villages where they left behind, due to subjective and structural factors such as 'level of education, economic situation, awareness of participation, unequal access to services and education, and rural bias and discrimination' (p. 92). Indeed, Lee (2007) discussed that their urban and rural experience with the authorities 'has convinced many that the political system is beyond their influence' (p. 230). In their search of factors behind migrant workers' community participation in cities, Palmer et al. (2011) found that education, neighbourhood interaction, and experience of help from community organizations contributed positively not only to their contact with, and frequency of seeking help from, community organizations, but also to their participation in formal meetings of the community resident committees.

Literature suggests the Janus-faced feature of political participation by Chinese university students. On one hand, Li (2009) reported that they engaged widely in the Chinese Communist Youth League, the youth wing of the CCP; and male students were interested in voting for representatives of the People's Congress. On the other hand, in his study of Chinese university students' political orientation, Chan (2000) observed that 'political apathy became a general trend on campus, as students avoided political activity' after the 1989 prodemocracy movements (p. 208). But he explained that although students' political participation shifted from active in the 1980s to inactive after 1989, what changed was not students' belief in values such as democracy which remained intact, but their perspective on how to realize those values. He discussed that university students actually changed from idealism to pragmatism by placing priority on practical and solvable concerns. Pragmatism can also be an explanation for university students' reported positive perception and experience of political participation. Students' expression of willingness to participate in politics such as voting might be little more than a politically correct response which is 'common for pragmatic youth' (Rosen 2010, p. 163). As Rosen (2010) pointed out in a review of existing survey studies, their engagement in the CCP including in its youth wing could be driven by an instrumental account of the membership which is 'widely desired and…valuable for one's future success', as few want to join the CCP because of the belief in communism and many 'have little knowledge or even interest in most party activities and goals' (p. 165).

Students' pragmatism is also discerned in their civic participation. Volunteering, which used to be a duty imposed from the top but has turned to be a free choice of individuals in society (Rolandsen 2008), is a form of civic engagement widely practiced by university students, with a reported rate of participation at 84.5% (Handy et al. 2010). While students now volunteer at will, their volunteer activities are subject to increased regulations by the party-state, with a 'disproportionately large number' officially organized and only 'a rather small part' initiated at the grassroots (Zhao 2014, p. 215). The key institution in organizing students' volunteering is China Youth Volunteers Association. Describing itself as an independent non-government association but in fact supervised by the party-state, the association, as Zhao (2014) commented, 'permeates every college campus and the surrounding communities' (p. 211). Enjoying limited degree of autonomy from state control, students are reportedly motivated to volunteer by, according to Zhao's (2014) review of existing empirical work, 'prominent' personal concerns such as life experience, social network, and job prospect, apart from idealistic altruism conventionally upheld by the authorities (p. 210).

Variations among university students regarding civic participation are reported. For instance, Li (2009) reported that female students and those with rural backgrounds are more likely to be committed to participation beneficial to community and society. Among the conveniently sampled Chinese volunteer students in the international comparative study of university students' volunteering by Hustinx et al. (2010), most were from low-income families and least from high-income families, as compared with other five studied countries of Belgium, Canada, Finland, Japan, and the United States. The reason behind such variations, however, remains unclear.

Compared with university students, migrant workers' volunteer participation is less studied in existing scholarship. One possible reason is that volunteering is not common to migrant workers at the first place. Given their workplace grievances and struggles for basic social rights referred to in preceding chapters, volunteer activities requiring time and money might well be beyond their reach. There might also be a cultural factor in it. According to Rolandsen (2008), the willingness of volunteering in the Chinese cultural context 'constitutes a break with the "family-first values" which have come to be associated with the Chinese societies'; and the act of volunteering is perceived as an embodiment of 'middle-class tastes and values' (p. 107).

There are also empirical studies suggesting that civic participation encourages political participation in Chinese society. By analyzing the data from a nationwide survey, Guo (2007) reported that participation in officially registered civic associations 'significantly facilitates' both officially sanctioned and unsanctioned political participation (p. 457). More specifically, in their study in Beijing on participation in neighbourhood affairs through homeowners' associations—the civic association initiated and governed by homeowners to safeguard their own property rights often infringed on by real estate developers and the authorities, Wang et al. (2015) found that such civic participation helped homeowners to develop not only democratic skills such as holding meetings, but also the awareness of rights and the sense of responsibility for the community built upon informal and formal social networks. Civic participation of this kind, they discussed, 'gave rise to political participation', as there were homeowners motivated to participate in local elections in order to influence government decision-making and make homeowners' voices heard (p. 17).

The review above gives a glimpse into what has been studied about political and civic participation in Chinese society. While the attitudes towards and the factors and reasons behind participation have been examined, the existing research leaves unexplored the extent to which the two kinds of citizenship participation are associated with the term *gongmin* used and understood in society. The extent is examined below with the empirical evidence from the two sub-studies.

At the Collective Level

The association of citizenship participation with the term *gongmin* at the collective social level was examined through the content analysis of the semantic connection of the term with participation in two newspapers, an influential nonofficial newspaper (*Southern Metropolis Daily*) in comparison with the CCP's mouthpiece newspaper (*People's Daily*). The nonofficial newspaper had less articles containing *gongmin* in connection with participation than the official newspaper in the examined period (9.5 vs. 14.0%), the difference of which was statistically significant [X^2 (1, N = 5001) = 24.307, p = 0.000, Phi = −0.070]. It meant that *gongmin* at the macro social level was less likely to bear participatory connotations when compared with the term in official discourses.

A further examination suggested that the difference tended to fall in political rather than civic participation. While the two newspapers similarly contained a low percentage of articles expressing *gongmin* in connection with the two kinds of

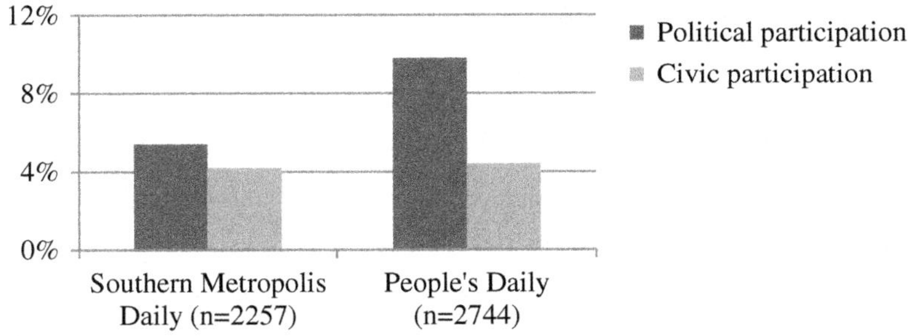

Fig. 6.1 Percentage of articles involving *gongmin* in semantic connection with two kinds of participation in the two newspapers. *Source* Chen (2013)

Table 6.1 Chi-square test result of articles involving *gongmin* in semantic connection with specific participation by newspaper (N = 5001)

Newspaper		Pearson Chi-square	df	*p*-value	Phi
Participation	Political	33.707	1	0.000*	−0.082
	Civic	0.237	1	0.626	−0.007

*$p < 0.001$

participation (Fig. 6.1), they were significantly different only in terms of *gongmin*-political participation connection (Table 6.1). The term *gongmin* was 1.81 times (5.4 vs. 9.8%) less likely to be mentioned in reference to political participation in the nonofficial newspaper than in the official one. The result indicated that neither political nor civic participation was salient in the meaning of *gongmin* in collective social discourses, as opposed to the relatively stronger connotation of political participation attached to the term in official discourses.

A paralleling of the current finding with the one in Chap. 5 that the term had significantly stronger connotation of political rights in collective social discourses than in official discourses gives the impression that the political implication of the term *gongmin* is floating in its official and macro social discourses. Yet this is not the case, as suggested by an observation of the ebb and flow of the number of articles containing the term *gongmin* in the two newspapers.

Figure 6.2 shows that the two newspapers shared a similar tendency in the monthly number of articles containing the term *gongmin* in the examined period. The number of collected articles similarly jumped up in Marches, when the two institutional avenues designed for collective participation in the political system, the PC and the CPPCC, hold their annual national gatherings. The two major and regular political events seemed to stimulate the mention of the term *gongmin* in both newspapers. The number of collected articles in both newspapers plummeted around Februaries, the Chinese New Year season. A reduction of pages covering political stories in the periods explained the decrease. Another ebb tide of the number of articles containing the term *gongmin* appeared in August 2008 for both newspapers, when Beijing hosted the Olympic Games. The lesser use of *gongmin* in

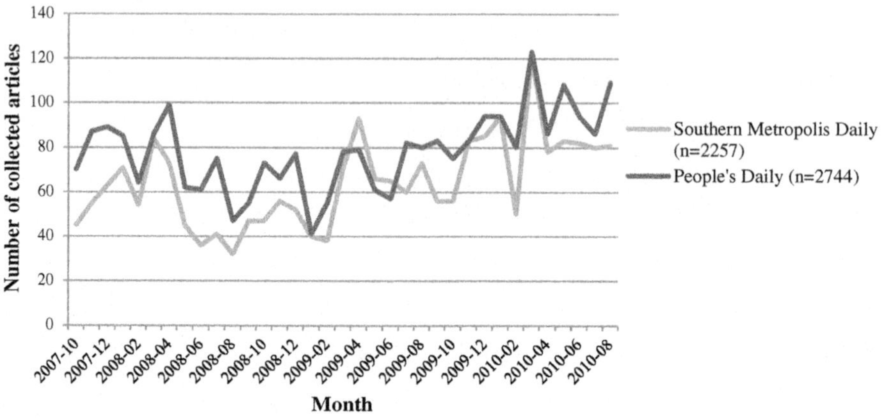

Fig. 6.2 Number of articles containing the term *gongmin* in the two newspapers across the examined months. *Source* Chen (2013)

the newspapers at the time was due to in part the focus on the Games and in part the lesser coverage on political stories probably as a response to the party-state's intention of decoupling the Games from politics. The ups and downs in the number of collected articles suggested that the term *gongmin* was embedded with political implications both in official and collective social discourses. The contradiction between those two findings is thus unlikely because the political nuance of the term *gongmin* is floating, but the difference between rights and participation in the meaning of the term. There are similar questions arising here as in the preceding chapter: Is the *gongmin*-participation association at the collective social level explained above faithfully reflected in the meaning at the individual level? Do the collective social discourses with public pedagogical function affect individual citizens' understandings of *gongmin* and participation? As the empirical evidence of Study II presented below will show, similar to the findings in the content dimension, individual citizens' understandings are not necessarily consistent with the collective discourse though which has a public pedagogical function.

At the Individual Level

The association of the term *gongmin* with citizenship participation at the individual level in society was examined through the investigation of university students' and migrant workers' perceptions of the practical attributes of *hao gongmin* (good citizen), or in other words, of what actions *gongmin* is desired to take. Figure 6.3 shows their degree of agreement on the nine listed desired actions. The result that none of the four demographic variables were found by Chi-square test to significantly affect the attitude of each group suggested that each group maintained a perceptual consistence on the *gongmin*-participation association.

Fig. 6.3 Degree of agreement (including strongly agree and agree) by students and workers on practical attributes of *hao gongmin* (good citizen)

Similarities were found not merely within but also between groups. More than 90% of student and worker respondents desired *gongmin* to obey the law, making it the most desired among the listed actions. The desire was similarly shared by the two groups (Table 6.2). Indeed, when asked about the attributes of *hao gongmin* (good citizen) in the interviews, many interviewees responded first of all that any

Table 6.2 Chi-square test result of respondents' attitudes towards listed practical attributes of *hao gongmin* (good citizen) by student/worker group

Student/Worker Group	Pearson Chi-square	df	*p*-value	Cramer's *V*	*N* of valid cases
Law-abiding	0.968[#]	2	0.616	0.043	518
Defend one's own rights when violated	6.303	2	0.043	0.110	519
Monitor government	44.302	2	0.000[*]	0.294	513
Defend other's rights when violated	4.979	2	0.083	0.098	517
Engage in local community affairs	7.829	2	0.020	0.123	518
Claim new rights for oneself	0.422	2	0.810	0.029	518
Influence government policymaking	22.274	2	0.000[*]	0.208	515
Claim new rights for others	31.849	2	0.000[*]	0.249	514
Volunteer	10.211	2	0.006	0.141	516

[*]$p < 0.001$
[#]1 cell has expected count less than 5

gongmin could be considered good as long as not breaking the law. This suggested that for students and workers legality is the first and foremost concern about *gongmin*'s desired participation. This echoes the finding in the extent dimension of *gongmin* that both groups similarly and overwhelmingly perceived *gongmin* as a legal identity.

Another perceptual similarity between students and workers was in the respect of *gongmin* and civic participation. As illustrations of civic participation, the two items of engaging in local community affairs and volunteering were similarly accepted by a majority of student and worker respondents, although, without statistical significance considered in the book, more students desired *gongmin* to take the former action while more workers to take the latter (Fig. 6.3 and Table 6.2). Workers' desire for *gongmin* to volunteer was recorded in the interview data. One worker interviewee commented that 'I would volunteer … once I am successful enough [by becoming a boss] to be counted as a *gongmin* [which now I am not]' (W2). This narration of civic participation desired and reserved for 'successful' *gongmin* echoed the privileged understanding of *gongmin* by some workers found in the extent and content dimensions. It is worth noting that volunteering was the least desired (58.8%) among the listed items by student respondents, with the considerably lower agreement than the engagement in local community affairs (73.8%). The two items seemed to be treated differently by students, despite that volunteering is often considered in theory as a form of community involvement. Unfortunately, no interview data were available to explain the seemingly different treatment in the perspective of students.

Similar to the other two dimensions of *gongmin*, there were differences as well as similarities in the perceptions of students and workers regarding *gongmin* and participation. One of the differences was about political participation. The association of *gongmin* with political participation was measured by two items, monitoring government and influencing government policymaking. While a majority of both student and worker respondents desired *gongmin* to take both actions, a significant difference was found between the two groups (Table 6.2), in the way that students were more likely to embrace while workers more likely to be uncertain about the two actions for *gongmin* (Table 6.3). Given the former action represents political participation following officially set rules and the latter one political participation in the making of rules, the result suggested that students were more likely than workers to expect *gongmin* to participate in political affairs, either following or making rules. But it is important to note that students' higher expectation than workers was still more on participation following rules, and less on rulemaking participation.

The reason behind workers' likely non-positive attitude towards political participation by *gongmin* could be illustrated by one worker interviewee's reasoning of her undecided attitude towards the act of monitoring government on the grounds that it was 'not what ordinary *gongmin* can do' (W11). Also, there were more than a few worker interviewees linking their uncertainty with their self-blamed lack of education, which was also a reason that worker interviewees referred to for their

Table 6.3 Respondents' attitudes towards attributes of *hao gongmin* (good citizen) significantly associated with student/worker group

		Disagree	Undecided	Agree
Monitor government				
Students	Count	15	26	253
	Expected count	14.3	55.0	224.7
	% within group	5.1%	8.8%	86.1%
	Adjusted residual	−0.3	−6.6	6.0
Workers	Count	10	70	139
	Expected count	10.7	41.0	167.3
	% within group	4.6%	32.0%	63.5%
	Adjusted residual	0.3	6.6	−6.0
Influence government policymaking				
Students	Count	18	69	205
	Expected count	23.8	89.0	179.2
	% within group	6.2%	23.6%	70.2%
	Adjusted residual	−1.9	−3.9	4.7
Workers	Count	24	88	111
	Expected count	18.2	68.0	136.8
	% within group	10.8%	39.5%	49.8%
	Adjusted residual	1.9	3.9	−4.7
Claim new rights for others				
Students	Count	17	87	188
	Expected count	25.6	109.6	156.8
	% within group	5.8%	29.8%	64.4%
	Adjusted residual	−2.7	−4.2	5.6
Workers	Count	28	106	88
	Expected count	19.4	83.4	119.2
	% within group	12.6%	47.7%	39.6%
	Adjusted residual	2.7	4.2	−5.6

understanding of *gongmin* in the extent and content dimensions, as shown in previous chapters.

Another difference between the two groups' perceptions was on the depth of understanding of participation, with students having a deeper understanding than workers. The depth of participation was gauged by four rights-related actions classified by two parameters, defending existing or claiming new rights, and for oneself or others. Figure 6.3 shows that student and worker respondents shared a similar approval tendency, most desiring the act of defending one's own rights when violated and least the act of claiming new rights for others, with either defending other's rights when violated or claiming new rights for oneself in between.

Among the four items, only the act of claiming new rights for others was found to be considered significantly differently by student and worker respondents, in the manner that students were more likely to embrace the act while, on the contrary, workers were more likely to hold an undecided and even negative attitude towards it (Tables 6.2 and 6.3). Given that claiming new rights for others is an action not contained within but beyond existing rules and not limited to oneself but extended to others, students' greater likelihood to expect *gongmin* to take the action demonstrated that they had a deeper understanding of *gongmin*'s participation than workers, though students still placed less weigh to the act than to the acts of defending and claiming rights for personal sake. Claiming new rights for others was the only item among the listed actions not agreed by a majority of worker respondents. One reason behind the uncertainty and even negativity was found in the interview data. That was their self-deprecation of ability as a migrant worker to take such action for others. This reasoning resonated with the influence of socioeconomic and sociopolitical experience and resources on the meaning of *gongmin* in the extent and content dimensions revealed in previous chapters.

There were four items in the list of participation desired for *gongmin* also listed and examined in the preceding chapter as must-have rights or responsibilities for *gongmin*. A comparison of the degrees of agreement by student and worker respondents on the four items in the two lists in Table 6.4 exposed the gap between right or responsibility awareness on one hand and participation desire on the other hand, suggesting that for the four actions, desire was not always on a par with awareness.

On one hand, both students and workers had higher approvals for monitoring government and particularly influencing government policymaking as *gongmin*'s must-have rights than as *gongmin*'s desired participation. Their awareness of the two items as necessary rights for *gongmin* seemed not to translate into their desire for *gongmin* to practice them. On the other hand, while student respondents expressed higher acceptance of the other two items as responsibilities that *gongmin* should have than as actions that *gongmin* is desired to take, worker respondents, by

Table 6.4 Degree of agreement on items listed both as must-have rights/responsibilities and desired participation for *gongmin*

%		Must-have rights/responsibilities	Desired participation
Monitor government	S	89.5	86.1
	W	62.8	61.5
Influence government policymaking	S	83.0	69.7
	W	54.4	49.1
Law-abiding	S	94.6	93.5
	W	90.7	94.7
Community involvement/Engage in local community affairs	S	78.6	73.8
	W	60.2	62.4

Note S = university students; W = migrant workers

contrast, considered the two more as desired actions than as necessary responsibilities. Taking into account the above-quoted worker interviewee's comment on the desire for *gongmin* to volunteer, it seemed that while both groups shared similarity in treating law-abiding as the primary action desired for *gongmin*, workers relatively refrained from considering law-abiding and community involvement as the necessary responsibilities to be shared by all *gongmin*, but as the actions desired only for 'successful' *gongmin*.

Social Implications

The findings from the two sub-studies disclose the association of *gongmin* with participation at the two social levels. The term does not bear salient connotation of participation, either political or civic, at the collective level. At the individual level, the term is on one hand similarly understood in the respect of civic participation by university student and migrant workers, and on the other hand associated with higher expectation in the respect of political participation and with deeper participatory connotation, in the sense of going beyond existing rules and for the sake of others, in the understanding of students, as opposed to workers.

The significant deviation between the official and collective social discourses on *gongmin*'s political participation is another evidence to the discrepancy in the meaning of citizenship between the two discourses, and furthermore, another testament to the autonomy of social discourses from the official stance despite persistent state-censorship. On the part of collective social discourses, the finding of the modest connotative link of *gongmin* to political participation—especially when compared with its much stronger link with rights reported in the last chapter—may appear counterintuitive, given the heightened political articulations and actions led by Chinese intellectuals in the late twentieth century (Goldman 2005) and the proliferation of social protests with political implications since the 1990s (Chen 2014). One possible reason behind the contrary could be the effect of state-censorship which led to lesser media coverage of those events. This needs to be tested by a further study on the reporting of grassroots political and social actions in nonofficial media. It could also be because that *gongmin* is not a term common to political participation without official sanction, given the legal connotation of the term which is officially and socially recognized. This reasoning corresponds to two other findings: firstly, the significantly stronger connection of the term with political participation in official discourses featuring expression and promotion of orderly political participation through official institutions; and secondly, the finding at the individual level that law-abiding, or legality, is the two investigated social groups' primary concern about participation desired for *gongmin*.

The confirmation of the political implication of the term *gongmin* in collective social discourses shows the potential of the term to serve as a vehicle for political expressions and struggles in society. The potential is supported by the found similarity of understanding within each of the two examined social groups. The finding at the individual level that students' and workers' understandings of *gongmin* regarding participation were not affected by their age, gender, education, and place of origin presents a picture different from the observations in previous studies of the effect of age, gender, education, and family income on citizenship participation (Hustinx et al. 2010; Li 2009; Palmer et al. 2011; Xu et al. 2010). The inconsistence supports the postulation raised in Chap. 5 that the influence of demographic backgrounds on citizens' understanding of *gongmin* may be contingent and changeable, keeping alive the hope to develop consensus on the understanding of *gongmin* at least within individual social groups.

In terms of university students, it is interesting to find that they desire *gongmin* to volunteer least among the listed actions, given their high participation rate in volunteering (Handy et al. 2010) often driven by personal concerns (Zhao 2014). Their relative unwillingness to associate *gongmin* with volunteering is perhaps their backlash against volunteering which is increasingly subject to official regulation and permeation, even to the extent of 'non-voluntary volunteering' that volunteering is rendered compulsory in education by some local authorities (Zhao 2014, p. 218). While students seem to keep *gongmin* away from volunteering, they do show a higher desire for *gongmin* to involve in community affairs. But their expectation of *gongmin*'s political and civic participation is still lower than their awareness of participation as right or responsibility of *gongmin*. The gulf between awareness and desire is arguably a reflection of what Chan (2000) discussed the pragmatism of university students. They value participation as *gongmin*'s necessary right or responsibility, yet do not assign corresponding expectation to its fulfilment at a time that citizenship participation is not free of constraint and control from the party-state. Nevertheless, their awareness of the inalienability of participation as right or responsibility to *gongmin* retains the possibility of students using the term to demand citizenship participation.

For migrant workers, community involvement seems to be less a responsibility shared by all *gongmin* but more a burden borne only by 'successful' *gongmin*, a label they kept distance. Such distance from, and at the same time desire for, community involvement in their understanding of *gongmin* echoes the existing observations that there is lack of participation in community affairs by migrant workers who are subject to economic and social constraints (Palmer et al. 2011), in the Chinese context that volunteering associates with middle-class lifestyle (Rolandsen 2008) which lower class groups like migrant workers would yearn for. The finding implies that what hinders the association of *gongmin* with civic participation in migrant workers' understanding might be again their socioeconomic circumstances, and, therefore, that the association could be strengthened through the improvement of relevant circumstances.

In contrast with migrant workers, university students are found more likely to expect political participation by *gongmin*, or in other words, to understand *gongmin* in stronger association with political participation. This is consistent with the finding in the extent dimension that students are more likely than workers to see *gongmin* as active political participants in the state. The two findings together give a negative implication that *gongmin* might not be an effective identity to boost the historical student-worker coalition for joint political participation in contemporary society. More generally, the two findings serve as evidence that the connotation of political participation in the meaning of *gongmin* is volatile at the individual level. The connotative volatility points to the uncertainty of the capacity of the term to facilitate either political participation by individual social groups or joint political participation by different social groups, even though the term does bear political implications at the collective social level. Furthermore, the finding of a majority of university students having, while a majority of migrant workers not, the expectation for *gongmin* to claim new rights for others gives the sign that the scope of participation—within or beyond established rules and for the sake of us or others—is also varied in the meaning of *gongmin* in society.

Previous studies reported that civic participation can facilitate political participation. The data from this study cannot tell, and thus future research is required to assess, whether that relationship also applies to civic and political participation in the use and understanding of *gongmin* in society, and furthermore, whether the participatory connotation of the term contribute to Chinese citizens' social and political practice in the name of *gongmin*. Nonetheless, drawing upon the findings from the two sub-studies, this and the preceding two chapters have unveiled the meaning of *gongmin* in three dimensions respectively. What are the implications of the disclosed contemporary social meaning of *gongmin* for the etymology of the term, for the state–society relation, for citizenship conception in East and West, and for Chinese citizenship education? This is the overall question to be addressed in the next chapter.

References

Chan, C. (2000). The political pragmatism of Chinese university students at the dawn of the twenty-first century. In S. Zhao (Ed.), *China and democracy: Reconsidering the prospects for a democratic China* (pp. 207–232). New York: Routledge.

Chen, S. (2013). The discrepancy of meaning of citizenship between the state and society in China: Implications for citizenship education and policymaking. *Education, Citizenship and Social Justice, 8*(3), 263–275. doi:10.1177/1746197913497660.

Chen, X. (2014). *Social protests and contentious authoritarianism in China*. New York: Cambridge University Press.

Goldman, M. (2005). *From comrade to citizen: The struggle of political rights in China*. Cambridge, MA: Harvard University Press.

Guo, G. (2007). Organizational involvement and political participation in China. *Comparative Political Studies, 40*(4), 457–482. doi:10.1177/0010414005285751.

Handy, F., Cnaan, R. A., Hustinx, L., Kang, C., Brudney, J. L., Haski-Leventhal, D., et al. (2010). A cross-cultural examination of student volunteering: Is it all about résumé building? *Nonprofit and Voluntary Sector Quarterly, 39*(3), 498–523. doi:10.1177/0899764009344353.

Hustinx, L., Handy, F., Cnaan, R. A., Brudney, J. L., Pessi, A. B., & Yamauchi, N. (2010). Social and cultural origins of motivations to volunteer: A comparison of university students in six countries. *International Sociology, 25*(3), 349–382. doi:10.1177/0268580909360297.

Lee, C. K. (2007). *Against the law: Labour protests in China's rustbelt and sunbelt*. Berkeley: University of California Press.

Li, J. (2009). Fostering citizenship in China's move from elite to mass higher education: An analysis of students' political socialization and civic participation. *International Journal of Educational Development, 29*(4), 382–398. doi:10.1016/j.ijedudev.2008.10.001.

Palmer, N. A., Perkins, D. D., & Xu, Q. (2011). Social capital and community participation among migrant workers in China. *Journal of Community Psychology, 39*(1), 89–105. doi:10.1002/jcop.20419.

Rolandsen, U. M. H. (2008). A collective of their own: Young volunteers at the fringes of the Party realm. *European Journal of East Asian Studies, 7*(1), 101–129. doi:10.1163/156805808X333938.

Rosen, S. (2010). Chinese youth and state-society relations. In P. H. Gries & S. Rosen (Eds.), *Chinese politics: State, society and the market* (pp. 160–178). Oxon: Routledge.

Wang, W., Li, H., & Cooper, T. L. (2015). Civic engagement and citizenship development: The case of homeowners' participation in neighborhood affairs in Beijing. *Administration & Society*. doi:10.1177/0095399715581041.

Xu, Q. (2007). Community participation in urban China: Identifying mobilization factors. *Nonprofit and Voluntary Sector Quarterly, 36*(4), 622–642.

Xu, Q., Perkins, D. D., & Chow, J. C. (2010). Sense of community, neighboring, and social capital as predictors of local political participation in China. *American Journal of Community Psychology, 45*(3–4), 259–271. doi:10.1007/s10464-010-9312-2.

Zhao, Z. (2014). Volunteer development in Chinese universities. In K. J. Kennedy, G. P. Fairbrother, & Z. Zhao (Eds.), *Citizenship education in China: Preparing citizens for the "Chinese century"* (pp. 208–221). New York: Routledge.

Zukin, C., Keeter, S., Andolina, M., Jenkins, K., & Carpini, M. (2006). *A new engagement? Political participation, civic life, and the changing American citizen*. New York: Oxford University Press.

Chapter 7
From *Gongmin* to Citizenship and Citizenship Education

The previous three chapters together have presented the meaning of *gongmin* in contemporary Chinese society based on the findings of the two empirical sub-studies. Having the unveiled social meaning of *gongmin* in hand, I shall discuss in this chapter its implications for, and by so doing situate the meaning into, the three relevant and wider contexts of Chinese citizenship, East-West citizenship and citizenship education.

A summary of the findings of the meaning of *gongmin* at the two social levels would be helpful for our discussion in this chapter. At the collective social level, *gongmin* is found to bear stronger connotation of rights, in discrepancy with its greater connotation of responsibilities and participation in official discourses. The collective social meaning, in which rights outweigh responsibilities whilst participation remains weak, is not invariably mirrored at the individual level. While university students similarly consider *gongmin* more about rights than about responsibilities, their expectation of political participation by *gongmin* is higher and deeper than migrant workers, who hold a relatively balanced view of rights and responsibilities. Also, while collective social discourses tend to highlight political rights more than social and cultural rights, individual understandings show an opposite tendency. The strong connotation of civil rights seems to be the only consistency between the two social levels. At the individual level, there are also similarities and differences between the two social groups in the understanding of *gongmin* as identity. The most salient similarities are their overwhelming approval of 'Chinese *gongmin*' as legal identity and of *gongmin* as collective social identity, and their strong acceptance of the identity of *gongmin* at the national and global levels. The main distinctions are that 'Chinese *gongmin*' defined in terms of ethnicity and culture is likely to be embraced by workers but denied by students, and that students also perceive *gongmin* as an independent identity and as a simultaneously active and subordinate entity vis-à-vis the state, while *gongmin* for workers is largely a subordinate identity in relation to the state. In short, it can be argued that the meaning of *gongmin* varies in contemporary Chinese society.

S. Chen, *The Meaning of Citizenship in Contemporary Chinese Society*,
Governance and Citizenship in Asia, https://doi.org/10.1007/978-981-10-6323-7_7

Gongmin: Past and Present

The term *gongmin* appeared in ancient Chinese literature, but only since the end of the nineteenth century did it enter Chinese academic and public discourses. As our brief review of the etymology of the term in Chap. 3 shows, in addition to its ancient uses, the term was used to bear certain political ideas and beliefs in the past centuries. Either from the Western experience of citizenship evolution shown in Chap. 2 or from the perspective that language as part of society is subject to socially conditioned production and interpretation (Fairclough 2001), the meaning of *gongmin* is variable according to changing social conditions. Do the connotations that the term earned in history sustain in its contemporary social meaning? What implications would its etymological legacies have for the contemporary use and understanding of the term in society? I shall discuss these two questions in turn as the attempt to bridge the research gap between past and present in the meaning of *gongmin*.

In its first appearance in Chinese literature where it was used as the antithesis of *siren* (private person), the term *gongmin* acquired the connotation of morally preferred publicness or non-privateness derived from the first character *gong* and collectivity or non-individuality from the second character *min*. The connotation of collectivity seems to sustain in, and indeed become an embedded part of, the contemporary meaning of the term, given the finding of the overwhelming endorsement by both university students and migrant workers of *gongmin* as members of society. But the moral preference for publicness over privateness seems to fade away in the contemporary meaning, which reconciles the ancient antagonism and is possible to be understood more or less as independent individual concerning personal interest yet not at the cost of public one, as shown in the understanding of the two social groups. In other words, the term can now serve as a vehicle through which individual or collective claims for personal or public purposes are articulated and compete. But it is important to add that the long established connotations of publicness and collectivity are nevertheless likely to prevent the term from evolving to be just another word of individualism.

Also traceable to the ancient connotative connection between the character *gong* and public and official institutions, *gongmin* earned the expectation of participation in public affairs such as local governance from the citizenship theories by reformists on the threshold of the twentieth century. About one century later, not only is the participatory connotation, either political or civic, found to be modest, especially when compared with the strong *gongmin*-rights connection, in the meaning of *gongmin* in collective social discourses, but also the participatory expectation seems to be unstable in the meaning understood by individuals, given the finding of the significant expectation gap between university students and migrant workers on *gongmin*'s political participation. Those century-old citizenship theories, Kang Youwei's work in particular, may be valuable legacies for contemporary advocates to revitalize the participatory implication and expectation in the meaning of *gongmin* in society. But the success would critically depend upon social conditions such as the availability and practicability of public and official arenas for participation by ordinary citizens, and social perceptions of the value, either as means or end, of citizenship participation.

In the ancient meaning of *gong* the connotation of public and official institutions was oriented towards another connotation of moral preference for publicness and moral commitment to universality and justice. Indeed, *gongmin* were also envisaged in Kang Youwei's theory to be participants in the utopian universal public realm beyond the state. Can these historically gained connotative associations be found in the contemporary meaning of *gongmin*? First, the finding that the identity of *gongmin* is well embraced at the global level by both university students and migrant workers suggests that the connotation of universality remains robust in contemporary times. The term thus maintains the connotative capacity to disassociate from the state. Second, while both students and workers are found unwilling to place on *gongmin* the responsibility of sacrificing individual interest to the collective good, students are nevertheless more likely than workers to hold deeper participatory expectations for *gongmin*, including taking actions not within but beyond existing rules and for the sake of not just us but others. These findings indicate that in the contemporary meaning the association with the commitment to justice is not lost, yet conditioned by personal interest and fluctuating in the understanding of *gongmin* amongst citizens. An implication from this is that questions such as for and against whose interest and to whom it is appealed need to be considered when justice is appealed through the term *gongmin* in contemporary society.

Gongmin and State-Society Relation

Whether continuing or changing from its etymological legacies, the contemporary meaning of *gongmin* in society is a product of contemporary societal conditions in which the party-state ascribes itself the leading role. Yet the Chinese state-society relation, as shown in Chap. 3, has become dynamic in the sense that there is space for both the party-state to maintain its ruling legitimacy and social forces to influence policymaking and governance. To reflect the state-society dynamics in the meaning of *gongmin* and in turn add empirical observations to contemporary state-society relation, in this section I shall compare the meaning of *gongmin* in society and the official account of *gongmin*, and then consider the implications of the social meaning for contemporary state-society relation.

The three primary focuses in the party-state's account of *gongmin* are rights, morality and political participation (Chap. 3). The findings of Study I, which examined the meaning of *gongmin* in nonofficial and official newspapers, provide evidence about the priority relationship between the three focuses, showing that when compared with collective social discourses, official discourses are more likely to pay attention to *gongmin*'s moral responsibilities and political participation but less likely on *gongmin*'s rights. The discrepancy between the two discourses empirically reveals that the meaning of citizenship in contemporary Chinese society is not in full convergence with the party-state's stance on citizenship. It supports the general observation that the state-society relation has been dynamized. The existence of divergence does not mean the elimination of convergence. In what follows I shall revisit the official perspective on the three aspects of rights, morality and political participation in turn in light of the found social meaning of *gongmin*.

Rights are one focus about *gongmin* in the official perspective which, according to Li (2007), does not assign equal importance to but hierarchize different rights, claiming social and economic rights more fundamental than civil and political rights. This observation appears contradictory to the finding in Study I that civil and political rights are in stronger semantic connection with *gongmin* and of higher concern than social and cultural rights in official discourses. One explanation for the contradiction is that for the party-state the term *gongmin* is more related to civil and political rights, though which are considered by the party-state less fundamental than social and economic rights in Chinese society. Indeed, employment, pension, education and health care, which we categorize as economic and social rights, have long been acclaimed by the party-state as the entitlement for *renmin*, the term charged in the Maoist years as the winner of the proletarian revolution and the owner of the socialist state. The contradiction between the current finding and the existing observation requires further research to trace the official expression of *gongmin* and, more substantially, to examine and compare the protection and, of equal revealing power, the violation of different rights by the party-state in order to better understand its stance on different citizenship rights. But if the authorities do view civil rights less fundamental, they need to take seriously the social perspective of *gongmin* in which civil rights are not only of the clearest expression at the collective level but also of affirmed necessity at the individual level. The issue of political rights is more complex. Although with lesser certainty over their necessity for *gongmin* by both students and workers when compared with other rights, political rights are of the second highest concern, after civil rights, in collective social discourses of *gongmin*. This has two implications for the state-society relation. First, the party-state is unlikely to face immediate pressure from university students and migrant workers for political rights in the name of *gongmin*. However, and second, there could well be social forces to demand claim for political rights in the name of *gongmin*, especially when the rights are downplayed or even violated by the party-state.

Another feature of the party-state's stance on citizenship rights is that rights are conditioned not to transcend the sovereignty of the state (Li 2007). Given the finding that both students and workers perceive *gongmin* as subordinate vis-à-vis the state—although students also assign *gongmin* an active role which arguably is itself a result of recent official policy regarding citizenship, the rhetoric of sovereignty may remain an effective tool for the party-state to shy away from issues about rights, at least for the two social groups, migrant workers in particular.

Having highlighted the state-society dynamics around *gongmin* and rights, it is important to remark that the *gongmin*-rights connection is well grounded in both perspectives of the party-state and society either at the collective or individual level.

The term *gongmin* is thus enabled to serve as a recognizable vehicle for rights negotiations between the two sides. This, however, might not be the case for morality and political participation, the other two focuses of *gongmin* in the party-state's perspective. For the finding of rights overwhelming responsibilities and participation in the collective social discourse of *gongmin* raises the risk of the latter two being overshadowed by rights and less discernible in the collective social meaning.

The moral virtues attached to and articulated via the term *gongmin* in official policies (Chap. 3) are a mixture of long propagandized socialist values and, more recently, politically charged traditional values. It remains to be explored if such amalgam is able to be incorporated into the understanding of the term in society. But at least one relevant implication can be drawn from two findings in the individual citizens' understandings of *gongmin*. The two findings are that, firstly, responsibilities do not always gain equal weight as rights do—university students are more aware of the necessity of rights than that of responsibilities while migrant workers have a relatively balanced awareness; and secondly, responsibilities are subject to personal interest, a feature shared by both students and workers. The implication is that the party-state's recent strategy to indoctrinate socialist values with the help of the term *gongmin* would hardly work if those values override citizens' rights and personal interest.

Similar to rights and morality, *gongmin*'s political participation in the account of the party-state is a course subject to its design and guide. Despite its recent rhetoric of 'enhancing *gongmin*'s orderly political participation', the observation that political participation sanctioned by the authorities is neither universally accessible in design nor obstacle-free in practice is testified in this study by university students' mention of lack of opportunity to excise political rights and migrant workers' disillusion generated in political practice. The either little or negative political experience led to their lesser certainty rather than a stronger assertion about *gongmin*'s political rights. This implies, in line with our discussion of political rights above, that the two social groups are unlikely to actively demand wider and substantial political participation through the term *gongmin*. But compared with workers, students do perceive *gongmin* having not merely a passive but an active role vis-à-vis the state, and show a higher expectation for *gongmin* to engage in political affairs and to claim new rights for others, or in other words, to go beyond established rules for the sake of others. This suggests that university students would be easier than migrant workers to join with other social forces in the name of *gongmin* to challenge the party-state's policies on political participation. But challenge against policy does not necessarily mean challenge against the CCP regime itself. As political participation recently widen by the authorities is observed in effect not weakening but strengthening the regime, university students' higher expectation of *gongmin*'s political participation may not be a threat to, and could play into the hands of, the party-state, especially given that *gongmin* may not be a term common to political participation without official sanction because of its salient legal connotation in society.

The social meaning of *gongmin* also bears implications for the relation of the state to the social sector and groups through which the meaning is studied in this book, namely the media, university students and migrant workers. The discrepancy in the meaning of *gongmin* between the nonofficial and official newspapers can be seen as a testament to the increased autonomy in the media sector to cater to readers' interests as a consequence of state-society decentralization since the late 1990s. Moreover, given that the party-state still has the final say on the contents of all newspapers through continuing state censorship and self-imposed censorship by media outlets, the discrepancy or more precisely, the significantly stronger *gongmin*-rights connection in the nonofficial newspaper seems to be within the tolerance limit of the party-state in the time period covered by the sub-study. With regards to students and workers, their unanimous consensus on *gongmin* as legal identity not merely accords with the legal status of the term in the constitution, but also suggests that the term can well serve as a vehicle for their citizenship communication and negotiation with the party-state, which has shown attempts to reconfigure its relations with the two social groups in legal terms.

This and the last sections have situated the found social meaning of *gongmin* into Chinese citizenship literature, bridging the research gap between the meaning of *gongmin* in society on one hand and the term in historical and official perspectives on the other hand. The other gap in Chinese citizenship studies that this book aims to address is the one between Chinese and Western citizenship conceptions, or more precisely, the question of to what extent the Chinese term *gongmin* embraces—or, in another word, binds—elements in Western citizenship conception. It is through the lens of Western citizenship that the meaning of *gongmin* in Chinese society is studied and unveiled in this study. This approach enables us to apply the found meaning to empirically address the above question and, furthermore, provide implications for East-West citizenship.

Gongmin and Citizenship

Given that citizenship, as a result of its contemporary reconfiguration, is recognized as a concept constructed in particular societal contexts, the meaning of *gongmin* in Chinese society is neither necessary nor expected to cover or convey every element and idea in Western citizenship theory. Yet at the same time, this does not mean that there should be no connection between Chinese *gongmin* and Western citizenship. In fact, Western influence can be traced in the meaning of *gongmin*. The use of the term in the work of exiled-to-Japan Kang Youwei echoed the connotation of the Japanese term with the same characters as *gongmin* in the Western-inspired Meiji reform era; and the legal status entailing rights and responsibilities, as which *gongmin* is constitutionally defined, is an institution of Western origin. Acknowledging their particularity and connection, in this section, I compare the found social meaning of *gongmin* with the Western citizenship conception outlined in Chap. 2 in the three dimensions of extent, content, and depth in turn.

Four observations can be made in the extent dimension about identity. First, the term *gongmin*, which is officially designated as legal state membership and found to be so understood in society, corresponds to the modern citizenship of legal nature. This suggests that the legal element can be a starting point for the dialogue between Western citizenship and Chinese *gongmin* not merely at the policy level but also at the social level. Second, while citizenship as a legal status in the state was mingled in its modern formation with people of the nation which often carried implications of ethnocultural homogeneities, the modern nation-state equation is decoupled in the contemporary conceptual reconfiguration of citizenship, leading to the detachment of legal identity from national identity and the recognition of ethnic and cultural diversity among people having the same legal state membership. The detachment, however, seems yet to be fully realized in the understanding of *gongmin* in Chinese society. For migrant workers are found to be likely to define 'Chinese *gongmin*' in terms of ethnicity and culture, a notion opposed by university students. The ethnocultural diversity among Chinese citizens, contributed by the dozens of ethnic groups and facilitated by globalization, arguably should also be recognized along with the common legal membership in the meaning of *gongmin*. In other words, *gongmin* as a legal identity should be detached from ethnic and cultural identities. It is beyond the scope here to theoretically explain why this should be done or to practically explore how this can be done in the Chinese context, but at least our review of the history of *gongmin* shows that the term does not have the etymological precedent of bearing ethnocultural implications.

Third, another important way to accommodate cultural differences among citizens is through reconfiguring citizenship to be a multi-layered concept traversing below and beyond the national level (Yuval-Davis 1999). The acceptance of the identity of *gongmin* in Chinese society is found in this study to be predominant at the national level and extendable to the global level, but conditional at the local level. This on one hand shows the potential of using *gongmin* as a vehicle in the Chinese context to develop a global identity to be shared with citizens in the wider world, on the other hand raises the question of how to develop *gongmin* as a local identity for citizens living in the same locality in the face of existing institutional obstacles such as the HRS.

Fourth, the overwhelming perception of *gongmin* as collective identity in Chinese society drags the term away from modern liberal citizenship which has individual independence and liberty at its core. But this is only part of the story. There is no lack of social perception of the term in a more individualistic vein, as shown in the understanding of university students. Nor the collective identity necessarily leads to community involvement and contribution, the essence of civic republican citizenship which is the other Western citizenship tradition than liberal citizenship, given that personal interest is found to be a significant concern in students' and workers' consideration about *gongmin*'s social and moral responsibilities. Adding further to the complexity of the story is the resemblance between the macro social meaning of *gongmin* and liberal citizenship in the way that both prioritize rights over responsibilities. It can be argued that neither liberal citizenship nor civic republican citizenship alone is adequate to fully represent the meaning of *gongmin* in contemporary Chinese society.

Turning to the content dimension, rights and responsibilities inherent in Western citizenship are found to be not merely integrated parts of *gongmin* in the constitutional definition and official policies, but also topics of concern in the collective social discourse of *gongmin* and deemed necessary in general in individual citizens' understanding of *gongmin*. Different rights and responsibilities, however, do not receive equal degrees of concern and necessity. On the part of rights, the varying degrees of concern and necessity add empirical evidence from the Chinese case to the discussion that citizenship civic, political, social and cultural rights are not necessarily ranked in the same sequence as they were historically developed in the British case outlined by Marshall (1998). Furthermore, cultural rights as the fourth and the latest wave of rights in Western citizenship development are well recognized in individual citizens' understanding of *gongmin*, while such rights seem to come short of concern in the collective social meaning of the term. This finding shows that the priority sequence can even vary at different social levels in one society. In a more general sense, the present study supports the postmodern understanding of the concept of citizenship that Western citizenship conception evolved and expanded from the political to the social and lately to the cultural sphere would not necessarily be followed by citizenship conception in other contexts. On the part of responsibilities, the momentum towards civic virtue in contemporary citizenship debates in the West, on one hand, might find resonance in the relentless campaigns for *gongmin*'s morality by the party-state, on the other hand, is less observed in Chinese society, especially when responsibilities are overshadowed by rights as in collective social discourses.

The importance of participation is widely recognized in Western citizenship debates, either as a way to protect individual liberty and rights or as the foundation of citizenship. While the participation dimension is one of the focuses of *gongmin* in the party-state's perspective, it is found to be not salient at the collective level and fluctuating at the individual level in the meaning of *gongmin* in Chinese society. The gap on the importance of participation between *gongmin* and citizenship cautions us not to take it for granted particularly in Chinese-Western comparative citizenship discussion. For individual citizens, university students are found to have a higher expectation than migrant workers for *gongmin* to monitor government, influence policymaking, and claim new rights for others. If measured by the typologies of citizenship proposed by Banks (2008) and Westheimer and Kahne (2004), *gongmin* in the understanding of workers seems to be closer to legal or personally responsible citizenship, while the term in the view of students resembles more the active or participatory citizenship, and even the transformative or justice-oriented citizenship featuring the most progressive level of participation of challenging existing unjust rules. The claim by Streich (2011) of extending the pursuit of justice for not just in-group but out-group members seems to be mirrored more in students' than in workers' understanding of *gongmin*. It can also be discussed that *gongmin* perceived by students is beyond what Almond and Verba

(1965) called 'subject' who participates within the establishment, echoing their definition of 'citizen' who engages in making the establishment. But it is important to remind that university students' relatively higher and deeper expectation about *gongmin*'s participation is unlikely to be unconditional, given their expression of concern, which is shared with migrant workers, about personal interest when considering *gongmin*'s responsibility of helping remove inequality in society. In this sense, the contemporary meaning of *gongmin* resonates with contemporary Western citizenship which, as Walzer (1995) soberly pointed out, is no more than one identity owned by citizens who have many other roles to play and care in private and public life.

The Western citizenship conception referred to in this study is admittedly just one side of the multifaceted citizenship debates in the West, and the ideas behind the conception are not free of controversy. Furthermore, citizenship as a constructed concept is subject to evolve along with changing societal circumstances. Treating the particular conception as the reference point, this section has nevertheless connected the found meaning of *gongmin* in Chinese society to Western citizenship amid ongoing conceptual changes and debates. This can be seen as an introduction with empirical details of the Chinese term *gongmin* to international citizenship discussions and debates and, furthermore, an intercultural communication and search for the possibility of common ground in East-West citizenship.

Gongmin and Citizenship Education

The inquiry into the meaning of *gongmin* in contemporary Chinese society in this book started from the party-state's attention on citizenship education in the name of *gongmin*. It is also guided by a model of citizenship education built upon the Western citizenship conception outlined in this study to give suggestions for how to promote this model with the term *gongmin* in and beyond schools in the contemporary Chinese context. Before specifying the citizenship education model and giving practical suggestions for its promotion, I shall consider in what respects the found social meaning of *gongmin* resembles and deviates from state-directed citizenship-related education, as a way to assess the impact of the latter on the former.

What featured Chinese citizenship-related education in the 2000s after the curriculum reform, as reviewed in Chap. 3, are the recognition of self and the increased appreciation for human rights and global awareness. The changes in citizenship-related education echo the perceptual difference about *gongmin* between migrant workers and university students, with the latter group found to have a more individualistic understanding of *gongmin* and to more saliently express *gongmin*'s rights and accept *gongmin* as global identity. Given that the university students investigated in this study were by age the recipients of the reformed school curricula and textbooks while the migrant workers averagely a decade older were not, it seems that citizenship-related education has an impact on individual citizens' perception of *gongmin*, though the data of this study could not prove the causal relationship between education and perception. Another clue to the impact of education on individual perception is the consistency between the long enshrined collectivism and patriotism (if not nationalism), both of which remain intact under the recent curriculum reform, on one hand, and the endorsement of *gongmin* as members of society and as national identity by both students and workers on the other hand.

While the self is recognized, collectivism remains a guiding principle in the reformed citizenship-related education. In other words, the party-state's educational stance remains encouraging citizens to submit the newly recognized self to the collective good. But such stance might not always be adopted by citizens, given that both students and workers in this study expressed their resistance to sacrifice personal interest for the sake of *gongmin*'s social responsibility, which is a key respect in the party-state's stance on citizenship. This illustrates that the impact of education on perception, if does exist, is not inevitable, and, more fundamentally, that state control on citizenship perception should not be taken for granted as it could be circumvented, contested and challenged in society.

It is inspired by such alterability that a model of citizenship education drawn from ideas in contemporary Western citizenship conception is put forward here. This model balances rights and responsibilities of citizenship, promotes inclusive citizenship so that no one is detained or deprived of rights and responsibilities because of age, class, gender, ethnicity, religion or ability, facilitates active and justice-oriented citizenship participation in social and political affairs, and encourages understanding and practice of citizenship that goes below and beyond nation-state. It is beyond the intention here to theoretically justify this model or to politically evaluate the possibility of its adoption and implementation by the party-state. Rather, with the understanding that state control on education as a result of power contestation is subject to challenge when power balances change, in what follows I shall draw upon the empirical findings of this study to suggest what needs to be done so as to achieve the model with the use of the term *gongmin* in contemporary Chinese society. There are eight suggestions.

(1) *Use* gongmin jiaoyu *as the overarching term for Chinese citizenship education.* The finding that rights are an integrated part of the meaning of *gongmin* at both macro and micro social levels raises the question: Can rights be effectively learnt, and rights and responsibilities be equally presented, under the long established moral education, which is interrelated to ideopolitical education despite appearing to be depoliticized and touch more rights issues in recent years? The morality-oriented nature of moral education poses conceptual and structural barriers to rights learning and to the content balance between citizenship rights and responsibilities. Instead of moral education which is often treated as citizenship education in China in recent literature, *gongmin jiaoyu* or citizenship education is arguably a broader term more capable to incorporate citizenship rights and responsibilities, and thus should be used as the overarching term under which moral education is side by side with rights education.

Moreover, given the shared legal implication between *gongmin* and citizenship, the use of the term *gongmin jiaoyu* for Chinese citizenship education would enable more nuanced cross-context dialogues on citizenship education.

(2) *Understand* gongmin jiaoyu *as lifelong education.* A key finding of this study is that the meaning of *gongmin* is not in the same mould but varies in Chinese society. This implies that not only is school citizenship education unable to build a consensus on citizenship in society, it has limitation in responding to varying citizenship understandings in the wider society. In order to facilitate citizenship understanding and encourage citizenship practice in society, citizenship education should not be constrained in schools but made available to citizens such as migrant workers in the wider society, serving as a platform accessible to all in society for citizenship learning, discussion and exercise. By widening the scope of citizenship education to be lifelong education, not only can in-school citizenship education be supplied with rich human and knowledge resources in the wider society, beyond-school citizenship education can provide citizens after leaving school constant learning opportunities for citizenship accommodating societal changes and developments. Moreover, given the variations of, and hence the tensions in, the meaning of *gongmin* between official discourses, collective social discourses and individual citizens' understandings, the role of public pedagogy in citizenship learning and understanding, which is in fact its original concern, should not be ignored. For instance, the varied types of media such as TV programmes and the Internet, which were indeed the key sources of information about *gongmin* for the university students and migrant workers (see Appendix), are also important platforms for citizenship (re)production, (re)construction and resistance in society.

(3) *Differentiate 'Chinese* gongmin' *from ethnic Chinese.* While Chinese *gongmin* as legal identity seems to be deep-seated in individual citizens' understanding, there are still citizens such as migrant workers likely to also understand the term as ethnic identity, typically in relation to the Han majority. The understanding of the term 'Chinese *gongmin*' in both legal and ethnic senses may lead to the marginalization and exclusion of dozens of ethnic minorities in China from being recognized as Chinese *gongmin* and, consequently, from legal rights and responsibilities that the status entails in law. Also, the particular understanding could be an obstacle to the inclusion of legal Chinese citizens of origin outside China. To prevent such potential exclusion and to develop inclusive citizenship, it is necessary to deliberatively differentiate Chinese *gongmin* as a legal status from ethnic Chinese, the Han majority in particular, in citizenship education. Only through this approach can the often-deprived identities of ethnic minorities be recuperated and protected not at the expense of legal status and rights. Practically, the differentiation could be done through public presence of diverse ethnic minorities as Chinese *gongmin*, and open expression, discussion and celebration of ethnic and cultural identity in citizenship education.

(4) *Take advantage of* gongmin *for global citizenship promotion.* The wide acceptance of *gongmin* as global identity positively suggests that, in accordance with the implication of universality from its etymological legacy, the term has the connotative capacity in contemporary society to carry the idea of global citizenship, though which, admittedly, is a highly contested concept. But given the found predominant identification with the term at the national level, there are questions for further exploration in the endeavour of global citizenship education using the term *gongmin*. For instance, what is the relationship between national and global citizenship? How does national citizenship influence the development of global citizenship? If global citizenship is understood as, for instance, a commitment to the human society, how to reconcile national and global citizenship when the two come into conflict in such cases as the pervasion of justice to global fellow citizens requiring the sacrifice of the interests of national fellow citizens?

(5) *Use* gongmin *in local contexts.* The conditional embracement, depending upon factors such as the official HRS, of *gongmin* at the local level by citizens despite living in the locality suggests that the term has difficulty in serving as local residential identity. At a time that the decades-long household registration policy is reportedly under reform,[1] it remains to be seen whether an official ease of HRS would boost citizens' acceptance of *gongmin* as local identity. On the part of citizenship education, more expression of *gongmin* in local contexts could be a practical way to increase the local relevance of the term, paving the way for the expression of local belongingness through the term *gongmin*.

(6) *Balance* gongmin*'s different rights.* The varying degrees of connection between specific rights and the term *gongmin* at the two social levels suggest that there is necessity to balance different kinds of *gongmin*'s rights in education so as to ensure that citizens do not narrowly focus on rights in their own interest but have awareness and understanding of other rights which could not merely be the concern of fellow citizens but influence their own rights claims. One case in point is the influence of political rights on other rights, as the latter is often earned through political participation, the exercise of the former.

(7) *Place more emphasis on* gongmin*'s participation.* The weak expression of participation in the macro-level social meaning of *gongmin* alerts that more emphasis on participation in citizenship education society-wide is required for developing active citizenship. Also, given the found varied understanding of *gongmin*'s participation between university students and migrant workers, behind which their socioeconomic circumstances could be a factor, active citizenship education needs to take into account different social groups' specific needs, concerns and challenges about participation as *gongmin*. Also, while

---

[1]See, for instance, the news report on China Daily 'Hukou reform under way in 29 regions across China', http://www.chinadaily.com.cn/business/2016-04/29/content_24966027.htm (accessed 16 November 2016).

there is participatory implication in the etymology of *gongmin*, further studies are required to explore how to revive the historical implication for contemporary promotion.

(8) *Uphold the value of justice*. It is interesting to find that there are a majority of university students and migrant workers expecting *gongmin* to claim for new rights, a way of seeking justice by challenging existing systems. Yet they expect much less the challenging action to be taken for the sake of others, especially in the case of workers. The concern about self-interest is detected in the two groups' consideration of *gongmin*'s responsibilities. Admittedly, it may be too heavy a burden for every individual citizen to take action to fight on a daily basis against injustice for others in the name of *gongmin* which, after all, is just one of many roles that people possess in contemporary private and public life. Nevertheless, the commitment to pursue justice not merely for in-group members but also for out-group members is still desirable, for the fundamental reason that justice, in the light of Rawls (1999), is an 'uncompromising' first virtue of human activities (p. 4). There is no lack of injustice issues in contemporary Chinese society; the discussed socioeconomic disadvantages facing migrant workers are an illustrative example. Like the preceding suggestion, a question for future exploration is how to galvanize the implication of justice rooted in the character *gong* to promote the value through citizenship education in contemporary society.

References

Almond, G. A., & Verba, S. (1965). *The civic culture: Political attitudes and democracy in five nations*. Boston: Little, Brown and Company.

Banks, J. A. (2008). Diversity, group identity, and citizenship education in a global age. *Educational Researcher, 37*(3), 129–139. doi:10.3102/0013189X08317501.

Fairclough, N. (2001). *Language and power* (2nd ed.). Essex: Longman.

Li, J. (2007). Human rights vs. state interests in China: Case studies. *New Zealand Journal of Asian Studies, 9*(2), 147–168.

Marshall, T. H. (1998). Citizenship and social class. In G. Shafir (Ed.), *The citizenship debates* (pp. 93–111). Minneapolis: University of Minnesota Press.

Rawls, J. (1999). *A theory of justice* (revised ed.). Cambridge, MA: Belknap Press of Harvard University Press.

Streich, G. W. (2011). *Justice beyond "just us": Dilemmas of time, place, and difference in American Politics*. Surrey: Ashgate.

Walzer, M. (1995). The civil society argument. In R. Beiner (Ed.), *Theorizing citizenship* (pp. 153–174). Albany: State University of New York Press.

Westheimer, J., & Kahne, J. (2004). What kind of citizen? The politics of educating for democracy. *American Educational Research Journal, 41*(2), 237–269.

Yuval-Davis, N. (1999). The 'multi-layered citizen'. *International Feminist Journal of Politics, 1* (1), 119–136. doi:10.1080/146167499360068.

Chapter 8
Conclusion: Possible Change, Necessary Work

Through the lens of Western citizenship conception (Chap. 2) and taken into account of the state factor (Chap. 3), this book has empirically unveiled the meaning of *gongmin* in contemporary Chinese society in three dimensions (Chaps. 4–6) and situated the meaning into the three relevant and wider research areas of Chinese citizenship, East-West citizenship and citizenship education (Chap. 7). Empirical study inextricably has methodological limitation. To compensate for the limitation of the current study, I shall consider in this concluding chapter the possible changes to the found meaning of *gongmin*. Moreover, the constructed and social nature of the meaning of *gongmin* determines that what this book has disclosed has its particularity in terms of time, space and people. The other purpose of this chapter is thus to suggest what future work needs to explore following the findings in this book to further understand the term *gongmin* in contemporary Chinese society.

On the relationship between language and society, critical linguist Norman Fairclough (2001) provided the revealing insight that language as discourse is a form of social practice, in the sense that language is a part of society produced and interpreted under social conditions of not merely the immediate and situational social environment in which language is used, but also the wider non-linguistic institutional and structural context. This insight gives three important reflections on the found meaning of *gongmin* in Chinese society. First, the discourse of *gongmin* is a social phenomenon, influenced by social convention and having a social effect. Second, the collective social meaning of *gongmin* glimpsed through the newspaper is conditioned by the situational and structural circumstances of the newspaper contributors as producer and the author of this book as an interpreter. Third, the investigated university students' and migrant workers' understandings of *gongmin* recorded in this study is the product of both the actual survey and interview settings and their social positions and experiences in Chinese society. The three reflections suggest, respectively, possible changes to the found meaning of *gongmin*.

First, and most fundamentally, the found meaning of *gongmin* seen as a social phenomenon is in effect a record of the meaning under the particular Chinese social

S. Chen, *The Meaning of Citizenship in Contemporary Chinese Society*,
Governance and Citizenship in Asia, https://doi.org/10.1007/978-981-10-6323-7_8

circumstances in the early 2010s. What *gongmin* means is therefore expected to change as social substances alter. One important social substance is the distribution of social power, which determines whose use and what kind of understanding of the term *gongmin* is powerful enough to become the social convention of how the term is used and understood, or in other words, to become the 'common sense' about *gongmin*. Seen from the other way around, the discourse of *gongmin*, which is confirmed in this study to bear political implications at both official and social levels, has maintaining or challenging effect on the distribution of social power. In short, the language of *gongmin* is, following Fairclough's (2001) observation on language in general, both a site of and a stake in social power struggle, for it is where social power is exercised and demonstrated and what helps distribute social power. This understanding of language suggests that the meaning of *gongmin* in Chinese society studied in this book in the perspectives of newspapers, university students and migrant workers is in close association with the social power possessed by the media sector and the two social groups, and hence that for other social sectors or groups with more, or less, social power, the term *gongmin* could have different meaning from the one presented here. Also, the use and understanding of *gongmin* in newspapers and by students and workers could contribute to their negotiation of social power in Chinese society. Whether this is the case and how it is done remain to be explored.

Moreover, the term *gongmin*, as Fairclough (2001) discussed the meaning of a word in general, 'is not an isolated and independent thing', but has a 'meaning system' which incorporates a cluster of words to define it (p. 78). In this study, the meaning of *gongmin* was examined through the three dimensions associated with Western citizenship conception. The approach by no means assumes that the meaning system of *gongmin* necessarily has only the dimensions about identity, rights and responsibilities, and participation. There could well be other dimensions or words in association with the term *gongmin* that are not found in Western citizenship conception, especially when the discourse of *gongmin* is considered as a form of social practice depending upon specific Chinese societal conditions.

Second, given the factor of the immediate and institutional conditions of newspaper contributors as language producer in the meaning of *gongmin* in the targeted nonofficial newspaper, the reported meaning at the collective social level could change, if the analysis covered a larger time span or more nonofficial newspapers and media platforms, and if there is new development in the media-state relationship in general in the future. Also, the meaning could alter if there were more researchers as language interpreter involving in the analysis process.

Third, for the meaning of *gongmin* at the individual level, the immediate social circumstances under which the study was done could influence the perceptions of the investigated university students and migrant workers. In particular, the fact that the survey and interviews were conducted amid heightened diplomatic tension between China and Japan due to territorial disputes in early 2012 and that the author of the book was affiliated to a Japanese university at the time might have impact on the students' and workers' perceptions of *gongmin* especially in relation to national identity and the state. Their perceptions revealed in this book could change if the study was done at other times or by an investigator of other background. Indeed, some migrant worker interviewees, who self-blamed the lack of education for their understanding of *gongmin*, were explicitly conscious of the academic background of the author. In the institutional context, conditioned by their social positions and relationships with the party-state, the understanding of *gongmin* of the two social groups could develop along with changes in social power distribution and in student-state and worker-state relationships.

The above possible changes and alterations to the meaning of *gongmin* found in this study necessitate three clusters of questions to be explored by further research on the meaning of the term in the Chinese context.

(1) In the media sector: What is the meaning of *gongmin* in other nonofficial newspapers and on other media platforms, the rapidly developing Internet in particular? Are there any differences to the meaning found in the book? How does the meaning evolve in the media? What are the forces behind the evolvement? How is the meaning in the media interpreted by ordinary citizens?
(2) In the university student and migrant worker groups: Are the understandings of the two groups in other parts of China similar to the findings of this study? Does students' understanding of *gongmin* change after graduation? How does migrant workers' understanding of *gongmin* develop under the household registration policy reform?
(3) In the wider society: What does the term *gongmin* mean to other social sectors and groups, particularly those having more social power, such as intellectuals and entrepreneurs, and those having less, including various minorities in terms of economic resource, ethnicity, culture, age, gender and religion? What are the meaning systems of *gongmin* in individual social sectors and groups? Are there any distinctive words and dimensions in their meaning systems of *gongmin*?

In light of the understanding that the discourse of *gongmin* is a form of social practice, what this book has focused upon is more the social side of the discourse, that is, its *meaning* in Chinese society, leaving unelaborated the practical side, that is, its *practice* by Chinese citizens. To understand the language in practice, it is helpful to draw upon Bourdieu's (1992) theory of language as symbolic capital. The theory sees the linguistic practice as 'a conjuncture, an encounter' between linguistic habitus and linguistic market (p. 37). Linguistic habitus is a set of linguistic dispositions that are inculcated and hence inscribed, structured and hence durable, and at the same time generative and transposable to other than the linguistic field in particular social context. The linguistic market is the field within which linguistic practice is performed; it is structured by social relations which are in turn determined by the distribution of different forms of capital. In this perspective, both linguistic habitus and linguistic market are shaped by social conditions, and so is linguistic practice. This theory is in line with, and indeed inherited by, Fairclough's (2001) view on language. What Bourdieu focused upon is the practice of linguistic habitus in the linguistic field where language serves as symbolic capital. A range of components in linguistic practice are identified, notably linguistic propensity, technical linguistic capacity, practical capacity in the sense of appropriate practice in specific fields, statutory capacity in the sense of entitlement to the practice, symbolic cognition by user and recognition by recipient of the language, and anticipation of the symbolic profit from the practice.

The meaning of *gongmin* in the media and among university students and migrant workers examined, reported and discussed in this book contributes to the understanding of their symbolic cognition and possible recognition of the language of *gongmin*. Following the above components in linguistic practice as signposts, there are a range of questions, from practical to theoretical, for future study on the practice of the term as symbolic capital in Chinese society: When and where do people use the term *gongmin*? Who are inclined to use the term? By and to whom is the term used? How does recipient respond to the use of the term by others? What linguistic profits does the user anticipate from the use of the term? What strategies does the user employ in the symbolic production of the term? What is the effect of the use of the term on the relation between user and recipient? How is the language of *gongmin* as symbolic capital converted into other forms of capital? And an ultimate question is: Can the linguistic practice of the term *gongmin* make a difference to social relations and conditions in contemporary Chinese society, and furthermore, to the Chinese society-state relation?

References

Bourdieu, P. (1992). *Language and Symbolic Power*. Cambridge: Polity Press.
Fairclough, N. (2001). *Language and Power* (2nd ed.). Essex: Longman.

Appendix
Data Collection and Analysis

Study I

The influential nonofficial newspaper *Southern Metropolis Daily* (*Nanfang dushibao*) in Guangdong Province and the CCP's mouthpiece newspaper *People's Daily* (*Renmin ribao*) were the two newspaper samples. I collected newspaper articles published between October 2007, when the need of citizenship education was remarkably articulated in the CCP's seventeenth national congress, and August 2010. For the regional newspaper, I only targeted the Page-A part which was published provincewide, ruling out those pages that were published exclusively in individual cities. I accessed to *Southern Metropolis Daily* via both its online version and hard copies in library and to *People's Daily* from its published CD-ROM database. Articles in which the term *gongmin* appeared were collected. A total of 5001 articles meeting the stipulated conditions were collected, among which 2257 from the regional one and 2744 were from the CCP organ newspaper.

This sub-study analyzed the term *gongmin* in the content dimension about rights and responsibilities and in the depth dimension about participation. The extent dimension about identity was not examined in this sub-study, because in most of the collected newspaper articles it was impossible to either identify whom the term *gongmin* was referred to or measure it in the three aspects focused upon in the identity dimension. Chinese terms that served as indicators in the content analysis were: *quanli* and *quanyi* (right); *yiwu* (obligation), *daode* (morality) and *zeren* (responsibility); and *canjia* and *canyu* (participation).

Krippendorff (1980) suggested that content analysis is a quantitative as well as qualitative research method, so that both explicit and latent meanings need to be taken into account (pp. 21–2). Following this suggestion, in the process of content analysis, I first of all analyzed whether each *gongmin* in each article was in positive semantic connection with the indicators, no matter whether explicitly or latently and if so, I further categorized the connected rights into civil, political, social and cultural, responsibilities into moral and legal, and participation into political and civic (nonpolitical).

The recording and analyzing proceeded on SPSS. Each article was treated as a case; each category in rights, responsibilities, participation and identity was set as a

S. Chen, *The Meaning of Citizenship in Contemporary Chinese Society*,
Governance and Citizenship in Asia, https://doi.org/10.1007/978-981-10-6323-7

variable. After recording the results of content analysis, frequencies of the variables were calculated and compared in and between newspapers. At last, Chi-square tests were run to measure the significance of difference of the frequencies between the two newspapers. To maximally avoid Type I errors, only differences with the p-value lower than 0.001 were considered significant.

Study II

Study II intended to investigate university students' and migrant workers' perceptions of *gongmin* in the extent dimension about identity, the content dimension about rights and responsibilities, and the depth dimension about participation. Specifically, it inquired six aspects: for the extent dimension, (1) the criteria for the identity of 'Chinese *gongmin*', (2) the identity of *gongmin* vis-à-vis state and society, (3) the capacity of *gongmin* as identity at the local, national and global levels; for the content dimension, (4) rights that *gongmin* should have, (5) responsibilities that *gongmin* should have; and for the depth dimension (6) actions that *gongmin* are desired to take.

The investigation was conducted through a questionnaire survey and in-depth interviews with willing and available questionnaire respondents. With the questionnaire I aimed to obtain the general perceptions with a relatively wide coverage, while I used in-depth interview to access to deep, detailed, personal and practical information behind the general perceptions.

Questionnaire

Questions in the questionnaire were initially devised in English, because the analytical framework of this study was based on Western citizenship literature, and then translated into Chinese, the native language of the respondents. Experience of encountering the term *gongmin* was specified as participatory condition on the cover page of the questionnaire to ensure that respondents had experience of the topic, as suggested by Denscombe (1998). The questionnaire was piloted before being distributed by three university students and two migrant workers who were also included in the final sample. Reflections from the pilot respondents confirmed that all the questions were understandable for both groups.

The questionnaire had two parts. In the first part, there were five background questions concerning four demographic backgrounds which might influence respondent's perception about *gongmin*. They were (1) birth year; (2) gender; (3) the location of primary school attended (rural/urban and in/out of Guangdong Province), which served as an indicator of household registration status (HRS) and (4) educational level (personal level for worker and parental level for student respondents). Also, there was a question in the first part asking where the term was encountered with a list of five possible types of media, from book, newspaper/magazine, radio, television program to the Internet.

A note is necessary on the inquiry of the location of primary school attended and the attendant HRS. As discussed in this book, the official HRS often entails social exclusion, the fear of which might hold migrant worker respondents in particular back from being candid in answering a direct question on their HRS. For this reason, I instead asked respondents the location of the primary school they attended, which could serve as a rough indicator of their HRS, because it has long been being officially determined by the latter. The controlled and limited HRS transferability is by and large out of reach of migrant workers; and while university students are allowed to temporarily transfer their HRS to the city where the university is located during the period of study, many do not bother changing it, at least for those studying in universities in Guangdong Province.[1] One reason is that even if they transfer their HRS, they are required to revert it to the original one upon graduation.

The second part of the questionnaire was a list of statements with a five-point Likert ordinal scale (strongly disagree, disagree, undecided, agree, and strongly agree) which allowed respondents' attitudes on the statements to be measured in a clear, ordered and ranked form (Denscombe 1998). Opportunities were provided for respondents to write down answers or examples that were not mentioned in the questionnaire. At the end, there was also space for comment on the whole questionnaire. The questionnaire also had a few statements irrelevant either to the above six aspects or to the Western lens of citizenship in the sub-study, which thus were not reported in this book.

I distributed the questionnaire in two universities and four factories between March and May 2012. Following the suggestion by Denscombe (1998) on the sample size of small-scale research, and with the consideration of the capacity of the sample universities and factories, I distributed 300 copies of the questionnaire in universities and factories respectively. The respondents in universities were restricted to undergraduate students with PRC citizenship (excluding Hong Kong and Macao) to minimize unexpected effects on respondents' perception. Through a personal connection with a staff member in one of the universities, an undergraduate student in her final year with experience of assisting in faculty-level social research was introduced to me and acted as my assistant. The student in turn introduced several friends with research assistance experience in the two universities to help distribute the questionnaires. Instructions on the process of questionnaire distribution and collection were given before distribution. With their help for which a small financial reward was provided, I successfully collected 294 valid questionnaires in total from the two universities with a 98% response rate. This might be because, first, the questionnaires were strategically distributed at night after lesson hours when students had spare time and in dormitories where they were

[1]See the news report 'Guangzhou's university students are no longer keen for big city's household registration' (in Chinese), http://www.chinanews.com/edu/news/2010/03-26/2192759.shtml (Accessed 26 November 2016).

assembled and easy to access to, and second, respondent's consent to voluntary participation was obtained before distribution and a small present was given as reward.

Same as in universities, 300 copies of questionnaires with small presents as reward were distributed in the factories. Using personal networks with their owners, I was introduced by them to factory directors or managers. Due to the restriction of the hard schedule of the machine shop and workers, I could not personally take part in the distributing process but asked the factory directors and managers—to whom I stressed the voluntary principle and instructed on how to answer the questionnaire before distribution—to take charge of handing out the questionnaires to and collecting them back from workers when they took a break between shifts or at lunch and dinner times. With their efforts, 256 completed questionnaires were returned with about 85 % response rate. While lower than that of the student group probably due to workers' limited break time and my absence at the scene for instruction, it was still an acceptable response ratio. To ascertain worker respondents' migration status, I excluded thirty questionnaires stating the location of attended primary school in urban area in Guangdong Province, because that implied those respondents might have local urban HRS in the city, from the final sample for analysis. In other words, I used the remaining 226 questionnaires as valid quantitative data from migrant workers in this investigation.

In-Depth Interviews

One-to-one semi-structured in-depth interviews were conducted to explore personal reasons and experience about the perceptions of the six aspects of inquiry. Interview questions included:

(1) What comes into your mind when you hear the term *gongmin*?
(2) What kind of people do you think can be designated as 'Chinese *gongmin*', why?
(3) What do you think is the relationship of *gongmin* with state and society, why?
(4) Why do you think that you are (not) a Guangdong/Chinese/global *gongmin*?
(5) What rights and responsibilities do you think *gongmin* should have, why?
(6) Why do you not agree that *gongmin* should have the right to X or the responsibility of X?
(7) What kind of people do you think can be called *hao gongmin* (good citizen), why?
(8) Why do you not agree that the act of X is an attribute of *hao gongmin*?

I arranged the in-depth interviews soon after all the questionnaires were collected. Interviewees were questionnaire respondents either introduced by the student assistant or selected from the pool of respondents who provided their contact information on the questionnaire as an indication that they were willing and available to participate in the interview stage. A small reward was provided for each interviewee. Interviews with worker respondents were arranged during duty time with permission of director or manager. I conducted the interviews in Chinese on university campus and in factory canteen, and tape recorded them with interviewees' consent. In each interview normally 30 min long, after a self-introduction and brief explanation of the purpose of the research, I asked the interview questions not in a fixed order and particularly inquired about the reason and experience of the interviewees in relation to their answers on the questionnaire. There was time left for comment at the end. I successfully interviewed twenty-two questionnaire respondents, half university students and half migrant workers.

Ethics

Ethics were considered carefully before and during questionnaire and interview data collection. I clearly stated the voluntary principle and guaranteed the confidentiality and anonymity of collected data on the questionnaire cover page and at the beginning of each interview.

Denscombe (1998) suggested that survey participants should be informed about the researcher's affiliation and research sponsor if any. In this sub-study, however, I provided the former information but not the latter although the sub-study was sponsored by a student research program in a Japanese university. Given the political nature of the concept of citizenship having close link with nation and state, and the timing of the sub-study, which was carried out amid diplomatic tension between China and Japan due to territorial disputes, the research might provoke unwillingness of participation and even antipathy against the research if I clearly stated the sponsorship. To minimize the potential side effect on the research while keep participants being informed, I identified myself with my Chinese name and as a doctoral student in Japan, and explained that the investigation was part of my doctoral thesis.

Data Analysis

I grouped respondents' birth years by decade which featured distinct political and social circumstances to examine whether the experiential difference between these birth cohorts had impact on the understanding of *gongmin*. Those born in the 1950s and 1960s grew up in the impoverished years of the early CCP regime, while those born in the 1970s suffered in childhood from the turbulence of Cultural Revolution and its aftermath; those born in the 1980s were the first generation affected by the one-child policy and came of age in the reform years at the turn to the twenty-first century, while those born in the 1990s were a generation exposed to the Internet from early ages.

The quantitative data collected from questionnaires was recorded and analyzed on SPSS. The analysis process involved two stages. At the first stage, descriptive analyses were conducted to calculate the proportions of different answers to each question and statement by the student and worker groups respectively. At the second stage, inferential analyses were performed to examine, first, the influence of each of the four demographic variables on the results within each group, and secondly, the difference of results between the two groups. A two-way contingency table analysis together with Chi-square test was employed to identify statistically significant association between variables. Similar with Study I, only associations with the p-value lower than 0.001 were considered significant. For the effect size of Chi-square test, Phi value and Cramer's V value were observed, the former for 2 by 2 crosstabulation table while the latter for crosstabulation table bigger than 2 by 2. For significant associations in crosstabulation table bigger than 2 by 2, cells with significant difference were identified through either pair-wise comparisons using the LSD method or inspection of adjusted standardized residuals having absolute value greater than 2 (Miller et al. 2002, p. 133).

The interview data analysis also contained two stages after transcription. I, first, picked up key words in answers to each question, and second, classified and extracted representative reasons and experience by the interviewees.

Background Information

Tables A.1 and A.2 show, respectively, the background information of student and worker questionnaire respondents, and interviewees, including birth cohort, gender, location of primary school attended, and parental or personal education level.

On one hand, the student respondents (mean age = 22.09, std. deviation = 1.246) were equally drawn from the 1980s and the 1990s generations; the majority was female (59.2%), received primary education in urban area (75.2%) and in Guangdong Province (83.3%), and with parents who had completed upper secondary education (49.8%). On the other, a typical worker respondent (mean age = 32.64, std. deviation = 9.237) was female (63.3%), born in the 1980s (36.8%), received primary education in rural area (97.8%) and in Guangdong Province (53.8%), and completed lower secondary education (51.8%).

Table A.1 Background information of questionnaire respondents

Valid %	University students (N = 294)	Migrant workers (N = 226)
Birth cohort	(n = 292)	(n = 223)
Born before the 1970s	0.0	13.9
in the 1970s	0.0	34.5
in the 1980s	45.2	36.8
in the 1990s	54.8	14.8
Gender	(n = 294)	(n = 226)
Female	59.2	63.3
Male	40.8	36.7
Location of primary school attended (an indicator of HRS)	(n = 282)	(n = 226)
Urban	75.2	2.2
Rural	24.8	97.8
	(n = 281)	(n = 225)
In Guangdong Province	83.3	53.8
Out of Guangdong Province	16.7	46.2
Educational level	(n = 293) (parental highest level)	(n = 222) (personal highest level)
Primary school or below	4.1	23.0
Lower secondary school	15.7	51.8
Upper secondary school or equivalent	49.8	18.5
Junior college or equivalent	16.0	6.3
University undergraduate	10.9	0.5
University postgraduate or above	3.4	0.0

In terms of the type of media where respondents encountered the term *gongmin*, on one hand, radio was reported similarly by both student and worker respondents as the least frequent source. On the other hand, the Internet and TV were found to be the two most common media for encountering the term for student respondents while the most common for workers were TV and books (Fig. A.1).

The result of Chi-square test for the association of type of media and student/worker group (Table A.3) indicates that students were more likely than workers to have seen or heard the term *gongmin* on the Internet and in newspapers/magazines and books. The result came as no surprise as university students were expected to have more opportunities to access these three types of media than migrant workers, given that university students are often exposed to the Internet at early ages, involved in education for more years than the generally less educated migrant workers, and thus have more time to read. Indeed, migrant worker respondents often vented grievance in the interviews against their hard working schedule which easily extended to more than ten hours a day.

Table A.2 Background information of interviewees

Interviewees	Birth cohort	Gender	Location of primary school attended (HRS)	Educational level[a]
Student1	1980s	Female	Urban-In Guangdong Province	3
S2	90s	F	U-I	4
S3	90s	Male	U-I	1
S4	90s	M	Rural-I	2
S5	90s	M	R-Out of Guangdong Province	2
S6	90s	M	U-I	3
S7	80s	M	U-I	3
S8	80s	F	U-I	4
S9	80s	F	R-I	3
S10	80s	F	R-O	2
S11	80s	F	U-I	3
Worker1	70s	M	R-I	1
W2	80s	M	R-O	2
W3	90s	F	R-O	3
W4	70s	M	R-I	3
W5	70s	M	R-O	3
W6	70s	M	R-I	2
W7	90s	F	R-I	2
W8	80s	F	R-I	4
W9	90s	F	R-I	3
W10	70s	M	R-O	2
W11	80s	F	U-O	3

[a]Parental highest educational level in the case of students and personal highest educational level in the case of workers. *1* = primary school or below, *2* = lower secondary school, *3* = upper secondary school or equivalent and *4* = junior college or equivalent

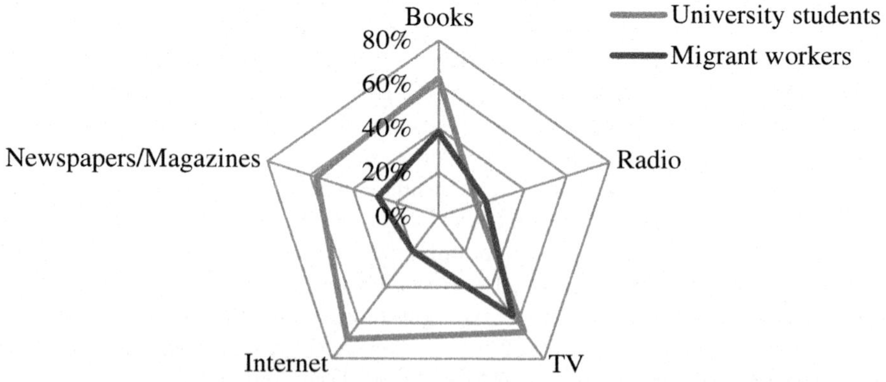

Fig. A.1 Media where respondents encountered the term *gongmin* (N = 520)

Table A.3 Chi-square test result of types of media by student/worker group (N = 520)

Student/Worker group*	Pearson Chi-square	df	p-value	Phi
Internet	123.663	1	0.000*	−0.488
TV	4.138	1	0.042	−0.089
Books	31.675	1	0.000*	−0.247
Newspapers/Magazines	42.963	1	0.000*	−0.287
Radio	1.595	1	0.207	0.55

*$p < 0.001$

References

Denscombe, M. (1998). *The Good Research Guide for Small-Scale Social Research Projects*. Buckingham: Open University Press.

Krippendorff, K. (1980). *Content Analysis: An Introduction to Its Methodology*. Beverly Hills, CA: Sage.

Miller, R. L., Acton, C., Fullerton, D. A., & Maltby, J. (2002). *SPSS for Social Scientists*. New York: Palgrave Macmillan.

Index

S. Chen, *The Meaning of Citizenship in Contemporary Chinese Society*,
Governance and Citizenship in Asia, https://doi.org/10.1007/978-981-10-6323-7

Printed by Printforce, the Netherlands